THE WORKS OF SRI CHINMOY

ANECDOTES & RECOLLECTIONS

VOLUME I

THE WORKS OF SRI CHINMOY

ANECDOTES &
RECOLLECTIONS

VOLUME I

★

RUN AND BECOME, BECOME AND RUN

LYON · OXFORD

GANAPATI PRESS

LXXXVII

ISBN 978-1-911319-11-5

See appendix for notice regarding this edition.

FIRST EDITION WENT TO PRESS ON 7 JUNE 2017

ANECDOTES & RECOLLECTIONS

VOLUME I

RUN AND BECOME, BECOME AND RUN

RUN AND BECOME, BECOME AND RUN

PART 1

RB 1. *The sprinter*

Around 4:30 in the morning I was completing my run. It was not twenty-seven miles like some of my disciples; it was only two miles.

As I was completing my two miles near the famous bus stop on 150th Street, a middle-aged white American said to me, "Man, you are a sprinter — not good for long distance!"

I thanked him and smiled at him, and he also smiled at me. See, his intuition was working so nicely!

RB 2. *The Grace protects*

I had only thirty or forty metres left to complete my mile that same morning, and I was struggling like anything. Then a car with three Puerto Rican youngsters made a right turn at the end of the street and started driving very slowly toward me. Two of the boys stretched out their hands through the window and screamed, "Hey, Sri, Sri!" Then such obscene words they started to use. It was the worst possible foul language — just absurd!

But the Grace was also there. The same middle-aged man who had spoken to me at the bus stop started running toward their car, using the same terms they had used. He repeated their mantra. When he repeated what they had said, they drove away very fast.

Then the man came over to me and I thanked him. He said, "Are you Sri Chinmoy? I am so happy that I am able to speak to you. I have heard so much about you. But I am not ready for the spiritual life, and I will never be ready." He smiled and smiled and thanked me.

This was an attack of the negative forces, but the Grace came to protect me. I would not have said anything to those youngsters. Who cares for them? But this gentleman ran ten or twenty metres and frightened them away by using the same absolutely foul tongue that they had used. This was my morning blessing.

Today's incident is so amusing. The older man had heard about me but had never seen me while those Puerto Rican boys definitely knew much about me.

Two weeks ago, on 150th Street, three black soldiers — cyclists — came toward me all riding together. But on that day I was very brave. I barked at them and they dispersed.

RB 3. *Big mouths*

Quite often a fat lady who walks with a cane greets me during my run. She has two dogs and she likes me very much. Whenever she sees me, she always has the same question: "Hey, don't you feel cold?" Each time I give her a smile and say, "No, no." By that time, I have run past her. Even if she sees me twice in the same day, she greets me with this same question, and I tell her the same thing.

This morning, at around 7:15 on our street, I saw this fat lady and her dogs having a real fight with another lady and her dog. The other lady was thin and seemed to be a little aristocratic. Let us say the fat lady is my friend, since she sees me every day and she likes me and talks to me. When the dogs started coming near each other, my friend said to the thin lady, "Don't you dare come near me." The thin lady replied, "Shut up, you big mouth!" Then, the fat one, my friend, threw her cane at the other one and said, "To hell with you!"

I finished my run and stood there watching them. As the thin one was leaving she said to her own dog, "You also have a big mouth!"

Now I had to sympathise with the fat lady because she was my friend. I went about 15 metres over to her cane and picked it up and gave it to her. She was very nice to me and said, "I knew all along you were a nice guy." She was giving me a compliment. By that time the other lady had gone away.

RB 4. *The power of a smile*

The first time I ever did seven miles, I was running alone in Flushing Meadow Park. After three or four miles an old man who was also running saw me and gave me a smile. There was such power in his smile that I went practically half a mile without feeling any pain, just joy.

Then, when I was coming back after having completed six miles, I was breathing heavily: "Ahh, ahh." An old, fat lady who was waiting for the bus saw me and started imitating me in a joking way: "Ahh, ahh." In silence I was saying, "Oh, if you had run six miles!"

The man was so nice and the lady was so bad!

RB 5. *Running late*

There is a very nice black lady who helps school children cross 150th Street. Every morning she sees me running and appreciates my style. The other day I was coming back from my run later than usual because I had run four miles instead of my usual two miles at that hour. She thought that I had run only two miles, but had taken more time because I was tired and exhausted. When I came near her she said, "What is wrong with you? Why are you coming so late?"

She had been talking to a man and she told me, "I was just telling my friend that today you have new shoes and you look so nice. Why are you late?" I went twice as far, but this lady thought that I should have come back sooner. She has her own time!

RB 6. *Child's advice*

One day while running, I was talking to myself in Bengali, in my Chittagong dialect: "I can't go any farther."

What could I do? I was dying! I kept saying, "I won't be able to go any farther."

Then, a child about eight years old came up to me and said, "Don't talk. It will make you more exhausted. Don't talk."

RB 7. *The Christmas run*

Early this morning I had run a mile and a half and had started coming back. I was at the 1200-metre marker when suddenly the Christ started running with me. While we were running, he showed me my presence inside his heart.

I said, "You can show me my presence inside your heart, and I can show you your presence inside mine." Then I started repeating his name in Bengali: "Jishu." He began repeating the Bengali word "ashu," which means speed, fastest speed.

I said, "You are mocking my running speed. But you should take a human body and then die here running."

"I am not mocking you," he said. "I am saying 'ashu' because you do everything on earth with the fastest speed."

"But here it does not apply," I said. "I have already run a mile and a half and I am dying, but you are in the subtle body. You are enjoying it."

Then we had a spiritual conversation.

RB 8. *The ambulance driver*

About six months ago when I was running on Union Turnpike around four in the morning, an ambulance driver asked me if I could tell him how to get to a particular place. He was drinking something — beer, I think — and going against a red light. Perhaps he was late. I thought to myself, "What is the matter with that fellow?"

I could not tell him how to get to his destination. There was also a truck driver nearby, but instead of asking the truck driver, he started saying bad words. Finally he said, "Hell with you!" I replied, "Heaven with you."

RB 9. *The direction-giver*

Once a taxi driver asked me how to get to Manhattan from Parsons Boulevard. I was so proud because, for the first time, I was able to tell someone directions. I said, "Make a left turn and then go straight."

RB 10. *Run within, run without*

Today I ran with two of my San Francisco children. I was so mean; I was running ahead of them. From time to time, the mischievous runner in me looked back to see where they were. I was happy to see that after covering one mile, the husband was somewhat behind me and his wife had stopped to take off her jacket.

We were running two miles. When there were 400 metres left, I was showing off like anything — running very fast. Then, after I crossed the finish line, I was breathing heavily, all out of breath.

I could not hear the husband's footsteps. That meant he was somewhere else. I saw that he was thirty or forty metres behind me, so I was very happy. That kind of thing is very bad, but it is due to the undivine human in me. The divine human in me would never have done that.

Actually, we had a wonderful time. As in the inner world we run together, so in the outer world we also run. In the outer world I have to keep my ears and eyes closed, because I know that most of my disciples are faster runners; I know what will be my fate. But in the inner world, I will be able to challenge all of them. So in the inner world I want my disciples to be as fast as I am. I ran with the husband and the wife as a token of my blessingful gift to the wife's birthday.

RB 11. *The severed head*

As you know, this spiritual Master wanted to experience the marathon world, so I began practising a lot. But each time I ran a marathon, my time increased. Even then I kept going on.

On one particular morning when I went out to practise, I was very tired. From the very beginning I said, "Today I have to fight against my mind. I will run at least two miles to fight against my mind."

O God, I started running, and then I ran one, two, three, four, five, six miles, and I became extremely tired. When I reached a very desolate place in the Woodhaven area, near a park, the park sign said, "No fishing, no bike riding, no roller skating, no dogs, no children, no everything." At the edge of the park were four or five cars very badly smashed, and right on the grass I saw a dead human body covered by a blanket. The head had been severed from the rest of the body and was lying a little distance away. I got the shock of my life to see that this man had been murdered, but what could I do? These things do happen in America. It is a daily story. I was horrified, but there was nothing I could do. There wasn't any telephone nearby. And besides, I would be the last person to inform the police. If I called the police, they would just harass me. So I said, "The best thing I can do is to pray for the soul of this dead person."

So I stood nearby, observing the dead body and the head and I meditated for seventeen minutes. I had a wristwatch, so I knew it was seventeen minutes. He was just an ordinary, simple soul, but I meditated and meditated and meditated. And I did much for the soul. Then I ran one more mile before turning around to go back home.

In all, I ran fourteen miles that morning. It was raining heavily. In those days, we used to have a gym, where I would go every morning to see my spiritual children and give out prasad. But on that day I came back from my run very late, so I did not go.

What things happen in America! Therefore, I ask my spiritual children to be very, very careful. No place is safe, no place. Of late, many unfortunate and destructive things are happening in the Jamaica area. So I wish my spiritual children to be extremely careful and to pray to the Supreme before they run and while they run, and afterwards to offer gratitude. And to do the same thing also when they go cycling.

RB 12. *The windy marathon*

The Western world always says that there is only one saviour and that is Jesus Christ. But I say that he is not the only saviour; there are many more saviours. Today I can prove that there are indeed many saviours; all my spiritual children are my saviours. Had you not been there, after two miles I would have saluted the race. As a bad carpenter finds faults with his tools, today — like a bad runner — I found fault with the wind. During the first six miles, before the disciples came to help me, you have no idea how hard it was. How I suffered! After two miles I had no strength left in my chest, arms or legs. Usually I have strength everywhere, but it was as if I were being pressed against a wall. After four or five miles, who could maintain his will power? It was like climbing up the Himalayas. There was so much obstruction that all joy, inspiration and aspiration went away. What remained was powerful disappointment, if you use a civilised word. The uncivilised word would be a curse. After two miles I was only looking around for the car, because the wind was so powerfully pushing me back.

I am so grateful when everybody began running with me, trying to block the wind. But actually, when it was a matter of relief, it helped very little. Today there was no relief.

The wind came from the front, the side and the top like a solid wall and weakened the runner. You people should have used your occult power to stop the wind. The Toledo marathon is nice. If there is a strong wind, they reverse the course so the runners don't have to run against the wind. Here they don't do that.

I was enjoying the way that one disciple would say one thing and another would inevitably and invariably contradict him. It wasn't that they were fighting. If one told the disciples running with me, "Go slowly!" then one second later another would say, "Go fast." For me, to go fast or to go slow was all the same; I was dying.

Those of you who sang the running songs along the route were so kind to me. You have also helped me so much. All those who have run with me and who have sung along the way, all those who have encouraged me in any capacity, please feel my gratitude-heart. I have finished the marathon because of you; otherwise, I could never, never have finished. It was self-imposed torture from beginning to end. Today, the best timing was 2:39; last year I think it was 2:27. So look at how bad the wind was! The second-best timing was 2:44.

Usually I select people — my running crew and a few others — to run with me. I tell the head of my running crew beforehand who the people are and he informs them at which mark they should join me. But today I told him that all the boys could join.

The organiser of the race was very nice. He gave me a special certificate and the mayor has also given me a proclamation. The organiser knew about us through the Montreal Centre. He has also heard about the Meditation Group that we have in Plattsburgh. Plattsburgh is so peaceful, soulful and beautiful. I have been admiring it since yesterday and appreciating the sincerity of the place.

RB 13. *Father's Day torture*

During the thirteen-mile run on Father's Day, I tried running at the pace of a few different disciples. There was one particular disciple, very fat, whom I was so proud of. I wanted to honour her and run with her, just because she was going to complete thirteen miles.

But then I discovered something new. It is infinitely more painful to run slowly. I tried to keep to her pace, but I couldn't. It was unbearable!

RB 14. *The Indian's pranam*

About a month ago I was nearing the playground at the Jamaica High School track when an Indian saw me running.

As soon as he saw me, he put down his briefcase and stood with folded hands.

RB 15. *The moving car*

This morning I almost had an accident. One fellow had stopped at a red light but his car was still moving as I was running across the street. He was just looking to one side and so I had to bang on his car, because he didn't know what he was doing. Of course, I banged on it very politely.

RB 16. *A close call*

I was running across an intersection in San Juan. One car was coming from one direction and another was coming from the other. One of them had a red light and one of them had a green light. At the intersection, the driver of the second car got inspired. All of a sudden, instead of waiting at the red light for the other car, which had a green light, he took a short cut through the intersection. I screamed.

A gentleman with a briefcase was crossing the street at the time. He started chasing the car and screaming, using all American vulgar terms. He even crossed the street and followed the car for 50 metres. Then he began cursing himself, saying that instead of running after the car he should have taken down its license number.

He came up to me and said, "I can see you are a nice guy." He said he also runs and a few days ago he had had a similar experience. How badly they drive in San Juan!

RB 17. *No red light*

At one place, it took me seven to ten minutes just to cross the street because of traffic. I kept saying, "O God, why is there no red light there?"

RB 18. *The race*

Today I saw one of my disciples running, about 200 metres ahead of me. Then my ego came forward and I said, "Just because her husband defeats me, that doesn't mean that she will defeat me."

So I ran past her, and then I ran practically 200 metres more.

Afterwards, a policeman smiled at me and spoke to me in Spanish.

RB 19. *"Master, when did you come?"*

There was a very big puddle about 400 metres from the Centre, near Lilo's Health Food Store. A lady was driving by quite fast, but she stopped her car in the middle of the street so that she would not splash me. Perhaps she had seen me somewhere — on television or in the newspaper. She asked, "Master, when did you come? How do you do?" The people waiting in the cars behind her were blessing her.

RB 20. *Ashford Avenue*

Every day, at about four in the morning, I run down Ashford Avenue, but it is so dark that I can never really see it. Then, during the day when I ride in the car down Ashford Avenue, it looks so different. I can't believe that I have run that far. I can only marvel and say to the disciples with me, "Look how far I have run!"

RB 21. *A precious morning*

On the way to Jamaica High School I saw a man about my age wearing a suit. He looked like a perfect gentleman, and he had a briefcase in his hand. As soon as I crossed the street and ran past him, he gave me a very, very broad smile.

You know I may be miserly in other fields, but not in offering smiles. So I also gave him a very broad smile, but I didn't stop running.

All of a sudden I heard someone running behind me. I turned around and saw the same gentleman running after me. This time he was almost shaking with a kind of reverential awe.

"Are you Sri Chinmoy?" he asked. Usually I can't speak when I run. It takes time for me to catch my breath. So I just looked at him and again gave him a very good smile.

Then he said, "What a precious man and what a precious morning!" I continued running. When I had covered another ten metres, I turned around and I saw him still standing there, looking at me.

RB 22. *Your best friend*

Today I saw a dog that I have seen a few times before. But for the first time I also saw the owner. It was an elderly woman, and she was holding the dog on a leash.

As I ran by, the dog blocked my way, so I just stopped and stood there. The dog was not barking at all and the lady said to me, "Don't worry, don't worry! She is as kind as any human being can ever be. She can be your best friend as well, if you want her to be."

I said to the lady, "Thank you, thank you."

Her dog can be her best friend, so true. After running a few more metres I turned around, and the lady was still looking at me.

RB 23. *The stopping place*

When I run up the hill on 150th Street, always I come and stop at a particular tree. I breathe in four times and then again I resume my running.

The other day, one of the disciples told me that she was parking her car near there when a lady said to her, "I saw your leader this morning. I see him every day. He goes running up the hill and he stops right by that tree. He looks so thirsty, I want to give him a glass of water, but I know I can't. Your leader is so terrific. You are so lucky to have such a good leader. He's such a wonderful man."

I think she is one of the ladies who had the fight with another lady and her dog a few months ago by the bus stop.

RB 24. *A tale from Flushing Meadow*

The other day I entered into Flushing Meadow Park and I happened to see one of the disciples. On other days when he sees me or when I see him, he runs quite fast. But on that particular day he was running so slowly. I said, "Today is not his day."

RB 25. *A display of strength*

Yesterday in Flushing Meadow Park a group of black and white girls were playing with a doll on the grass. I was running by on the street when all of a sudden one of the black girls came into the street. She was quite fat and short, and she stood blocking my way and showing her muscles. I stopped running and went two metres to the right, and then I started running again. How she was flexing her muscles!

RB 26. *Flushing Meadow blessing*

Ten minutes later I was running near the start of the Road Runners' 100-mile race. I was running slowly. Near the bridge there were five or six young boys and one girl, all black. When I came by, they started using all their American slang and pointing at me, but I didn't pay any attention.

But O God, one girl didn't stop at just cutting jokes. In two minutes' time she started running side by side with me. All American rubbish language she was saying, but I was deaf and dumb, absolutely not answering. She ran with me for about 150 metres. She was holding a baton or small stick. Finally, she threw it at me, but fortunately it did not strike me. Then she ran back to her friends.

That is why I ask my disciples, especially the women, to be very, very careful while running. I am an older man and yesterday I was wearing a running outfit and looking smart, too. But still they were joking and disturbing me. So please be very, very careful when you run.

RB 27. *The intersection-haven*

Yesterday I was returning home after having covered only two miles. Suddenly, somebody from behind said, "Hey, hey! Hello, hello! Hello, Guru!" Now, you guess who it was. It was one of my disciples.

Then I told him to run according to his own speed. So he ran very fast, but he halted at an intersection. I continued running and I came very near him — 100 or 150 metres away. I was watching him. There was no car there, no red light, nothing. Even then he was waiting there. I said, "Oh, he is my perfect disciple. He can say that he is at an intersection, so it is all right to take rest there."

RB 28. *The silent dog*

The day before yesterday, around 5:30 in the morning, three dogs came running after me. One little dog ran very fast and came within a metre of me. He wasn't barking; he was just running. I didn't even see this dog until it tried to bite my ankle. Luckily, a car went by and the noise scared the dog away.

RB 29. *A cooling friendship*

This morning, while I was running near the Grand Central Parkway, a man said, "Wait!" So I stopped and waited, but I didn't know what he wanted. Then he said, "This will be cooler," and he sprayed me with a hose.

He asked me where I was from. I told him, "India," and I asked him where he was from. He said, "Ireland." He was very happy to learn that I had been to Ireland a few years ago and had met the President. On my way back I again saw him working in his garden. I waved to him and he said, "Good morning."

RB 30. *The dime*

One day, after running eleven miles, I stopped to watch some children who were looking for something. One of them had dropped a coin, and they were all looking for it. So I also started looking. Finally, I found a dime and pointed it out to the child who had dropped it. He said, "Thanks a lot." Then he gave me a smile and I gave him a smile.

RB 31. *Who is that guy?*

Once I passed by an old man and a little child. The old man was looking at me with admiration. The child said, "Daddy, who is that guy?" The father answered, "He is a great man."

RB 32. *Too fast*

Yesterday at noon, when I was returning from my run, a little boy and a little girl came out of their house. The little boy ran and followed for fifty metres. He said, "Boy, you run quite fast." Then he stopped and gave up.

RB 33. *The hill*

Yesterday, after I had run about three and a half miles, I stopped for a couple of seconds while running up a hill. At that time another runner — a man of about my age — passed me and said, "Come on, you can make it. You are not that old." So I started running and then I passed him. He gave me a broad smile and said, "I told you so." He was very happy that he had inspired me. Then I made a right turn and he made a left turn and we parted.

RB 34. *The fisherman's request*

One morning, after I had run ten miles, I saw a fisherman catching fish. He said, "Man, you have run a lot. Now give me a hand." He wanted my help, but I just smiled and kept running.

RB 35. *How many miles?*

The other day my road crew was following me in a car as I was running. After I had run only six miles, a fisherman started screaming at me, "Keep on running, run faster." Then he asked, "How many miles have you run?"

The boys are such jokers. I had run only six miles, but they told him twelve miles.

RB 36. *I am working*

On Parsons Boulevard construction men were digging a big hole and a very fat man was inside the hole up to his eyes. As soon as he saw me he smiled at me and clapped. Then he started grumbling, "Oh, I am here working and you are running and enjoying yourself."

RB 37. *The slow runner*

Once, a 60 or 70-year-old man was following me during a run. Then he said to me, "Young man, what is the matter? Why do you run so slowly?" For fifty metres he ran with me, but then he gave up. He was so out of breath.

RB 38. *The garbage collectors*

This morning I was running by three garbage collectors, two white and one black. One of the white ones said, "Boss, what do you doing?" instead of what are you doing. So I smiled at him. The black one said, "He's a smart guy." I also gave him a broad smile.

RB 39. *The drunken driver*

Yesterday I was running at five in the morning near Thomas Edison High School. At a little traffic island I had to stop for the cars. All of a sudden a car came right into the island, stopping just thirty metres from me. The man seemed drunk. If it had not been for the trees, it would have been a very close call.

RB 40. *The showoff*

As I made a left turn off 150th Street, I noticed an old man on the corner, looking at me. I looked at him and said, "Good morning." In a few seconds he felt inspired to also start running. I said to myself, "O God, what is he doing?"

As he approached me, the time came for me to show off. I ran fast, but then I cursed myself. Usually, if people pass by me, I say, "Oh, perhaps he is doing only one or two miles and I am doing eight or nine." This time I felt sorry for my stupidity.

For 200 metres we ran together. Then he made a right turn and I made a left turn.

RB 41. *Good job!*

Yesterday while I was running in the morning near the old Greek Deli which burnt down, a gentleman said to me, "Good job, good chap!"

RB 42. *The barking girls*

Before the bus left for the triathlon, around midnight, I went for a three-mile run. After 600 metres I crossed the street. There were five girls sitting on the curb. As soon as they saw me, they all stood up and started barking the way dogs bark.

When I came back, they were still there chatting. Again, as soon as they saw me, they got inspiration to stand up and bark.

RB 43. *The chase*

After one and a half miles, when I was returning from my three-mile run, I passed by a group of four or five Puerto Rican boys. They were looking at me. Then all of a sudden one got inspiration to run with me. It was almost as though he was chasing me. I ran quite fast for 300 metres and then he gave up.

RB 44. *An invitation*

This afternoon some workers were digging up the ground in the middle of the street. They were listening to the radio. When they saw me, they gave me a smile and one said, "Come and join us and listen to the radio."

RB 45. *Don't be a fool*

This morning an old lady with a dog said to me, "You are tired?"
I said, "Yes, I am tired."
"How many miles?" she asked.
I answered, "Six and a half."
She said, "Kidding? Don't have to kill yourself. Don't be a fool, honey."
This was the first time I had ever seen her.

RB 46. *The storm*

One night I wanted to go for a sixteen-mile run. I started about 3 a.m. at Flushing Meadow Park and my road crew was following me in a car. After I had gone six miles, it started raining heavily. It was a real torrential downpour which lasted the whole night. But still I went on, went on, with my faithful crew.

RB 47. *The running machine*

Last year I was practising on my running machine early one morning when a former disciple's soul visited me. The soul said, "I wish I could run as fast in the inner world as you are running on this machine." That night, this particular seeker visited the Jharna-Kala Gallery, seeing me for the first time in a few years.

RB 48. *The sprinkler*

At about five-thirty one morning, a husband and wife were in front of their house. The husband was putting garbage in the garbage can and the wife was watering the lawn.
Suddenly the wife got inspiration to water me with the sprinkler. Her husband said to her, "Honey, why did you do that?

Do you think he appreciates it?" Then she laughed and laughed. Actually, I don't like the sprinkler at all. As soon as I see one I run away.

RB 49. *The blessing*

As I was finishing a six-and-a-half-mile run and coming back to the starting point, a black man said to me, "The Christ will bless you."

RB 50. *The extra mile*

My road crew is very good, but sometimes when I give them a job, they forget to do it. Then, I bark at them like anything.

Yesterday I wanted to run only 400 metres, and when I didn't see any mark, I said, "Perhaps I made a mistake." I went on running farther and farther. Finally it became one mile — 800 metres one way and 800 back. My road crew had forgotten to measure that route.

Afterwards, I had them drive that way in a car and we discovered that I had run one mile extra.

RB 51. *Join us*

One day, after running a few miles, I started walking for a while. Some workmen saw me and asked, "Why aren't you running? We enjoy seeing you run."

These same workmen once asked me to join them for a beer.

RB 52. *The taxi driver*

Today, another taxi driver asked me for directions. Since I could not give him directions, I just folded my hands and said I didn't know.

RB 53. *The fat man*

One winter morning I went out to run thirteen miles. Right after I started, I saw three young girls on their way to school.

I am not fat, I have to say, but when I wear a down vest to keep warm, I do look heavier.

So one girl said, "Hey, fat man, you are doing well! Fat man, you are doing well." Another girl said, "Fatty, carry on, carry on! Fatty, carry on, carry on!"

RB 54. *An unexpected encounter*

Once, as I was running about five-thirty in the morning, I saw a young man waiting for the bus.

As soon as he saw me, he became so happy and he ran with me for thirty or forty metres. Then he went back to the bus stop.

After I had covered one mile and was returning, past the same bus stop, the young man ran with me again.

He was so happy to run with me. He said, "You are a good runner."

RB 55. *A running companion*

Today after I had run a mile and a half, a little dog.... it was so ferocious.... suddenly jumped at me and tried to bite me.

O God, what could I do? I was running in the street and there were a lot of cars coming. If you go that side, you will end up inside the car and if you go this side, the dog will bite you. Either way is dangerous.

But that is not the story. While the dog was trying to bite me, an elderly woman was enjoying it. And it was her dog! I had to change the position of my legs, scream something and pretend I had a stone. For twenty metres the dog chased me, and the old lady was enjoying it like anything.

I am not an American, and I don't know your American slang. But you people would have gone up to that lady and insulted her. But I just walked in the street, staying as far from the sidewalk as I could. It was very difficult.

From the spiritual point of view, a dog symbolises faithfulness. If a dog bites you, they say that you have lost faith. When have I lost my faith? No, I have not lost it. It was just an attack by the hostile forces. They can act through a dog also. So a dog is supposed to be a divine instrument, but it can be very undivine as well. Here I am having such a serious problem, and the woman is enjoying it.

People should not run in the street. If they do, a dog will come from a house and create such problems! Out of the blue they come, sometimes three or four at a time. Some bark beforehand and some do not.

Almost every day I have problems at various places with dogs.

RB 56. *The escort*

It was drizzling, and I was running back slowly along the same road where the dog had attacked me earlier. An old lady, over seventy years old, was standing on the sidewalk. Her umbrella was a plastic garbage bag. When she saw me she shouted, "Hey, stop!"

I said to myself, "O God, another old lady!" But I am obedient, so I stopped. There was a red light there, and I enjoyed stopping and resting at the red light. Sometimes even at a green light I enjoy rest.

The old lady said to me, "Do you know the Grand Central Parkway?"

I said, "Isn't the Grand Central right here?"

She said, "No! What do you know?"

There were many cars coming by and she asked me, "Can you come with me?" I thought that she was asking me to carry her bag, so I said, "I will gladly carry it."

I was observing her to see if she was really crazy. I felt sorry for her. Perhaps she felt sorry for me. When I took her to the other side of the Grand Central, she just stood there. I didn't know if anything was going on inside her mind. She was not smiling, but at least she didn't scold me.

RB 57. *Observations from a bus stop*

A few days ago I was running past the bus stop on 150th Street. A black man and a white woman were standing there waiting for the bus.

Because of the construction there, I can't run very fast and I always have to go from one side of the road to the other. When the lady saw me, she said, "Good going! You are going so fast."

The man said, "No, he's not. I could have run much faster when I was his age."

The lady said, "No, you couldn't have."

Poor man, he was jealous of my running ability.

RB 58. *Three car experiences*

The day before yesterday, in the morning, I had covered about two miles when a car with a little girl and her father approached me. The man said, "Look, look, Sri Chinmoy is running!" When the child looked outside the window, she was so delighted and excited to see me running.

Fifteen minutes later I was running near Bohack. Very slowly a car came toward me and finally stopped. A black lady and a black man were inside the car. The black lady was driving. She said to me, "Hi, Sri Chinmoy. You are running, you are running!"

One minute later another car with two middle-aged men slowly drove by. The driver asked me where a particular street was. I said, "Sorry, I do not know."

The man said, "Damn you." So I said, "Thank you."

RB 59. *The divine cheerers*

Five minutes later I was running on the street where the Greek school is — the one which leads to Agni Press. As I was running, I passed a young girl of sixteen or seventeen who was riding a bike. She came up to me and said, "Hi, Sri Chinmoy." She was smiling and smiling. Then for about 150 metres she rode beside me, and then she pedalled away quite fast.

When I came up to Agni Press, I saw her talking to a few of her friends, some boys. As soon as I came by, they all started shouting my name, and clapping and jumping with such cheerfulness. They were cheering me at every step: "Sri Chinmoy! Sri Chinmoy!"

When I got home I asked one of my disciples to bring me twelve apples and twelve oranges immediately. But he didn't hear the word "immediately." Twenty minutes passed and I said, "By this time those divine children will have disappeared." So I asked another disciple to drive me in the car. Then I saw the first disciple. He was walking very slowly. I said, "What are you doing? I asked you to come 'immediately'." He said, "Guru, I didn't hear the word 'immediately', I just heard 'go and bring'."

Anyway, I went to the spot to see if those children were still there. To my great surprise, the girl was sitting on the steps in front of the Greek School, with a friend of hers. Since both of them were girls, I didn't think it would be proper to go and speak to them. "Best thing is for us to go to Guru Stationery and bring some girls," I said. So we brought back two girl disciples who were working there to the spot where the two girls were talking.

When the girl saw our car approaching her, she stood up and jumped towards the car. "Sri Chinmoy, Sri Chinmoy," she said. She and her friend were both jumping for joy.

I said to them, "Can I give you some fruits?"

The girl who was then standing beside the car said, "Of course. You are such a sweet, nice man. Can I kiss you on your hand?"

I said, "Oh, no!" I gave them each an orange and an apple. Then I asked, "Where are your friends?"

They said, "We'll go look for them." They went into the school, but their friends were not there. When they came out, the other girl said how happy she was to see me running. She was also a runner, and she said that she had run in one of our ten-mile races in Connecticut. She had come into Guru Health Foods that morning to ask when our next race would be. Both girls were excited.

I asked if they would see their friends soon, so they could give them apples and oranges, but they said, "No, we will not see them." I said, "Then I would like to give you again another orange and apple."

A young boy was watching the scene. He was not one of those who had cheered me, but he said, "Can I also have an orange? I don't care for apples, however." He came up to me all excited, and I gave him an orange.

RB 60. *Two crazy fellows*

Last night, after six and a half miles, I was returning at one-thirty in the morning near the Grand Central Parkway. A car came slowly toward me. I was going away, but it went right against the red light. I said, "O God, what is he doing?"

The driver was smoking and his wife was sitting beside him. The man leaned out the window and said to me, "Please come near me. I shall not harm you. You don't have to be afraid." It was a very respectable looking couple, so I went over to the car. The man said, "Tell me, why are you running at this hour?"

I said, "I like it, I enjoy it."

The man said to his wife, "Every day I also run at this hour and you call me crazy. Now, here is somebody else who is running."

The lady said, "Yes, another crazy fellow like you!" Then she said to me, "Young man, go home and sleep. If you don't sleep, you will die soon. But if you don't run, you are not going to die soon."

The man said, "It is better to die sooner than to live with a wife like you."

The lady pushed her husband and knocked his cigarette out of his mouth. It fell down on the street, coming very close to my leg. But fortunately it didn't hit me.

I started laughing, and then both of them started laughing and laughing. Finally they said to me, "Thanks a lot."

RB 61. *Street nuisance*

Yesterday I was running in Flushing Meadow Park when an old, fat lady came from behind me and with her left hand gave me a very good push on my shoulder. A thin old man dressed very smartly in a running outfit was approaching us and observing the scene. He said to her, "Street nuisance!" O God, I thought that I was about to enjoy seeing a very good fight. So I increased my stride and ran away quite fast.

RB 62. *The lawn-mowers*

Yesterday as I was finishing a five-mile run I passed two men mowing their lawns. One of them came up to me smiling and said, "Are you Shry, Shry?" The other one said, "It is so nice that you are running."

RB 63. *Happy Birthday*

Yesterday, while I was running, a young girl came up to me on a bicycle. She said, "Hi! Happy Birthday, Happy Birthday!" Her friends were all looking at me and smiling and cheering me. Then, many of them joined her and sang "Happy Birthday," for about three or four minutes, until I had run so far that I could no longer hear them.

My birthday, however, wasn't until nine days later.

RB 1. *(p. 5)* 12 August 1978
RB 2. *(p. 5)* 12 August 1978
RB 3. *(p. 6)* 5 December 1978
RB 4. *(p. 7)* 5 December 1978
RB 5. *(p. 7)* 5 December 1978
RB 6. *(p. 8)* 5 December 1978
RB 7. *(p. 8)* 25 December 1978
RB 8. *(p. 9)* 25 July 1979
RB 9. *(p. 9)* 25 July 1979
RB 10. *(p. 9)* 30 January 1979
RB 11. *(p. 10)* 12 May 1979
RB 12. *(p. 11)* 12 May 1979. Plattsburgh, N.Y
RB 13. *(p. 13)* 17 June 1979
RB 14. *(p. 13)* 25 July 1979
RB 15. *(p. 14)* 11 July 1979
RB 16. *(p. 14)* 11 July 1979
RB 17. *(p. 15)* 11 July 1979
RB 18. *(p. 15)* 11 July 1979
RB 19. *(p. 15)* 11 July 1979
RB 20. *(p. 15)* 11 July 1979
RB 21. *(p. 16)* 21 July 1979
RB 22. *(p. 16)* 21 July 1979
RB 23. *(p. 17)* 21 July 1979
RB 24. *(p. 17)* 21 July 1979
RB 25. *(p. 18)* 21 July 1979
RB 26. *(p. 18)* 21 July 1979
RB 27. *(p. 19)* 21 July 1979
RB 28. *(p. 19)* 25 July 1979
RB 29. *(p. 19)* 25 July 1979
RB 30. *(p. 20)* 25 July 1979

RB 31. *(p. 20)* 25 July 1979
RB 32. *(p. 20)* 25 July 1979
RB 33. *(p. 20)* 25 July 1979
RB 34. *(p. 21)* 25 July 1979
RB 35. *(p. 21)* 25 July 1979
RB 36. *(p. 21)* 25 July 1979
RB 37. *(p. 21)* 25 July 1979
RB 38. *(p. 22)* 25 July 1979
RB 39. *(p. 22)* 28 July 1979
RB 40. *(p. 22)* 28 July 1979
RB 41. *(p. 23)* 28 July 1979
RB 42. *(p. 23)* 30 July 1979
RB 43. *(p. 23)* 30 July 1979
RB 44. *(p. 23)* 30 July 1979
RB 45. *(p. 24)* 30 July 1979
RB 46. *(p. 24)* 7 August 1979
RB 47. *(p. 24)* 7 August 1979
RB 48. *(p. 24)* 7 August 1979
RB 49. *(p. 25)* 7 August 1979
RB 50. *(p. 25)* 7 August 1979
RB 51. *(p. 25)* 8 August 1979
RB 52. *(p. 26)* 9 August 1979
RB 53. *(p. 26)* 20 January 1979
RB 54. *(p. 26)* 20 January 1979
RB 55. *(p. 27)* 11 August 1979
RB 56. *(p. 28)* 11 August 1979
RB 57. *(p. 28)* 11 August 1979
RB 58. *(p. 29)* 15 August 1979
RB 59. *(p. 29)* 14 August 1979
RB 60. *(p. 31)* 15 August 1979
RB 61. *(p. 32)* 23 August 1979
RB 62. *(p. 32)* 24 August 1979
RB 63. *(p. 32)* 18 August 1979

RUN AND BECOME, BECOME AND RUN

PART 2

RB 64. *Run and become*

Run and become.
Become and run.
Run to succeed in the outer world.
Become to proceed in the inner world.

— Sri Chinmoy

RB 65. *Shry and John McLaughlin*

Two Puerto Rican boys were in a car driving the wrong way on a one-way street as I came running down. One boy said, "Hi, Shry, Shry, Shry. I love you." The other boy said, "Hi, John McLaughlin. I love you."

RB 66. *No objection*

Along one of my running routes a little girl of five or six and her father were entering into a car. The father was getting into the driver's side and the daughter was getting in the other side. As I ran by, the daughter said, "Hi, Guru!"

The father said to her, "Call him by his real name: Sri Chinmoy." Then he said to me, "I have no objection to her calling you 'Guru', but I just wanted her to know your real name. We have some tenants who always talk about you."

RB 67. *I miss my youth*

When I went out running I saw a short, thin, old man with a hat and cane sitting on the edge of a wall, waiting for the bus. I didn't pay any attention to him, but when I came back from my seven-mile run, the same old man was still waiting there. He said to me, "How I wish I could get back my youth."

I said, "I too miss my youth."

"How old are you?" asked the man.

"Forty-eight," I answered.

"I am seventy-three," said the man.

I stayed there with him for two or three minutes and then I finished my run.

RB 68. *I can beat you*

As I was running up 85th Avenue, a little boy said to me, "Hi, Shry Chinmoy. You can't run. I can beat you."

I said, "Easily."

The little boy said, "Easily, I bet!"

RB 69. *The ticket-giver*

While I was running about four or five days ago, I passed a man who was giving a parking ticket to a car — God knows what he is called. I was very tired, and when he saw me he said, "Young friend, you have run enough. Now take rest."

After writing out the ticket, he himself sat down at the foot of a tree. He was a very old man, a very nice soul. I asked him, "Do you get joy by giving tickets to cars?"

"No, never!" he replied. "But will you give me my bread and butter? Daily I have to give at least ten or twelve tickets in the morning. If I do not, then my boss will fire me. He will not give me my bread and butter."

So we sat down and both rested for about five minutes — this is how I run — and then we went our own ways.

RB 70. *Stride instruction*

Yesterday when I was finishing a six-mile run on 150th Street, a young boy came up to me and said, "Nice style, but you need longer strides."

He began demonstrating, saying that after each stride I should pause and press the ground with my toes. "In this way your stride becomes longer."

He was very nice and demonstrated this for two minutes or so. I did not tell him that I know all the different stride techniques.

RB 71. *The nice guy*

Around 4:30 in the morning, after running three and a half miles, I passed a very old man who was in his seventies. He was carrying a bag which had some food inside it. This happened between Queens Boulevard and Main Street.

He asked me, "Excuse me, which way is the subway?"

I said, "I'm very sorry. I don't know."

The old man said, "Never mind, you are a nice guy."

After I went on about 200 metres, I remembered: "Oh, he is walking towards the highway. How is he going to get the subway there?"

So I ran back to get him. O God, he was coming back; somebody else had already told him to head towards Queens Boulevard.

But when he saw I came back to help him, he said, "I knew you were a nice guy."

RB 72. *How the world exists*

There are bad people, there are good people and there are very good people on earth. I don't care for pizza at all, but some of my disciples enjoy pizza like anything. A few months ago I said, "Let me please my disciples!" So I went to the pizza parlour and asked for eight pieces. The man asked me to take a whole pie. It would be a matter of ten minutes, he said, for him to get it ready.

Instead of waiting in the hot pizza parlour, I went outside to do some jogging. After thirteen minutes I went back inside.

The man didn't have it ready yet. He said, "I didn't trust you. I thought you wouldn't come back." So I waited there, and in five minutes he gave me a pie to take home.

Yesterday I was running while some of the girls were working in the Jharna-Kala Store. Since I know my disciples like baklava, I entered into a store that sold it and asked the man if he could cut twenty pieces in half. He said yes and started cutting. He had cut only two pieces when I told him I would be back. Then I ran a mile and a half.

When I returned, the man was surprised to see me. He said, "I am giving this to you for fifty cents less because I am so surprised to see you." In his case I was late, but he had it ready for me.

He asked me for ten dollars. I said to myself, "Each piece is 40 cents and there were twenty pieces." Fortunately, a lady standing behind me said to the man, "That should be eight dollars." The man said, "Oh, yes, yes. Sorry."

Now we come not to better but to best. Three weeks ago I received an anonymous letter deeply appreciating what I am doing for mankind, along with a bank check for one thousand dollars. It was a check from Citibank, but for some reason it had been mailed from Maine. So there are, indeed, good people on earth. This is how the world exists. Otherwise, the world would collapse.

RB 73. *Who will feel sorry for whom?*

Sometimes someone is ten or twenty metres ahead of you in a race. If you look at that person, you see that he is running so slowly. You can't believe that you are running slower than him, but you are.

In our last ten-mile race, two older women were running near me. Who will feel sorry for whom? But they finally went ahead of me, even though they seemed to be going so slowly, and I couldn't catch up to them again.

RB 74. *The insurmountable hill*

I will never allow the Centre to sponsor a race with the same kind of hilly course that we had in today's ten-mile race. Even my road crew driving alongside me in a car knew what we were going through. Each mile had at least one hill or even more, and there were three hills that were almost insurmountable.

When I saw one particular hill, my reaction was immediately to collapse. Then I saw two of my girl disciples running together in front of me, literally running and jumping up the hill.

I said, "If they can jump like that, why can't I drag my body up the hill?" And I did finally reach the top.

RB 75. *"Look, mom!"*

The day before yesterday I was running by the Indian grocery near our old gym. An Indian family was standing beside the grocery. As I came by, a young boy of eight or ten began calling his mother, "Mom, look, Sri Chinmoy is running, Sri Chinmoy is running! We haven't seen him for a long time."

He called his mother, but I had disappeared before she could come out of the store.

RB 76. *The race*

This morning at 4:30, when I made a turn off 150th Street onto the Grand Central service road at the half-mile mark, I passed a very thin, old man who was half drunk and very dirty.

He said to me, "I can beat you walking." I smiled at him. Then he started walking very fast for forty metres, but I was still a little ahead of him.

Then I told him, "*You* run. I can beat you walking."

So he started running and I started walking. I stayed behind him deliberately; otherwise, I could have easily defeated him.

He said, "Oh, now we are even." He could not defeat me when he was walking and I could not beat him when I was walking.

RB 77. *"One, two, three!"*

This morning a fat lady, my neighbour-friend, was standing with her two dogs near my house. She saw me run by and then she started walking slowly across the street. By the time she reached the other side, I was back from running around the block. She said, "You run so fast. One, two, three, and you are here!" She could not cover fifteen metres in the time I took to run 400 metres.

RB 78. *"Don't stop"*

At four in the afternoon, after running a half-mile, I stopped for two seconds in front of an old man, an invalid who was sitting in a wheelchair in front of his house.

He said to me, "Don't stop, don't stop! It is not allowed. Keep going, keep going. Don't stop, it is not allowed."

I thanked him, and then I ran a mile and a half. When I was returning, I thought that the old man would still be there and give me the same advice. So about 100 metres before his house, I stopped for a few seconds and thought of him. Immediately I saw a flash and heard him say in the inner world, "That's perfect."

When I saw him 100 metres later, I smiled and he said, "That's perfect." He didn't know that I had stopped 100 metres before.

RB 79. *"Run softly!"*

After I had run about two miles and was near my tennis court, I saw an old lady who had just mowed her lawn. Leaves and grass were lying on the sidewalk. When I was about to run by, she said to me, "Please run softly and gently. Don't make a mess!" When I heard this, I immediately jumped into the street. "Such a nice guy!" she said.

RB 80. *"No, never!"*

When I was running the day before yesterday, I felt such tiredness in my body. The body was so undivine, not receptive at all. After 200 metres, I stopped for no rhyme or reason. After 400 metres, again I stopped. This time I got mad at myself. "Is it tiredness or is it something else?" I asked.

Inwardly I said a few times, "I am not going to stop, I am not going to stop." Then I began chanting out loud, at every step, "No, never! No, never! No, never!" In this way I covered one mile. If people had heard me chanting in the street, they would have said: "Insane!" Luckily, no one was around. Then I ran all the way back home, feeling quite happy.

RB 81. *"You are beautiful!"*

Early yesterday morning around seven o'clock, as I was running towards Parsons Boulevard, I saw an elderly man sitting on a chair across the street. As I came by he raised his hand and said to me, "Hey, your style is beautiful. You look beautiful. You are beautiful, beautiful, beautiful!"

When I came back from running around 7:30, one of the disciples came to my house to drive me to the playground. As soon as she opened the door and saw me on the porch she said, "Guru, you look so beautiful!" She used the same words as the old man. So in silence I blessed the soul of my laundress for my beautiful outfit.

RB 82. *The old runner*

In the afternoon at three o'clock I was running along the street near the turn-off to Guru Stationery. Many children were coming home from school at that time.

A little girl, eight or nine years old, said to a little boy, "Look, look, Shry is running!"

The boy said, "His name is Sri."

The girl said, "He runs like an old man."

The boy said, "He is not old."

The girl said, "But he runs like an old man."

RB 83. *The saint*

After I had run 400 metres more, I saw a group of boys standing opposite one of my disciples' houses. One white boy was so excited to see me running. "Oh, Sri Chinmoy!" he said.

A black boy said, "No good, he takes away everybody's money."

The white boy said, "No, my father said he is a saint like our Christian saints. He never charges any money."

I didn't want to enter into their conversation, so I just kept going.

RB 84. *The missing water bottle*

At night, one of my disciples was driving us along the route where one of my spiritual daughters, A., was going to run thirteen miles the next morning, so we could leave bottles of water there. She was saying that she wanted to get rid of all her old running shoes. Another of my spiritual daughters, B., who was in the car with us, said, "Why do you have to get rid of them?

There will be many people to buy them." But she used some American slang expression.

A. said, "Nobody will buy my shoes."

B. said, "Why don't you give them to Casey to sell in his flea market? People will be happy to buy running shoes at a cheap price."

A. put bottles of water at the three-mile, five-mile and six-mile marks. On the bottles it was written, "This bottle is for a runner. Please do not remove!" or something like that.

The next morning A. was supposed to start running at six o'clock. At five o'clock I was out running along the same route. A little before the three mile mark, I said to myself, "Let me go and see whether the bottle is still there." I knew she had put it near the sidewalk at the base of a drinking fountain. I stopped there to look, but the bottle was not there. "Wonderful, wonderful" I thought sadly. "Somebody has removed it."

I was about to start running again on the street when one of my inner beings said, "My Lord, please run on the sidewalk." I didn't ask why. After 100 metres, right at the 1,500-metre mark on the sidewalk, I saw the bottle standing straight up. Someone had removed the bottle and put it on the sidewalk. Had my inner being not asked me to run on the sidewalk, I would not have seen the bottle since it was quite dark.

I picked up the bottle and ran back to put it in the original place. Then I continued my run.

RB 85. *Seven dollars talks*

At the four-mile mark I saw a middle-aged, innocent looking lady in trouble. She was having problems with her Volkswagen and had opened the hood. She said, "Can you give me a hand?"

O God, I know nothing about cars. I said, "I know nothing about mechanics, but please wait. In ten minutes I will be able to send you my chauffeur." She didn't understand my English, so I said, "My driver, my driver."

Then I began running quite fast to look for a telephone booth to call the disciple who drives me around. After 200 metres, I saw an ambulance driver asleep in his ambulance. As soon as I passed him he woke up and said, "Hey, such a beautiful, cool morning. Don't you know how to enjoy sleep? You woke me up."

I said, "Friend, can you do me a favour? A girl is having trouble with her car."

He said, "Pretty girl?"

I said, "Middle-aged lady." This man was a real joker. I never carry money when I run, but this time I happened to have seven dollars with me. I gave him the money, and the seven dollars talked. He immediately turned on the motor and made a wrong turn down a one-way street heading towards the lady. When I saw him finally talking to the lady, I said, "Now I have done my part. He is a joker, but he will fix her car." So I continued running.

RB 86. *The policeman*

Twenty metres away from the five-mile mark there was a parked police car with two policemen in it. One of them was asleep. The other one said to me, "Sir, how I wish I didn't have duty at this hour. Why don't you go and rest? Why do you have to run at this hour?"

I said, "I enjoy it."

He asked, "Where are you going?"

I answered, "Somebody has put water at this spot to drink."

The policeman said, "Don't you want to drink it? Aren't you thirsty?"

I said, "No, I am not thirsty."

"Go home and sleep," he said.

RB 87. *A great runner*

When I had run another mile and a half, I stopped for a second or two. Immediately a tiny dog came and sat by my right foot, wanting me to caress it and give it a little kindness. I never do this kind of thing, but this time I bent a little to touch the dog's head. The owner, who was bald-headed, wearing a grey coat, came over to me and said, "My Dolly has fallen in love with you."

I kept caressing the dog. The owner said, "Dolly, do you want to become a great runner like this gentleman?"

I said, "How I wish I could become a great runner!"

RB 88. *The mysterious hat*

On my way back I wanted to see if the first bottle of water was still there. I was wearing my Pepsi Cola Bicycle Marathon hat and I put it under the bottle to see if my spiritual daughter A. would find it. Later, A. told me that some crazy person had put a hat under her water bottle and she had just left it there. Her intuition wasn't working. I didn't tell her whose hat it was.

RB 89. *The show-off*

I had just started running very slowly and I passed a little boy about six years old playing with his older brother on 150th Street. The younger boy said, "What are you doing? Just showing off?"

His older brother said to him, "Don't say that. He is a very great man."

The younger one said, "My daddy is far greater."

The older boy said, "Our daddy is not as great as he is."

The younger one said, "No, he is just showing off."

"Don't say that, don't say that, don't say that!" the older one told him.

When I was coming back after covering one mile, the two children were still playing. The little one again said to me, "You are just showing off. Go home, go home!"

The older brother got furious and shouted, "Don't say that! Don't say that! Don't say that!"

RB 90. *The priest*

As I was running by Queensboro Hall, a very big building on Queens Boulevard, I saw a priest crossing the street in front of me. He was about 60 years old and wearing a black robe. Suddenly he said, "Damn you!"

I stopped and said, "Father, why do you swear?"

The priest said, "Why not? All the time I see people like you running, running, running. Why don't you run inwardly? You don't believe in Heaven? By running in the street, do you think you will be able to go to Heaven?"

I was in a joking mood so I said to the priest, "I will find Heaven everywhere except inside your tongue."

He said, "Who are you, after all?"

"I am an ordinary man," I answered. "As you see, I am just a runner."

The priest said, "Why do you have to run?"

I said, "I am getting ready for the New York Marathon."

"You dark fool!" he shouted. "Look at your head, look at your head."

"It seems I have more hair than you," I said.

He said, "Like you, thousands and thousands of fools will be running in the New York Marathon. Go back to your running. I shall pray for your salvation."

I said, "Perhaps you need salvation more desperately than I do."

Then the priest swore again, "Damn you!" and crossed himself.

RB 91. *The queue*

The journey to Greece, where I was going to run the marathon, took about nine hours. For me to sit for that long on a plane — especially with my right leg problems — was a difficult task. At one point, I got up to go to the bathroom. I was standing in line for about fifteen minutes but the line did not move. So very gently I was stretching my right leg while standing.

An elderly lady saw me and came up to me. "I am sure you are going for the marathon," she said. "Look, my husband too is going for the marathon."

Then she called her husband over and introduced me to him. I had a long talk with him. He came from Cleveland, and this was going to be his seventeenth marathon. Sixteen times he had run, but this was going to be his first time in Greece. He told me his time in his first marathon was 4:17. Now he does it in three hours or 3:15.

He was advising me to do hill work. "You must do hill work if you want to become a good runner. Nobody can become a good runner without doing hill work. If you want to increase your speed, if you want to strengthen your legs, if you want to have long strides, then hill work is the only answer."

I thanked him deeply.

RB 92. *The Philadelphia man*

Then, at the airport in Athens, a tall, fat gentleman came up to me and caught me by the shoulder.

He said, "Friend, are you going to run the marathon?" I smiled at him.

Then he said, "I am going to run. I come from Philadelphia."

I said, "Philadelphia gave me a very sad experience. I went to Philadelphia to run the marathon."

He said he was also there and gave up after thirteen miles. I said, "At twenty-one miles I gave up."

So in the same marathon where I gave up after twenty-one miles, he gave up after thirteen miles.

He had run one other marathon somewhere else, he told me; his timing was five and a half hours. So my ego came forward. I said, "I am not so bad." O God, in two more days what would happen!

Then we talked for a long time. Since my timing is a little better than his, I felt quite at ease talking to him.

Then the Cleveland man came up and joined our conversation. He was very sincere; he was not bragging, only advising us what to do.

RB 93. *My Japanese companion*

My first evening in Greece I went out to run. It seems that taxi drivers and car owners there are insane, especially at night. How badly they drive!

At every moment you are at their mercy, even in the park. I don't know how, but they manage to drive right into the park itself. There is no street or anything; far from it. But they drive right into the park, and so speedily. Then they leave their cars there while they go to a party or some place. And we are trying to run there!

Inside the park an old Japanese man — very short, very skinny — started following me as I was running. I thought I was shorter than the shortest, but he was practically at my shoulder. And he was very old.

With such affection, such affection, he started running with me. Then we started talking. He told me all about his running experiences. I was very happy.

He was about 70 years old and he said he had come all the way from Japan for the marathon.

He was staying at the same hotel that I was. There were quite a few Japanese staying there. They all had come to run.

The following day also we ran together. I always make complaints about my strides, but his strides were shorter than mine. I ran two miles with him, very slowly.

I saw him once more after the marathon. He took seven hours and fifteen or twenty minutes. He was so delighted that he had completed it. Who would not be proud of him!

RB 94. *Looking over the battlefield*

Later that day, which was the day before the marathon, I took a cab and went to the marathon starting point. I was disappointed, frightened, to say the least, when I saw the whole course.

I said, "Since I came all the way, best thing is to die on the battlefield."

But when you are in the car, the battlefield is not a real battlefield. Only when you start running, when you are on the ground, is it a real battlefield.

When I saw it in the car, I still had a little hope that I would be able to manage it. Secretly I had a little hope that I would be able to finish it. O God, the actual day was something else!

RB 95. *Well-wishes from a friend*

About ten minutes before the race, my Cleveland friend all of a sudden came up to me. He didn't say hello or anything; he just grabbed my hand and started shaking my hand.

He is a far better runner; I was so honoured.

Then he started giving me advice. He said, "You have to drink a lot, drink a lot."

It was so hot — really very, very hot. Everybody had told me that the weather would be very cold. But no, it was really hot.

So my Cleveland friend said, "Drink a lot, drink a lot; otherwise, you won't be able to make it."

My Philadelphia friend — God knows where he was! But he would appear very soon.

RB 96. *Caught by surprise*

They started the race at least two minutes early. Believe me, my New York time I always keep perfect, and I had got the New York time transferred into Greek time. But they started at least two minutes early.

Many people were surprised. They were just chatting and all of a sudden they heard a sound: "Boom!" Many people were murmuring, "It is not time, it is not time." But we ran.

RB 97. *The loop*

After two miles there was a loop that brought you back again to the main road. Look at their divine stupidity! Instead of making the loop cross the main road further up, they brought it back so it overlapped the first part of the route.

Some were running at a five-minute pace, and others were running at a 13-minute pace. So the fast runners who were finishing the loop were blocked by the slow runners who hadn't reached the loop. They could not go fast because we were blocking the way. I felt sorry for them.

After two miles I saw my Cleveland friend. I was only 200 or 300 metres inside the loop, and he was completing it. He was practically 1,200 metres ahead of me. He had made the loop, but he was being blocked by the slow runners. He was almost furious. I don't know, but his face was not normal at that time. Even then, when he saw me he waved. I was so grateful to him.

Now the fool in me — I don't know how or why — also started running fast. When it was three miles, my time was under 21 minutes. I said, "Is it possible?"

When I completed the loop, I looked back and, O God, there were so many people behind me — hundreds of people. At that time all my pride came to the fore! "I am a great runner, because so many people are behind me." I thought some had not even come to the loop. "I am completing three miles and, God knows, still they haven't completed two miles." And at least 300 or 400 were way ahead; God knows where they were.

But I felt sorry for the excellent runners, because they had to cross through the bad runners like us. We were disturbing them on the way.

RB 98. *Terrible! Terrible!*

As soon as I reached five and a half miles, I saw the first hill. For at least 1,200 metres it went up. It was not yet six miles, so still I had strength.

The next 200 metres were not downhill but flat, and then again it went up for practically half a mile. Next it went down — this time not even for 100 metres — and again up.

Like this, when I came to nine miles, I felt miserable. I said, "What am I going to do?" Luckily, at that time it went downhill for about 800 metres. I was so delighted, so happy; at last there was an oasis in the desert.

O God, after 800 metres it went up again.

From five and a half it started, and for the next fourteen miles it was only hills. And you won't believe me, but there were no downhills. At most it would be flat for 100 or 200 metres and then it went up, up, up. There were three hills that were at least, *at least*, one mile long.

People were cursing and dying.

One young man was lying right on the street — not on the sidewalk but right on the street — massaging his knee and saying, "Never in this lifetime will I run again." Terrible! Terrible!

RB 99. *Some fast walkers*

Some were running fifty metres and walking fifty metres. You won't believe it, but three elderly men walked faster than I could run. I was running — "Huh, huh!" — and they were walking, but my running was not as good as their walking.

One of them was mischievous enough to laugh at me. He was laughing at me because I was running and he was beating me while walking. But after two miles I saw him; he had become so tired that he went to drink ERG or water, and he did not appear for a long time.

RB 100. *Quick, quick, quick*

There were runners poorer than me. I felt sorry for them. And the people who were going ahead of me, I was admiring like anything. No jealousy, absolutely none! I was adoring them. It was an impossible task they were performing.

Sometimes old people — at least ten or fifteen years older than me — were going ahead of me. There was no competitive spirit on my part; only my admiration was coming forward. "These people are older than me and look how they are doing." They had such short strides — about half the length of my strides — but quick, quick, quick.

RB 101. *The exerciser*

One man was running with his wife. Every fifty metres she stopped and twisted herself. She bent down, touched her toes and did all kinds of stretching exercises. Then for fifty metres she would run again. Each time I would pass her while she was stretching, but when they ran they caught up with me. When they ran, they ran fast. This went on. Finally they stopped or fell behind me.

RB 102. *Ruhhh, ruhhh, the motor man*

One man was following me for at least two or three miles making noise: "Ruhhh, ruhhh, ruhhh." People around him were laughing at him. "Ruhhh, ruhhh." For three miles he went on making that noise.

I didn't have the capacity to go ahead of him, and I didn't want to decrease the little speed that I had. So I said, "No, let me go at my own pace."

For about three miles, he went on making that noise. Then afterwards he disappeared. He didn't go ahead of me; perhaps he stopped running.

RB 103. *The Philadelphia man's victory*

At about eleven miles, I heard somebody screaming my name. It was my Philadelphia friend. He knew my name, Ghose, and had remembered it. He was inside the bus that was carrying the dying soldiers, and he was waving at me. He had won his "victory".

After eighteen miles there was another bus. All together, there were two or three buses carrying those who had dropped out. Another bus invited me to enter, but I said, "No! It is better to die."

RB 104. *The chorus*

At eighteen miles my first attack came: my hamstring revolted.

When it was twenty-one miles, out of the blue, five songs I heard all at once. It was absolutely a chorus; the music was on! How can I get five cramps at a time? The pain was excruciating. I was helpless, flat, dead! Some of the disciples were helping me. One of them was seated and, with a sponge, was pressing my leg with cold water, while another was pushing my toes forward. How hard, how quickly, the first one was massaging me! And afterwards, four or five times he did it again. Even now it frightens me when I think of the pain — excruciating!

After that experience I started walking. Slower than the slowest, a quarter mile I walked. Again the pain, so again I walked.

Running is forbidden now. Just walk, walk as slowly as possible. When it was twenty-three miles, another new friend came — right here in the neck. I couldn't breathe in; neither nostril was functioning.

O God, this was really unbearable! With the previous pain, at least I was able to breathe in, so I felt that there was something going on. But when it started in this muscle, I was not able to breathe even. Too much, too much!

Some people — I think, nurses — came up, but we didn't take their help. I said, "I have got my help."

When it was twenty-five miles, a strong desire arose: "Oh, let me run at least the last mile." It was a desire, nothing else. As soon as I tried, all the cramps said to me, "Where are you going? We are still alive." Such pain!

I thought 800 metres, 400 metres, 100 metres I would run. Finally, when it was only twenty metres, the officials were asking me to run. I tried, but I knew if I had run, I would have dropped right there and fainted, so I just dragged myself. I wasn't even walking — just dragging my body. Anyway, I managed to finish.

RB 105. *Stop!*

The management of the race was far from perfection. Sometimes the water stations were on the right side of the street, sometimes they were on the left side. It didn't bother me, because my disciples were supplying me with ERG. But others I saw. Sometimes they were running on this side of the street and they had to cross to the other side.

And a horrible thing! They allowed the vehicles to run along the same route. After eleven miles it was so difficult to run. When we had only six miles left, we had to run in the city of Athens. There it was infinitely worse.

You are running this way when, all of a sudden, from the side street cars will enter. Policemen hold the runners and let the cars pass. Here we are dying to reach the destination one minute sooner, and the policeman will say: "Stop!"

RB 106. *The rogue*

After I finished, I waited around for practically an hour. I was enjoying watching the people coming in after me. I thought that I was one of the most unfortunate runners, but people kept coming in.

One man who came in was a rogue. He was about sixty. He came in quite fresh and did three somersaults. He was so happy.

He was jumping — one, two, three. Most of the people didn't believe that he had run the whole course. His number was missing, but he said that he had the number. God knows!

RB 107. *Brrrr!*

This morning I left about a quarter to four to go running. I ran a few blocks without gloves or a hat. After 500 or 600 metres, I was absolutely frozen to death. I went back home and got my gloves and hat, and then I went out again to run. How difficult to run in such cold!

RB 108. *"Stop, my son!"*

The day before yesterday, in the evening, I was running on 150th Street, near the bus stop. An old lady affectionately said to me, "Stop, stop!" so I stopped. Then, with such affection she said, "My son, my son, cold, cold, cold!" She had on a heavy winter coat and fur hat. I gave her a very broad smile and continued running.

RB 109. *The garbage-can man*

I was running around four-thirty in the morning when I saw a tall, thin black man was running ahead of me. When he saw a garbage can, he went over to it, removed the cover and threw it onto the owner's lawn. Then he went on to the next one. After he did this to four houses I said, "O God, I am not going to run with him," and I went in another direction.

RB 110. *The lost taxi driver*

When I was running on the Grand Central service road near Jamaica High School, a taxi driver very pathetically asked me how to find Atlantic Avenue.

I am the one who never knows anything about giving directions. I said to myself, "O God, save me, save me!" Then I said to the taxi driver, "Make a right turn and go to Jamaica Avenue, and then ask people there how to go to Atlantic Avenue."

The driver said, "I see the Van Wyck Expressway and Atlantic Avenue when I come from Kennedy Airport."

I said, "Yes, you have to make a right turn."

I was so proud of myself that I was able to give him the correct information.

RB 111. *The mockers*

About a week ago I was running near the Jamaica High School track. Some mischievous boys on their way to Thomas Edison Vocational and Technical High School called out with tremendous mockery, "There he goes: the great spiritual Master!" It was not with any kind of good feeling that they were saying this.

RB 112. *The big man*

Today B. was running on a street near my house. A neighbour noticed that she was wearing our new *Sri Chinmoy Marathon Runner* shirt, and he said to her, "So, the big man is preparing for the marathon too?"

RB 113. *The sub-three marathoner*

Today one of the disciples was telling me that he met a very good runner while running in Flushing Meadow Park. This man had told the disciple that he often sees me running and that he thought I was a sub-three-hour marathoner because I was so thin and I looked like I was in such good shape. The disciple was very polite and told the runner that I was hoping to break three and a half hours in the New York Marathon. He didn't tell him my previous bullock-cart marathon times.

RB 114. *The devoted jogger*

Yesterday while I was running on 150th Street I saw a girl of 14 or 15 also running. When she came near me, she said, "Sri Chinmoy." Then she gave me a big smile, folded her hands and stopped running. After I ran past her, she continued her running.

RB 115. *The lost child*

Right after I passed the young girl runner, a little child came up to me and asked how to find 140th Street. He was lost. When I told him which way to go, he ran in that direction very fast.

RB 116. *Well-wishes from the bus driver*

That afternoon I went shopping to bring back some food for the disciples. When I entered into the bus, the driver said to me, "Why didn't you run this morning? What were you doing?"

He was a very nice, bearded black man. I said, "Are you talking to me?"

The driver said, "Yes. Every day I see you running before five o'clock in the morning. I see you at least two or three times every day, but I have not seen you for a couple of days. What is wrong with you?"

I explained, "I am relaxing before the New York Marathon."

He said, "Good luck! I see you don't give a damn about cold or rain. People enter into my bus cold and frozen and I save them, but I see you running in such cold. For the last couple of days I have not seen you."

I said, "This is on my route, but recently I have been running very few miles."

When I was leaving the bus he said, "Lots of luck to you."

RB 117. *A gentlemanly bow*

I was about to cross the street when a small school bus stopped in the middle of the street. One of the disciples saw me waiting there and came running to carry my bags. Then I saw a thin man take off his hat and bow down. This kind of thing only the Harry who works at P.S. 86 used to do. When I came nearer I saw that it was Harry, so I also bowed down.

RB 118. *The Con Edison worker*

When I was running early in the morning, a little after five o'clock, I saw a fat, black Con Edison man working near C.'s house. I heard someone call out, "Guru?" absolutely the same way the disciples call my name. Then I saw it was the Con Edison worker.

What is a Con Edison man doing calling me like that?

Who is my disciple in Con Edison?

RB 119. *The sanctioned prayer*

Quite often I see the two soldiers, H. and T., running along the street. As soon as H. sees me, even at a distance, he puts his right hand on his heart. T. either folds his hands or gives me a smile. H. smiles through his eyes and T. smiles through his teeth.

Today I was returning home after running only one mile. When I had only five hundred metres left, I saw someone running very fast on the other side of the street. In silence I said to him, "I am not envying you. Go ahead." I looked carefully and saw it was T. But this time he didn't greet me. I thought, "Had it been H., he would have greeted me."

As usual I was going very slowly, at my Indian bullock cart speed, so T. passed me and continued on his way. When I finished, I saw somebody practically hiding at the foot of a tree across the street. He gave me the biggest smile and folded his hands. I said, "My prayer has been sanctioned." It was T.

RB 120. *An invitational run*

While I was in Japan, I was running in a park. At one point I saw ten or twelve American boys about to run short distances. The coach, a Japanese, said to me, "Come along. Run with us."

I said, "No, I can't run with you. You will run fast. I am running long-distance."

So I watched them. They were starting with one hundred or two hundred metre dashes. It was their morning run. Every day they run and many people in the park watch them. Their strides are quite good.

RB 121. *Dogs are everywhere*

When I ran during my second day in Japan, there were many, many people in the park. At one point I said, "Here is the place where I will not be disturbed by dogs." In two minutes I saw a gentleman running with his dog on a leash. He bowed to me and I saluted him.

RB 122. *The Japanese tradition*

That morning I ran about six miles. During the run at least twenty other runners I encountered along the way bowed to me in the traditional Japanese manner. Ten or twelve times I also bowed to them. But after that it was too much for me. When they bowed I would just raise my hand to salute them.

Then, when I was really tired, I saw an old lady about sixty years old running. She bowed down, and in her case I felt that I had to bow down also.

RB 123. *The Madras run*

When I was in Madras, I ran twelve miles in the Madras heat. Afterwards, I went to a store to get some soda.

One, two, three, four, five, six sodas I drank one by one. The owner laughed and laughed.

I said to him, "Why are you laughing? You go and run twelve miles!"

He said, "I won't be able to run even half a mile."

RB 124. *Harry runs, you jog*

Yesterday, around five o'clock, I ran three miles. Two out of the three miles were hill work. After the hill work, I wanted to run one more mile to make three miles.

An old man waiting for the bus saw me and said, "Oh, you look like my friend Harry, only he is taller than you. But you are not running; you are jogging. My friend Harry runs, but you are not running."

RB 125. *The miserable runner*

When K. sees me running, at least she smiles at me. V. is so horrible. Either she ignores me or, if she looks at me, she won't smile.

The other day I saw V. and, as usual, she did not smile. A few minutes later I saw K. and she did smile. When V. runs she is not irritated, but she is miserable. Once I even shouted at her when I saw her running, but still she ignored me!

RB 126. *Mistaken identity*

The more I practise the slower I become. So I decided to cut down on my distance and only practise speed work.

Today I started my speed work. This morning I was running a very short distance, and in front of C.'s house I saw someone who looked exactly like T.

I said, "T., T., T." three times. Then I said to myself, "It can't be T. If I call him three times, how is it that he won't answer? The strange thing is that he didn't even nod. I came near him and, O God, it was a different person.

RB 127. *My puddle experience*

Last winter I ran fourteen miles with four members of my road crew. After four or five miles I said to two of them, "You go ahead and clear the snow." After one hundred metres, one of the two could not keep up with the other, so like a gentleman he slowed down and ran with us.

After five miles, one of the boys running with me became tired and didn't want to run any farther. While I was barking at him, I ran into a puddle. For five or six steps it was so cold! Such agony!

When we completed seven miles, that same disciple said, "Now can we go?" I said to him, "We will take a taxi," but in the back of my mind I knew we would run another seven miles.

Now, one of the boys was wise. He saw a diner. So he said, "I wonder if they have hot chocolate." Three of them stopped and had a hot chocolate, and then we started running again. The disciple who had said he was tired was running behind us. All of a sudden he became inspired and started going ahead. So I barked at him. "Either run fifty metres behind me or ahead." Again, I ran into the same puddle going back the other way.

Two or three miles later I saw that disciple and another of the disciples. They had taken off their jackets and left them on the street. People didn't care for their jackets, so they picked them up on the way back.

RB 65. *(p.37)* 31 August 1979
RB 66. *(p.37)* 2 September 1979
RB 67. *(p.38)* 3 September 1979
RB 68. *(p.38)* 5 September 1979
RB 69. *(p.38)* 21 September 1979
RB 70. *(p.39)* 21 September 1979
RB 71. *(p.39)* 21 September 1979
RB 72. *(p.40)* 23 September 1979
RB 73. *(p.41)* 23 September 1979
RB 74. *(p.41)* 23 September 1979
RB 75. *(p.42)* 26 September 1979
RB 76. *(p.42)* 26 September 1979
RB 77. *(p.42)* 26 September 1979
RB 78. *(p.43)* 26 September 1979
RB 79. *(p.43)* 26 September 1979
RB 80. *(p.44)* 29 September 1979
RB 81. *(p.44)* 29 September 1979
RB 82. *(p.45)* 29 September 1979
RB 83. *(p.45)* 29 September 1979
RB 84. *(p.45)* 29 September 1979
RB 85. *(p.46)* 29 September 1979
RB 86. *(p.47)* 29 September 1979
RB 87. *(p.48)* 29 September 1979
RB 88. *(p.48)* 29 September 1979
RB 89. *(p.48)* 30 September 1979
RB 90. *(p.49)* 30 September 1979
RB 91. *(p.50)* 7 October 1979
RB 92. *(p.51)* 7 October 1979
RB 93. *(p.51)* 7 October 1979
RB 94. *(p.52)* 7 October 1979

RB 95. *(p.53)* 7 October 1979
RB 96. *(p.53)* 7 October 1979
RB 97. *(p.53)* 7 October 1979
RB 98. *(p.54)* 7 October 1979
RB 99. *(p.55)* 7 October 1979
RB 100. *(p.55)* 7 October 1979
RB 101. *(p.56)* 7 October 1979
RB 102. *(p.56)* 7 October 1979
RB 103. *(p.57)* 7 October 1979
RB 104. *(p.57)* 7 October 1979
RB 105. *(p.58)* 7 October 1979
RB 106. *(p.59)* 7 October 1979
RB 107. *(p.59)* 11 October 1979
RB 108. *(p.59)* 16 October 1979
RB 109. *(p.60)* 16 October 1979
RB 110. *(p.60)* 16 October 1979
RB 111. *(p.60)* 16 October 1979
RB 112. *(p.61)* 16 October 1979
RB 113. *(p.61)* 16 October 1979
RB 114. *(p.61)* 18 October 1979
RB 115. *(p.61)* 18 October 1979
RB 116. *(p.62)* 18 October 1979
RB 117. *(p.62)* 18 October 1979
RB 118. *(p.63)* 18 October 1979
RB 119. *(p.63)* 19 October 1979
RB 120. *(p.64)* 1 November 1979
RB 121. *(p.64)* 1 November 1979
RB 122. *(p.64)* 1 November 1979
RB 123. *(p.65)* 1 November 1979
RB 124. *(p.65)* 18 November 1979
RB 125. *(p.65)* 24 November 1979
RB 126. *(p.66)* 24 November 1979
RB 127. *(p.66)* 24 November 1979

RUN AND BECOME, BECOME AND RUN

PART 3

The other night, Sudhir, Scott, Casey, Peter and I ran fourteen miles. After four or five miles I said, "You go ahead and clear the snow."

Scott and Casey are "excellent" runners, so it was Sudhir and Peter who went ahead. After one hundred metres, Peter could not keep up with Sudhir, so like a gentleman he started running with Scott, Casey and me.

After five miles Casey was tired; he didn't want to run anymore. While I was barking at him to keep running, I entered into a puddle. For five or six steps, it was so cold. Such agony!

Then we went on and completed seven miles. Casey said, "How can we get back?" I said, "We will take a taxi," but in the back of my mind I knew we would run back — another seven miles.

Scott is wise. He saw a diner and he said he was wondering if they had hot chocolate. Secretly he was hoping I would say to stop.

We turned back. Only Scott, Casey and Sudhir were still with me. Casey was behind us. All of a sudden he got inspiration and he wanted to go ahead. I started barking at him, "Either be at least fifty metres ahead, or stay behind." While barking at him, again I entered into the same puddle which I had run through going the other way.

Sudhir was very nice, always running far ahead of us. After two or three miles, I saw Casey and Sudhir putting on their jackets. They had taken them off on the way and left them by the side of the street. Luckily, people didn't care for their jackets, so Casey and Sudhir got them on the way back.

RB 129. *Mother and daughter*

When I was little, my mother used to give me money if I had eaten my food. If Madhuri takes most delicious things to Radha and tells her it will give her more strength, then Radha will become bigger than Madhuri. Then Madhuri can defeat her. If Madhuri feeds her, Radha will become three times as fat as her mother. Then it will be easy for Madhuri to defeat her.

During the New York Marathon, Radha saw me twenty times. Her stride was useless, but she had such determination to go ahead of me. She was absolutely grinding her teeth, and she did defeat me.

RB 130. *A new theory*

After running, now I walk one mile. I like it very much. I have formed a new theory that if you walk fast, you will have more stamina and you will be able to run better.

RB 131. *First among the girls*

Yesterday, while running by the canal in Honolulu, I saw Susan the Great first among the girls.

Susan is a great runner. She went ahead of me. Madhuri and Annette were right behind her by the canal, but I didn't see them.

Before I greeted Susan, I looked at the time. It was four minutes to six. I said, "How can she do this? She is not allowed to run alone until after six o'clock."

Then, ten metres behind, I saw the other two I said, "All right."

RB 132. *One good competitor*

I am so proud of myself. An old man was running about fifty metres ahead of me. I said, "I have to prove I am a good runner." Then I went far ahead of him.

After each minute I looked behind to see if he was catching up to me. But no, he was getting even farther behind. When I reached the end of the canal, he was still staggering.

I said, "At least I have one good competitor."

RB 133. *Got a match?*

I was running at about five o'clock by the canal. A young boy came up to me and asked me for a match. Then he asked if I had a cigarette. I just smiled at him.

RB 134. *The lost runner*

Yesterday, while running near my hotel in Hawaii, I got lost for about fifteen minutes. Then again today, I got lost for about twenty minutes. But now I won't make a mistake. I know the name of the street well. If I can remember the name of my sister Lily, then I will remember the street name. Previously, I tried to remember where my hotel was by the small house with two trees in front. But then I saw that four or five houses had two trees in the front yard.

RB 135. *The look-alike*

I think people run on alternate days. The day before yesterday, many people ran. Then again today, there were many people. Some disciples run so fast.

One lady looked from a distance like Ila. She really looked like Ila and I was about to call, "Ila!" But then I saw it was somebody else.

RB 136. *The fast runner*

I wonder if some people are clever like me. When they see I am coming, they go fast. That's what I do when I see some people. I don't want them to see that I am running so slowly, so when I come near them — about thirty metres away — I increase my speed. I keep this speed for about twenty metres after I pass them. Then, when I think they are out of sight, I slow down.

RB 137. *The tennis shoes*

Today, my bad luck started right from early in the morning. I have two pairs of running shoes, but they were all inside the car. So I was running in my tennis shoes. My tennis shoes are heavy. They kept striking the ground while I was running, hurting me like anything.

I ran five and a half miles. Then I said, "Why run anymore?" Then I walked two miles.

RB 138. *Doing his duty*

When I went out to run, about 4:30 in the morning, the man at the hotel desk was doing his duty — absolutely in the other world. I opened the door very quietly, and he was still in the other world.

RB 139. *Morning blessing*

Even around four-thirty in the morning, people bless me. Old people will walk side by side, holding tiny flashlights, and not permit me to run past them.

RB 140. *The friendly runner*

Before the start of our five-mile race, a black man said to me, "So good to see you." Afterwards, when I was at the two-and-a-half mile point and he was at the same spot completing four miles, he greeted me again.

RB 141. *Incognito*

The other day in Hawaii, we were eating at the Pancake House. A man and his wife were sitting in the next booth. The man was talking about the Sri Chinmoy Marathon.

I looked at Ranjana to say that I was facing him, but he didn't know it was me. Ranjana was whispering to Lucy about it, but the man still didn't recognise me. He must have been reading someone's T-shirt.

RB 142. *Today you are running*

Today I was running and somebody said to me, "Oh, today you are running and not jogging."

That means every day I jog.

RB 143. *You look fine!*

An hour later, I was running to the tennis court. A young boy was standing there, holding some books. He was about seventeen or eighteen years old.

He said, "Guru, you look fine. Guru, you look fine." Then he noticed a tennis racquet in my hand. "Oh, you play tennis as well?"

RB 144. *A dog's life*

This morning around 5:30, a lady came out of her house with a little dog. I was going down 150th Street, running very slowly. She said, "Hi!" Then I said, "Hi." She said, "I was talking to my dog, not you."

I went on running. About fifteen minutes later, as I was running very slowly up the hill, I saw the same lady in her front yard. I didn't pay any attention to her. I didn't want to be insulted by her again.

She said, "Hi!" This time I absolutely remained silent. She said, "What is the matter with you? You don't know how to talk?"

This was my morning blessing. I thought she was saying "Hi" to me, but her dog is better than I am. Then she insulted me again, fifteen minutes later. This is how the lady blessed me.

RB 145. *Why are you quitting?*

Two hours later, when I was running again, I ran only 800 metres. A middle-aged man said, "I just started. Why are you quitting?"

I said, "I am very tired." He had just started running, and I was stopping.

RB 146. *Six hooligan cars*

Yesterday, at two o'clock in the morning in Queens, I was walking very fast. Six cars — not one, but six — were bothering me like anything. They were driven by young boys, blacks and Puerto Ricans. They were going against the light and going the wrong way down a one-way street. They were screaming and doing all kinds of absurd things.

Then they drove onto the sidewalk to bother me. So I tried to get the license numbers. Then they got frightened and said, "Sorry, sorry, we won't do it anymore."

RB 147. *The smiling runner*

Savita was smiling all the time during the marathon. Usually, when you see people running, you can tell who are the helpers: they are the ones smiling. But Savita smiled for twenty-six miles.

RB 148. *Hashi's blessing*

For fifty metres during the inspiration Marathon, I was blessing Hashi like anything. How? I was ten or fifteen metres behind her. Each time I saw her shadow, bang! I put my left foot on her head. For fifty metres I did it. It was at the twelve-mile point.

I was ten or fifteen metres behind her. She is so short, but her shadow was quite long. Then, the second time Hashi started running with me, she went so fast.

RB 149. *Two competitors*

In the Vermont Inspiration Marathon, the first time I saw Gangadhar, at sixteen miles, he was smiling. Simon was behind him. The second time I saw them, Simon was ahead of Gangadhar. Simon was so happy that he was ahead and had taken the lead.

When I started running at the twenty-one mile mark, I saw Simon again. He was very glad to see me and said, "Guru, Guru, Guru!" Gangadhar was nowhere near him. I was always waiting to see if I would hear Gangadhar's footsteps, and I kept looking around. But the only footsteps I heard behind me were not a man's. It was Prataya. Gangadhar was walking.

Then I saw that husband and wife were going together — Gayatri was inspiring him.

The first time I saw him at sixteen miles, he was quite happy. Then at twenty-one miles, he was not smiling, but Simon was so happy.

RB 150. *I run and they run*

I was on 150th Street, returning from my morning run. I had just passed a few of my girl disciples.

As I was approaching the bus stop, a woman with thickly painted lipstick said to me, "Master, Master, why do you have to run? Why can't your disciples run for you?"

I smiled at her and said, "I run and they run too."

Had one of the disciples whom I had just passed run by at that moment, I could have said to the woman, "Here is the proof. I am running, and they are running too."

How do these people know me? I'm sure this lady was Puerto Rican, or else she wouldn't have used the term "Master."

RB 151. *Hello or something*

When I was coming back from my walk, I saw an elderly man waiting for the bus. As I was approaching him, he said "Hello," or something. I didn't pay any attention. Then he said, "Why are you so nasty? I said hello to you. You can't say hello?"

RB 152. *Why are you walking?*

Yesterday morning I was walking at about 5 o'clock. A middle-aged man saw me two different times. He asked, "Why are you walking and not running?" I gave him a smile.

RB 153. *You look so beautiful*

Yesterday, around eight o'clock, I was walking quite fast when an elderly lady came out of her house. Who she is, God knows. She must live on that street, but I had never seen her before.

She said, "Sri, you look so beautiful."

Five or six steps passed before I said, "Thank you," but by that time she didn't hear.

RB 154. *Go home*

This morning I was walking, and Scott and Casey were clearing the road. Snow and water were all over, and I felt sorry for them. So I told them, "I am going home. You go home too!"

RB 155. *God speaks through me*

Sometimes God speaks through me. This morning God saved me. Otherwise, I would have been proved a liar.

At seven o'clock I went out to run. O God, with such difficulty I ran one mile. When I was nearing the starting line again, an old man shouted, "Hey! Good morning!" He was screaming and looking around.

I thought to myself, "Perhaps he is just looking around and not speaking to me." But again he screamed, "Hey! Good morning!" So I answered, "Good morning."

He had a cane. Next he shouted, "Come here!"

O my God, morning command has come! He was commanding me, "You help me cross the street. I was waiting for the bus, but the bus wouldn't stop for me."

He was on the wrong side of the street. Why should the bus stop or go on the wrong side to get him? He was an old man of about 80 and he walked very slowly as I helped him across the street. He said, "What is your name?" in a commanding way.

I said, "Ghose!"

"Ghose? I had a friend named Ghose. He is dead."

I said, "I am alive."

After we crossed the street, he commanded, "Now you wait with me here until the bus arrives." I have to wait for the Sunday bus? But if I say no, then where is my sympathetic heart? So I said, "I can do something else. I have many students here. I will send one of my students in three minutes."

"Three minutes?" he said.

"Five minutes," I promised. "In five minutes one of my students will be here to wait with you."

He said he had to get breakfast on Sutphin Boulevard and then go out shopping. On Sunday, what kind of shopping will he do? Anyway I had promised to send someone in five minutes, but I was unable to walk even. I was getting such pain!

I tried to run, but as soon as I took two or three steps, I saw a car come and stop in front of the old man. It was Nathan, and Vinaya was driving. So God speaks through me.

I shouted to them, "Stop!" but they had already stopped. I asked them to take him for breakfast. As I am lame, the old man could barely get into the car. Finally, Nathan took his leg and lifted it into the front.

The old man never believed that I would send someone. He thought that I would just go home, but I would have called Ashrita to get someone. He didn't believe me, but God wanted him to see my sincerity.

This man lives in Ranjana's building, behind her apartment.

RB 156. *The lady and her dog*

While I was running, I saw an old lady and her dog. The old lady was walking the dog, and the dog was on a leash. The dog came up to me, as usual, and the lady could not do anything about it.

RB 157. *The hit-and-run driver*

I was running about half a block from the house in Hawaii. All of a sudden a car went against the light, made a wrong turn — everything. He ran into me and I just fell down. But I was so lucky. One foot away there was a pole, and I fell against it. Otherwise, my whole head would have been smashed.

At that time, I did not think of getting his license number. The accident seemed like nothing. But when the shock was over, about two minutes afterwards, I could not see anything.

RB 158. *Go, Sri, go!*

During the ten-mile race, the boys on my road crew were cheering me on: "Go, Guru! Go, Guru!"

Then some other runners started saying: "Go, Sri! Go, Sri!"

RB 159. *Starting fast*

When we were lining up for the race, John was saying that those planning to run a five-minute-a-mile pace should stand here, and so forth.

I saw Charles there, so I said, "Let me go and stand there too."

RB 160. *An honour to run with you*

During the seven-mile race today, one man was with me for the entire time. I followed him and he followed me.

After three miles he took two glasses of ERG and offered one to me.

At one point, he went five or six metres ahead of me. I said, "Where is he going?" Then I ran fast and caught him.

He finished just a little ahead of me.

Then he shook hands with me and said, "It was such an honour to run with you."

RB 161. *The soul of Jesse Owens*

We ran twelve and a half miles. Nathan was ahead of me and Casey was behind me.

Casey was breathing so heavily: "Huh! Huh!"

And Nathan, was he walking or running? God alone knows.

After we ran five and a half miles, all of a sudden I saw Jesse Owens' soul around my head, looking at me. It was full of love, softness and tenderness, and I stopped to help it.

When I came back from running, one of the disciples gave the news that Jesse Owens had died.

RB 162. *The accident*

Around 3:20 this morning I was running on Main Street, coming back from Flushing Meadow Park. Suddenly I saw a blue car and a beige car have an accident. It was only fifty or sixty metres away from me. In the blue car were a black man and a white man, and in the beige car was a white man. Both the cars were badly damaged, but strangely enough, nobody was injured.

The two men in the blue car came out and started finding fault with the white man. Only one word which they used was civilised: 'stupid'. The rest were beyond my vocabulary. Such a foul tongue they had.

The white man said that his daughter was in the hospital, so he did not know what he was doing. The others said, "Before your daughter dies, do you want us to die?" and all kinds of rubbish things.

For ten minutes it went on. I was sympathising with the man from the beige car, because of his daughter, and I was also sympathising with the other two because their car was badly damaged. Fortunately, I was quite safe because I was sixty metres away.

I was thinking how they could not get along with one or two in a car, and now you have to have three persons in the car during the transit strike. Let us see what happens.

RB 163. *Long strides*

This morning, around five o'clock, I was running near the corner of our street. Somebody drove up to the corner, stopped and started honking. I knew that he wanted someone to come out of the building, so I paid no attention to him. I was running and running, practising short stride and long stride.

At one point he came out of the car. He was a very nice black gentleman. Finally I saw a lady come out of the building. He was telling me he would like me to teach his son how to run.

I was smiling and laughing, and telling him that I am the wrong person to teach his son.

He said, "No, your stride is pretty good."

Occasionally I take long strides and fool people.

RB 164. *Slow joggers*

During the 10-kilometre walk in Central Park today, I saw a man and a woman jogging. They were running and I was walking but I was going ahead of them.

RB 165. *An unexpected companion*

This morning I was running up 150th Street, doing hill work. All of a sudden, a nice young man who had been running up the hill behind me started running with me. When I started walking, he started walking. When I began taking measurements with my feet, he began taking measurements with his feet. Then I did speed work, and he also did speed work.

This was going on, going on; he was doing everything that I was doing. I thought, "What kind of crazy fellow is he?"

One of my disciples spoke to him afterwards, and the man asked him when I was going to have the next public meditation. That means he was not a madman after all.

RB 166. *Name and fame*

I was running on Kissena Boulevard. It was very far, and I was running on the grass. I had just finished my marathon running and I was going along rather slowly.

A young man ran nearby very fast and screamed, "Sri Chinmoy, Sri Chinmoy!"

I did not recognise him and my road crew did not recognise him. But since the man recognised me, that means I am greater than he is.

RB 167. *My best disciple*

Jeremy is my best disciple. I see all my disciples while they are running the Long Island Marathon, and I greet all of them. But Jeremy enters into serious trance. His trance will really take him to the hospital.

RB 168. *A guilty conscience*

I started running in the Long Island Marathon at seventeen and a half miles. I was feeling sad and miserable because I had so much energy. People around me were so tired, and I felt so guilty because I was deceiving those people. There was a small hill, and I was going up so easily, because I had just started. Everybody else was dying. Of course, they did not know that I was only running a few miles with some of my disciples to inspire them.

RB 169. *Two blind disciples*

I wanted to run with Shephali and Amy. For two miles, I kept coming up behind them. At least eighteen times I did it, but I always remained two steps behind. They didn't see me at all. Like that, it went on. They were so blind! Sometimes they took water and poured it over their heads, and I was only two metres behind them. But still they didn't see me!

So many times I went five metres ahead of them and turned around. Shephali came, but Amy did not come. After twenty-three or twenty-four miles, one was on my right side and the other was on my left side. Then I saw that Jane was helping them, so I knew they were all right.

You should have seen Shephali's face — it showed so much pain!

RB 170. *Long-lost friend*

At one point during the Long Island Marathon, I was walking towards the runners for about half a mile. They were yelling, "Hey, Sri Chinmoy!" and "Sri" and "Master." It went on like this and didn't stop for the entire half a mile.

Then, three strong black men stopped running and captured me. One put his arm around my head. He was perspiring like anything. The other said, "How are you doing, Sri Chinmoy?" They said that they never saw me, so now they were getting a chance to see me.

RB 171. *Which one is Sri Chinmoy?*

Shephali and I were finishing together. Six hundred metres from the end, they asked me to run outside the chute, because I didn't have a number.

A husband and wife were watching. The husband said, "Look! Sri Chinmoy and his T-shirt."

The wife looked at Shephali, who was wearing our Centre T-shirt, and at me, and asked, "Which one is Sri Chinmoy?"

Shephali and I were very near them at the time, but Shephali didn't hear.

RB 172. *The silent handshake*

I saw someone running with a T-shirt saying "Cahit Pacers." The next minute I saw John running by. Suddenly somebody came and stood in front of me and shook my hand. He didn't say anything. It was Cahit Yeter.

RB 173. *The hidden disciple*

At one point, a man was running alongside Nishtha. I am sure she was desperately trying to look at me, but she didn't go either one step ahead or one step behind this man. So I couldn't see her.

RB 174. *The waving bus driver*

This morning I was running along 150th Street and a bus that was passing by kept honking at me. Finally, I turned to see what all the commotion was about. The bus driver, a very nice black man, was waving at me. He had been making all that noise just to get my attention. This was the same bus driver who had asked me once why I wasn't running any more.

RB 175. *The blessing*

When I was finishing the three-mile race in Seattle, a man came up to me and said very imperiously, "I want your blessings. I am going to Pakistan." Then he told me the name of the place. It is in West Pakistan, near the Chinese border. Since he will be leaving in a few weeks, he wanted my blessing.

RB 176. *Suspicious characters*

Yesterday, around one o'clock in the morning, I took six or seven boys with me while I went out for a run. They were standing along 150th Street, helping me. They were so calm and quiet, but somebody called up the police and made complaints against us. They said some suspicious characters were outside.

A policeman came to see what we were doing. He was so sympathetic. He knew us well. He asked me whether I had run the Long Island Marathon. He said that if the rest of the people in the neighbourhood would be my disciples, then he would have no problems.

RB 177. *I wish to meditate like you*

While I was running during my visit to Seattle somebody in a car shouted, "Sir, Sir." I thought he was going to ask me directions, so I said, "I don't know the way." Inwardly I said to myself, "I know the inner way, but the inner way will not solve your problem."

Then the man stopped the car and said again, "Sir." He looked like a nice man, so I went up to the car.

He said, "You looked so beautiful and you meditated so beautifully at the concert you gave here. How I wish I could meditate like you." He was appreciating me for my meditation.

I asked him, "Would you like to have a book on meditation? Please give me your address."

While he was writing down his name and address, he said, "Believe me, I am one of your true lovers." Then, as he was giving me the piece of paper, he grabbed my right hand through the window and kissed it. He wouldn't let go.

I gave the Seattle disciples the address to send the man a copy of my meditation book. They said they know the man well. He belongs to the Theosophical Society and he sent me his greetings and love through one of the Seattle disciples when he came to New York.

RB 178. *A warm reception*

When I was warming up before the three-mile race in Seattle, somebody came up to me and stood right in front of me. He looked at me and said, "Can't you recognise me?"

Do I know these runners? Then I remembered him. He had lost so much weight. I said, "Frank."

He said, "Yes, yes, it is Frank Bozanich."

I said, "I saw you when you came to our place with Don Ritchie."

He was talking and talking about the different runners. He spoke about so many runners, but what do I know about runners? He was telling me that today he was going to run in our three-mile race, the next day he was going to run forty miles and the next day one hundred miles. I thought he would win a prize in our race, but he didn't get any place.

At the end of the race, Frank was waiting for me, and again he started talking. I went and sat in my chair. He followed me. Our conversation never ended. Then, when I was about to give the prizes, whom do I see? Somebody has to come and shake hands with me. That was the final time. He said he had to leave.

RB 179. *The best mile*

It is no joke to run a seven-minute pace. Today, in the three-mile race in Greenport, Long Island, by the time the race started at ten o'clock, it was so hot. After the first six hundred metres, I was feeling very hot. My head was so hot, I couldn't breathe and I was dying of thirst. Still, in my first mile, I did my fastest time since I have been in America: a 6:35 pace.

RB 180. *The worried sixty-year-old*

After the three-mile race today in Greenport, Long Island, an old man of sixty came up to me. He was worried because I had finished before him. He thought I would take first place in his category — sixty and over. This man did stand first.

RB 181. *The silent Brahmin*

One girl was with me all the time during the three-mile race. I was breathing so heavily, but from her there was no noise at all. She was the silent Brahmin. I felt miserable that I was disturbing her consciousness. She was the better runner, so she should have gone ahead, but she stayed right by my side.

Then, when we were 800 metres from the finish, she disappeared. But I could not go any faster.

RB 182. *Such a wonderful brother!*

There were two children running the three mile race — a brother and sister about seven or eight years old. All of a sudden, the sister got a leg cramp and couldn't even walk. The brother waited for her. I said, "Such a wonderful brother! He is waiting for his sister."

RB 183. *The problem-makers*

In the race, the young children were the problem-makers. They had indomitable energy. As soon as I saw a child, I would say to myself, "I am surrendering." When children run, they don't know how to become tired. They smile, and their strides are so wonderful. They go this side and that side, running back and forth.

RB 184. *The San Francisco meeting*

Just before the Sri Chinmoy Marathon in San Francisco, I was warming up. A former disciple of mine was near me, but I could not recognise him. He was taking Chinese exercises. Finally, one of my San Francisco disciples told me, "This is Devashish." I had been pretty sure, but then I went closer and I did recognise him.

I said to him, "Do you recognise me?"

Immediately he blessed me, placing both his hands on my feet. His eyes were flickering and moving around. I blessed him and told him that his soul had come to me so many times. He was smiling and full of devotion, but his eyes defeated my eyes like anything in flickering. Because his present wife, or girlfriend, was blessing me inwardly — or rather, cursing me inwardly — I left.

At about two and one-half miles into the marathon, there was a turn, and as I was entering the turn, I saw him on his way back. He saw me from about 500 metres away and he raised both arms. I signalled him when we passed each other.

Afterwards, he came up to me and showed me how many exercises he knew. Each time he did a punching motion, it reminded me of his monkey incarnation.

RB 128. *(p. 73)* 11 February 1979
RB 129. *(p. 74)* 19 December 1979
RB 120. *(p. 74)* 21 December 1979
RB 131. *(p. 74)* 21 December 1979
RB 132. *(p. 75)* 21 December 1979
RB 133. *(p. 75)* 21 December 1979
RB 134. *(p. 75)* 21 December 1979
RB 136. *(p. 76)* 21 December 1979
RB 137. *(p. 76)* 26 December 1979
RB 138. *(p. 77)* 26 December 1979
RB 139. *(p. 77)* 26 December 1979
RB 140. *(p. 77)* 4 January 1980
RB 141. *(p. 77)* 4 January 1980
RB 142. *(p. 78)* 4 January 1980
RB 143. *(p. 78)* 14 January 1980
RB 144. *(p. 78)* 14 January 1980
RB 145. *(p. 79)* 14 January 1980
RB 146. *(p. 79)* 14 January 1980
RB 147. *(p. 79)* 20 January 1980
RB 148. *(p. 80)* 20 January 1980
RB 149. *(p. 80)* 20 January 1980
RB 150. *(p. 81)* 22 January 1980
RB 151. *(p. 81)* 30 January 1980
RB 152. *(p. 81)* 30 January 1980
RB 153. *(p. 82)* 16 February 1980
RB 154. *(p. 82)* 16 February 1980
RB 155. *(p. 82)* 2 March 1980
RB 156. *(p. 84)* 22 March 1980
RB 157. *(p. 84)* 22 March 1980
RB 158. *(p. 84)* 30 March 1980

RB 159. *(p. 84)* 30 March 1980
RB 160. *(p. 85)* 30 March 1980
RB 160. *(p. 85)* 31 March 1980
RB 162. *(p. 85)* 1 April 1980
RB 163. *(p. 86)* 2 April 1980
RB 164. *(p. 87)* 13 April 1980
RB 165. *(p. 87)* 3 May 1980
RB 166. *(p. 87)* 3 May 1980
RB 167. *(p. 88)* 4 May 1980
RB 168. *(p. 88)* 4 May 1980
RB 169. *(p. 88)* 4 May 1980
RB 170. *(p. 89)* 4 May 1980
RB 171. *(p. 89)* 4 May 1980
RB 172. *(p. 89)* 4 May 1980
RB 173. *(p. 90)* 4 May 1980
RB 174. *(p. 90)* 6 May 1980
RB 175. *(p. 90)* 12 May 1980
RB 176. *(p. 90)* 12 May 1980
RB 177. *(p. 91)* 12 May 1980
RB 178. *(p. 92)* 12 May 1980
RB 179. *(p. 92)* 17 May 1980
RB 180. *(p. 93)* 17 May 1980
RB 181. *(p. 93)* 17 May 1980
RB 182. *(p. 93)* 17 May 1980
RB 183. *(p. 93)* 17 May 1980
RB 184. *(p. 94)* 3 June 1980

RUN AND BECOME, BECOME AND RUN

PART 4

RB 185. *Not so bad*

Yesterday, while I was running during the 33-mile race, a member of my road crew was talking to some spectators who were watching from the other side of the fence. One of them said, "The old man is not so bad." That means that although I was running with the young boys, I was not so bad.

RB 186. *To be like you*

After I stopped running last night, I was watching the rest of the 33-mile race. A little boy came up to me. He was very nice to me and said, "How I wish I could be like you."

Then he said, "Did you hear me calling you 'Guru'?" He was only ten years old.

RB 187. *A Woodstock experience*

In September or October of 1964, I was running in Woodstock, in a place called Yerry Hill. Believe it or not, my Beloved Supreme began running with me, right in front of me. He was holding a golden wand — like a magic wand. You can call Him my highest part or my separate part, but I was overwhelmed with Light and Delight. This was my first running experience in America. From this concert hall it is only half a mile to where I had that experience.

RB 188. *The grilled cheese mishap*

The day before yesterday, after running about five miles, I was tired and hungry. So I went into a cafeteria for a grilled cheese sandwich. The grilled cheese sandwich was cut into halves, and there was a toothpick in each side. I was reading the Olympic athletes' times in the newspaper, and I didn't see the toothpicks. One toothpick got stuck in the roof of my mouth. How I suffered! The owner of the store, a middle-aged lady, got frightened when she saw my face. I didn't know what had happened. If this experience had lasted a few minutes more, I would have thought about joining my Father in Heaven!

RB 189. *Time passes*

In 1944, when I ran 400 metres, I did it in 56 seconds. In 1946, it was 54 seconds. Then, for years, it was always 53.6 seconds or 53.8 or 53.9. Now, O God, it takes me so long.

I used to do 100 metres in 12.1 or 12.2 seconds. Then, when I was finished I used to laugh and smile and go away. Now, I'm taking 19 or 20 seconds, and I'm not laughing when I finish.

RB 190. *Two madcaps*

At four o'clock in the morning, I got inspiration to go run. There was another madcap out at the same time; he was roller-skating. Either he is crazy or I am crazy. He was going up and down the 150th Street hill with his dog. The dog followed and chased him up and down the hill. The skater was going this way and that way, zigzagging all over the road. It was very dangerous.

RB 191. *A deceptive ten miles*

This morning, starting at about four o'clock, I ran ten miles. Sometimes when I am tired, I enter into Peter's car. But this morning I ran the whole ten miles. I thought I was going fast, but my timing was not good. So I was disgusted.

Around two o'clock this afternoon, Casey all of a sudden said to me, "The measurement of the ten-mile course you ran this morning is all wrong." Three years I have been running that course! Casey said that after the third mile, fifty metres was added. And it was after the third mile that I noticed my timing was becoming worse. Then, after that, there are more mistakes.

I asked, "How is it that you are only telling me now?"

Casey said, "I heard it at the Smile a long time ago, but I was in another world at the time. I am only now remembering it."

Peter said, "That is what I heard too."

Ashrita said, "Yes, we found the mistake a long time ago, but we didn't have time to correct it."

At two o'clock this afternoon they were telling me the news, and I had run early in the morning! When I first used to run the ten-mile route, I didn't care for timing. But now it is a different story. My road crew knew that the measurements were wrong, but they were too frightened to tell me or their sincerity didn't come forward.

RB 192. *The intelligent crew*

A few months ago, I asked four or five members of my road crew to watch the side streets while I ran down the 150th Street hill. Each time I ran down the hill, Sanatan drove behind me in his car. Then he would bring me back up the hill. So Sanatan I can't blame. But the other members of my crew are such good, intelligent people — so full of wisdom! If it is a one-way street, the cars will only come from one side. But our boys stood on the other side instead. That is how they were guarding me! That night they were all idiots!

What was worse, Peter and Danny were supposed to take movies. Danny came late, so it was not his fault. Peter was using Ranjana's movie camera, but whenever I came near him, he was in some other world. He was talking to someone. Even when I screamed, he did not hear me. Finally, he started taking movies.

Peter's stupidity never ends. I was running in the left lane. He also should have been on the left side, so that the cars wouldn't obstruct his view. But he was in the wrong place. Each time I came by him, a car was also passing, so he could not shoot the movie. Once, twice, thrice I went by; but Peter wouldn't come to the other side to take my picture. My photographers are so brilliant!

RB 193. *The flying glass*

It is so unsafe to run — no matter which hour of the day or night you go out! Right after midnight I was going down the 150th Street hill. Three Puerto Ricans were in a car enjoying their music, making unbearable noise. That was not enough! One of them had to throw a large piece of glass at me. I was going very fast down the hill and did not really see what was happening. The glass fell and broke only two or three metres ahead of me. I saw something coming, but luckily it didn't strike me.

Then I was brave enough to go near them and ask, "What are you doing?" I was very serious. They all became like the silent Brahma.

Members of my road crew were so useless. Eight or nine boys from the crew were there, and there were also two or three girls watching. Everyone was standing on the top of the hill. The girls are not to be blamed, but I started barking at the boys:

"Idiots! You people all stand there, but no one is at the bottom of the hill." So some of them went to the bottom of the hill, and some stayed at the top.

I said to Peter, "How is it that you didn't go there before?" Peter had the ready-made answer: "We were watching the girls. I had to take care of the girls."

RB 194. *The real Susan Hoffman*

Garima's name is Susan Hoffman. When they announced that Susan Hoffman won second place in our triathlon, I couldn't believe it. Then another Susan Hoffman appeared for the award.

RB 195. *Lament of a garbage can owner*

This morning, around five-thirty, the funniest thing happened. I crossed 150th Street and ran my straight one-mile course. When I got to Queens Boulevard and Main Street, an elderly woman began screaming at me. I was running on the street, not on the sidewalk or on her lawn. I wondered, "What have I done at this hour?"

When I finally approached her, I discovered that she was not actually screaming at me. But she wanted me to hear her complaints. Somebody had taken away the cover of her garbage can. She had put all her garbage in the can and now the wind was blowing it away because the cover was missing. I went there and sympathised with her. What could I do?

RB 196. *The crazy runner*

There is an old man who likes me very much. He lives on 150th Street, and he is partially lame. Whenever he sees me running, he has to say something. The other day, about two weeks ago, he stood up from his chair and said, "You are crazy! In this heat you have to run?"

RB 197. *Saved by a name tag*

During our Games Day, I went out for a run and got lost. I saw a girl ahead of me, but I said to myself, "What am I going to ask her? I don't even know the name of the school or the street. Maybe I should say, 'Have you seen hundreds of people playing tennis and other games?'"

I decided just to run by her. Then I noticed that she was wearing a name tag. So I went back and asked her what Centre she was from.

She said, "Connecticut."

Then I asked, "How long have you been a disciple?"

She answered, "One month."

The disciple directed me back to the school. I had to make a few turns, but it wasn't far. So you see, you should all wear name tags. Then, if any of you ever get lost or something happens to you, you will know whom to ask for help.

RB 198. *Can't they run?*

Yesterday, at four o'clock in the afternoon, I went running on 150th Street. As you know, construction is going on there. When the construction started, we know; but when it will end, we don't know. A middle-aged man said to me, "Boss, why do you

have to run? You can't make your boys and girls run for you?"
Then he ran with me.

RB 199. *The photographer-runner*

As I was running, three young girls came and stood in front
of me. They asked, "Can you please take our picture?" I was
running, and they had to come and stand in front of me with
an Instamatic camera!

Since I have that kind of camera also, I didn't have any difficulty using it. They stood together and I took their picture. But
that was not what they had in mind. They wanted something
else. "We want you to be in the picture with us," they said.

So I stood with them, two at a time, while the other one took
the picture. They know some of the disciples and they have been
wanting to meet me for a long time. So they were all very happy
and they thanked me.

RB 200. *Who is last?*

In my latest racing adventure in Prospect Park — a two-mile
race — I got the first prize because there was no competition in
the Masters' category. There was a group of people who were
excellent runners ahead of me. But not even one girl was ahead
of me. Behind me were other runners.

Danny knows how to flatter me, and I am full of receptivity
for his flattery. Recently, he videotaped a race for half an hour,
but he taped only three seconds of my running. So I scolded
him.

This time, he wanted to show more of me running, and less of
others. So, at the finish line, he video-taped all the runners ahead
of me. But, according to Danny, behind me nobody existed!
Danny showed that I was the last runner!

RB 201. *Don't run so fast!*

I was running in the afternoon at a seven and a half or eight-minute pace. An old man with a pronounced moustache was watching me. He said, "Don't run so fast! You will get tired."

RB 202. *Monkey street*

On one street, three or four boys and two or three girls are real monkeys. Each time they see me running, they stand up. They don't cheer me; they boo: "Boo, Guru!" That kind of thing they do! They are bad people, bad people. I pray to God, when I come back, that I don't see them, and God listens to my prayer. When I come back, I don't see them.

RB 203. *Woof! Woof!*

When I was running a few months ago, three or four girls who were standing near the street started barking. Human beings started barking at me! Very bad! There are so many nice people in this area, but God's creation is so vast. Always He has to have a mixture of good and bad. Four or five girls and boys are so unkind to me. Each time they see me they have to make fun of me. Again, most of the others are very nice.

RB 204. *Stop and watch!*

This morning I was running on the left side of the street. On the right side a car passed me. It was in the other lane, but just because I heard it coming, I stopped. A stout black man was driving. He gave me a smile and said, "You are right. Always you should stop and watch."

RB 205. *A flat two-mile course*

I have been asking the boys to find me a two-mile course to run — flat, without sidewalks and side streets and no more than ten minutes away by car. Nobody has been successful; perhaps nobody ever will be successful. Vinaya last week told me he had found a place. I believed him, and he took me there. God! It was a useless road! He wasted my time, but I forgave him.

Then, three days ago, he said he had found Heaven on earth. Those were his words. I said, "To find Heaven on earth is really something!" So I went to see his Heaven. It was Heaven, according to Vinaya — our old course at my seven-mile mark. His course was full of small pebbles and stones, and it was not even clean. It was very bad, very bad! The other day Lorne took me to a place that he said was extremely beautiful. He said that Kanan was the witness, that Kanan had taken him there. So I went to see the place. O God! It was almost like a highway, with a tiny path for cyclists on the side. Thousands of cars were going by very fast. So how could I run? That was Lorne's place. Like that, many people tempt me to go and see their discoveries, but their discoveries always frustrate me.

RB 206. *Shorter than the shortest*

This morning I was worshipping Anupadi's feet as I was running behind her. She was running with such short strides that I was thanking the Supreme that there is at least one girl disciple who has shorter strides than I do. That is why I was worshipping her feet.

RB 207. *You make me tired*

About a week ago I was running up and down 150th Street. A gentleman was watching me. Two or three times he saw me run up the big hill. Then he said, "Sri Chinmoy, you are making me tired. Stop, stop!" He was only watching me, and he said I was making him tired.

RB 208. *The pretender*

At four o'clock this morning I ran four and a half miles. As usual, my pace was 8:40. Two girls were helping the road crew and holding markers at every quarter-mile. Each time they held up the sign, I was pretending that the numbers indicated a full mile, not just a quarter-mile. They put up the number one marker, and I pretended I had run one mile. But when it was sixteen, I had only run four miles — not sixteen. Then I had to stop pretending.

RB 209. *The mad cyclist*

Yesterday Pahar and Lorne were running side by side, right in front of me. I was just two steps behind. A young boy rode his bike so fast right in between them. Pahar and Lorne were furious — there was very little space between them, and I was just behind them. This is how bad some young boys are!

RB 210. *The slow runner*

The other day, I saw Anupadi running. She was dressed in all her winter clothes, trying to lose weight to pass the weigh-in. Had she been a better runner, I would have invited her to run with my road crew and me. But we were planning to run quite fast. If I had been running by myself, with just one driver, she could have trained with us.

RB 211. *The correct pace*

Today I compelled the members of my road crew to run with me at a ten-minute pace. I was barking at them when they went faster.

The other day we ran first a nine, then an eight and a half, then an eight, then a seven-forty-five and, finally, a seven-thirty pace. I tell them the pace, and they go on, go on.

RB 212. *The nice boss*

Monday, when I was visiting my students' offices in UNICEF, I had a soulful conversation with Chandika's boss. Then, this morning, before I went out running for the second time — around six o'clock — I meditated on him. For nice people, quite often I do something special in the inner world, even if they are not my disciples. Yesterday her boss showed gratitude and today, also, his soul came to me.

After meditating on him, while running I was getting a very good response from his soul; it was all gratitude. His soul is a combination of dynamism and softness. Usually, dynamic people do not have any soft qualities; but his main attributes are his dynamism and softness. He is a very luminous soul.

RB 213. *Hi, Pop!*

Yesterday I was running on the street facing Thomas Edison High School. A young black boy said to me, "Hi, Pop! Hi, Pop!" Then he said, "Hi, Shry! Hi, Shry! Don't get a heart attack." In this way he was asking me not to run. He added, "Your children are not here."

Then two teachers turned around and saw me. They stood aside and showed me much respect.

RB 214. *Howdy*

This morning while I was running I saw Robin. He said something to me that sounded like "Good morning." He spoke in such a low, flat voice, but I saw that it was Robin. Robin told me later that he didn't know it was me, and he said, "Howdy."

RB 215. *The unlucky runner*

Every day, sometimes twice a day, I see Madhuri and Joyce running. They are so lucky. But Tanima is so unlucky. She runs with them, but each time, one second before I come by, she goes somewhere else.

RB 216. *I want to jog with you*

This afternoon, around two o'clock, I was running near the school opposite Lucy's street. Three or four little children came out of the school. One of them, a little girl of five or six, got the inspiration to run with me. So she crossed the street, since I was on the other side, and came running up to me with her books, saying, "Sri Chinmoy, I want to jog with you." She had perfect pronunciation. For her, it was 'jogging'. I had been running quite fast, but as soon as she started jogging, I had to slow down. She ran with me for forty metres and she was so delighted.

When she stopped, I gave her a smile and I continued my run.

RB 217. *The secret fans*

I was running by the construction on 150th Street, right in front of Ranjana's house. Three or four Filipino children were hiding in one of the big holes, so I didn't see them. I was running by at an eight-minute pace, and all of a sudden I saw three or four heads. The children had been hiding, waiting for me to go by. They were so delighted, so excited to see me.

In this area everybody knows me. Sometimes they call me 'Sri Chinmoy' or 'Shry'; sometimes they call me 'chief' even. I hear that one of our disciples is teaching in the school right across from Lucy's street, so many children learn about me from that person.

RB 218. *Early morning inspiration*

Just the other day, around four-thirty in the morning, I was running right behind my house. A young man came out of his house and said, "Good morning, Sri Chinmoy. How nice to see you running." He saw me running early in the morning, so he was very inspired.

RB 219. *Unwanted help*

In one house on 150th Street there are two ladies who are dead against us. They are very rude. Recently, I was trying to help one of them who was having difficulty getting her car out of her driveway because there were too many cars going by. Finally, I signalled to her that she could go. Sometimes when we help people, our help is accepted. But she ignored me completely.

RB 220. *The smiling friend*

Some people are always nice to me when they see me running. One fat lady, my friend with the two dogs, is like that. Even if she sees me running three times during the day, she will greet me and smile. Sometimes I slow down when I go by her. She is always smiling.

RB 221. *Simplicity incarnate*

The first woman in our Oregon 30-Kilometre Race was the well-known runner Martha Cooksey. She had come to our meeting the previous day to meditate with us, and she had been very, very moved.

When she was on her thirteenth or fourteenth mile, the other women runners were far behind her. I was in the car, as I had run only seven miles, and I waved to her. She was so delighted to see me waving from the car.

Then, when I gave her the prize, there was only one foot between her existence and my existence, but she grabbed my left elbow and whispered to me, "I enjoyed it. I enjoyed the race very much! " She is so short, but still she bowed down. Of all the women runners I have met, she has the most simplicity. She is very simple, very cheerful and very kind-hearted. If people are champion runners, very often there is something in them which you call pride; or they have a certain way of expressing themselves because they are champions. But in Martha Cooksey's case, she is absolutely simplicity incarnate.

RB 222. *Jogging with the Mayor*

Just before the start of the race in Oregon, the Mayor of that town came up to me and said, "I am the Mayor here. I am so happy and honoured that you are here, Sri Chinmoy."

Three or four minutes later the race started. I started jogging, and the Mayor also started jogging with me. He was quite fat. I wanted to go at a ten-minute pace, and he ran with me. We were last. After eight hundred metres, the Mayor said, "I am now going home." Eight hundred metres was enough for him. Also, the eight-hundred metre mark was right in front of his home.

RB 223. *The wheelchair racer*

In our Oregon race, a man in a wheelchair stood first. He defeated the first runner, a top-ranking runner, by sixty metres. I couldn't believe how fast the man in the wheelchair was going. Then Dayal told me it always happens like that.

The prizes were so cute. The winners got big pies, which were the same size as their medals. They had a special prize for me, which I wanted to give to the man who was in the wheelchair. When I went near him, he immediately started shedding tears. He was so moved that I was giving the prize to him.

RB 224. *Dead dog*

Everywhere I run there is a dog problem — even here in Tobago. As I was running this morning, two dogs came and started barking and barking. I thought they were barking because of my red T-shirt. But then I saw that there was a dead dog lying there by the road.

RB 225. *No life!*

Yesterday a man saw me running and said, "Dad, Dad, put some life into your running." Then he began showing off, pumping his arms.

RB 226. *Everybody makes progress*

This morning I saw Haridas come out of the hotel and start running quite fast. Two years ago, I used to laugh when I saw him run, saying, "Maestro, you are so great." And today, he runs at an eight-minute pace right from the beginning. So everybody makes progress.

RB 227. *You need spring!*

Two young boys were running. The first time they passed me, they didn't see me. Then, when I turned around, one boy told me, "You need some spring, man. You need some spring."

RB 228. *Not a disciple*

I went out to run after seven o'clock this morning, and I saw a girl running alone. I thought it was Hladini. It was on the tip of my tongue to bark at her, because here in Tobago the girl disciples are not supposed to run alone. But when I came nearer, I saw that the girl was uncivilised. Since her uniform was immodest, I said, "No, no, it cannot be a disciple."

RB 229. *The shy disciple*

I saw Agraha running this morning. I was admiring his style, but as soon as he saw me, he went on another street.

RB 230. *The pumpkin hole*

At the start of our seven-mile race, even before one mile, inside my chest was a pumpkin hole. There was nothing inside my chest. I couldn't breathe.

RB 231. *She is ahead*

At the start of the seven-mile race, I saw Sarah go way ahead of me. I said, "Oh, she is so far ahead of me!" But she dropped dead before the one-mile mark. She had to stop running after one mile, but that I didn't see.

RB 232. *Peter's soul operates*

At the one-mile mark during our race, one person said, "8:07." Then, after one step, another person said, "8:11." Peter's soul is working through everyone! During one marathon he would say the timing, and four metres later he would say a completely different timing.

RB 233. *The discouraging timekeeper*

At the fifth mile, Dolores said the time, and I got mad at her. She saw that I was walking, so why did she have to tell me my timing and discourage me?

RB 234. *The disciple surrenders*

Before the first mile was over, I was ahead of Nirvik, and I was so delighted. Then, after two miles, he went ahead of me. I said, "Oh, he was fooling me."

After three and a half miles, I was only looking for Nirvik, but I couldn't see him. For five miles it went on like this. But later I surrendered. By the time we reached seven miles, he was following me.

RB 235. *Silence conquers sound*

Yesterday I had my dog problems again. At a certain place along my running route here in Tobago, if you run, they bark. If you walk, they bark. What can you do?

As soon as you come in sight, three or four dogs come from their houses. You have to walk as slowly as possible, pretending you are not even walking. Then they become frightened. Silence conquers sound; here is the proof. While you are running, they chase you. While you are walking, they bark at you. But when you stop walking, they also stop. This is the proof that our silence can conquer sound.

RB 185. *(p. 99)* 12 July 1980
RB 186. *(p. 99)* 12 July 1980
RB 187. *(p. 99)* 26 July 1980. In first edition, the hill's name was misprinted as "Cherry Hill"
RB 188. *(p. 100)* 1 August 1980
RB 189. *(p. 100)* 4 August 1980
RB 190. *(p. 100)* 9 August 1980
RB 191. *(p. 101)* 9 August 1980
RB 192. *(p. 101)* 9 August 1980
RB 193. *(p. 102)* 9 August 1980
RB 194. *(p. 103)* 10 August 1980
RB 195. *(p. 103)* 16 August 1980
RB 196. *(p. 104)* 16 August 1980
RB 197. *(p. 104)* 16 August 1980
RB 198. *(p. 104)* 16 August 1980
RB 199. *(p. 105)* 16 August 1980
RB 200. *(p. 105)* 16 August 1980
RB 201. *(p. 106)* 18 August 1980
RB 202. *(p. 106)* 18 August 1980
RB 203. *(p. 106)* 18 August 1980
RB 204. *(p. 106)* 18 August 1980
RB 205. *(p. 107)* 18 August 1980
RB 206. *(p. 107)* 8 September 1980
RB 207. *(p. 108)* 12 September 1980
RB 208. *(p. 108)* 13 September 1980
RB 209. *(p. 108)* 23 September 1980
RB 210. *(p. 109)* 23 September 1980
RB 211. *(p. 109)* 23 September 1980
RB 212. *(p. 109)* 23 September 1980
RB 213. *(p. 110)* 1 October 1980

RUN AND BECOME, BECOME AND RUN

PART 5

What an experience I had in Hawaii with a good man and with a bad man! I will start with the bad man. I had been running every day — three times a day. Of course, my running is really jogging, but there were people there who were worse than I am. I was so happy, so delighted that there were worse runners: their legs were crooked, their muscles were no good. I enjoyed watching them. I wanted to take movies of them so that I would be able to watch them at home and amuse myself.

So I went to a camera store while Savyasachi went into another store. When I talked to the owner, he was so nasty — very bad! O God, I really wanted to say something. How could someone be so mean? He must have been taught by God or the devil. Finally he started writing out the bill. Usually, in a restaurant or store, people get nice at the end. Even if they have been nasty to the customers, they get nice when it is time to get paid. But this man was nasty to the end. When I was about to give him the money, still he was showing such an unkind face. So I said, "You are such a hopeless fellow," and I didn't take the camera. I didn't even feel sorry for him. I just left, without waiting to hear what the man had to say.

There were no other camera stores in that particular mall, so Savyasachi took me to a different place to find another camera shop. Here we had just the opposite experience. The man in the camera shop was so kind — explaining everything on his own. Such a nice man! I decided I would definitely buy something there. And his prices were much cheaper. Then he gave me the bill, and I saw that he had charged me eleven dollars too much. He was not trying to deceive me; he just made a mistake.

Since he was such a nice man, I wanted to give him the extra eleven dollars without saying anything. O God, when he went to the cash register, he found the mistake. He said, "Please excuse me. I have charged you eleven dollars too much." Then he came over to me and gave me back the eleven dollars. So, if a store owner or anyone is kind and nice, people will want to buy things or give things to him. Just before, in the other camera store, I left without giving any money because the man was so nasty.

Bad luck! The day I wanted to take pictures, my friends were not available. Very few crooked legs I saw. But in general, people usually have very peculiar styles. Out of sixty or seventy runners that I see in a day, only four or five will have a good style. The rest will be all bad, all bad!

RB 237. *A trip in the sauna*

I was running this afternoon near the tennis court where Malati teaches. I went there while having my sauna in Vinaya's car. Vinaya takes me here, there and everywhere with the heat turned up to about a hundred and twenty degrees, and it is so hot! We happened to be near Malati's court when I got out of Vinaya's sauna-car and started running. I didn't see Malati, though.

RB 238. *Running perils*

Today I rode in Vinaya's sauna-car for about an hour and a half. Chetana also came with us. When I finally got out of the car to run, some dogs came and frightened me, so Chetana got out to frighten the dogs. She was shouting at the dogs, "Get away!"

Not only dogs, but also children were so bad today, throwing snowballs at me! One snowball just missed my head and fell on my hand instead.

RB 239. *Early morning drivers*

When I am running early in the morning, I can't believe the way some people drive. Sometimes they even go up on the sidewalk, and you have to run almost into someone's house to avoid them!

RB 240. *Apartments for rent*

The other day at about five in the morning I was running near Flushing Meadow Park. A man stopped his car to ask me if there were any apartments available near there. What do I know about apartments? I said, "I don't live around here." He said, "Damn you!" No "Thank you!" or anything. He was so mad at me — absolutely furious. What was he doing at five in the morning looking for an apartment?

RB 241. *The defeated runner*

I told my sister over the phone that all the girl disciples had defeated me in the Inspiration Marathon. She laughed and laughed and laughed. Then I told my brother the same thing. They both enjoyed my story. They were asking, "Do they know how old you are?"

RB 242. *Shoes can't run*

I am not a good runner, but I have a very good selection of shoes. Unfortunately, the shoes can't run for me!

RB 243. *A morning walk*

What kind of humiliation you go through when you see movies of yourself running! The movie of the Inspiration Marathon shows that at one point while I was running, twenty metres behind me some girl runners were enjoying a morning walk. Yet they were keeping up with me. If they had started running, they would have gone ahead of me. If I had realised they were walking behind me, I would have turned around and barked at them to go ahead of me.

RB 244. *Running like thieves*

Yesterday morning Lucy the Great, Nilima the Great and I the Great ran eight miles. Savita and Pranika happened to see us and ran behind us secretly. When we turned around to come back after four miles, they hid in the bushes until we passed. Then they came out and ran behind us like thieves. None of us saw them; only later they told us about it.

RB 245. *Such sympathy*

During the Prevention Marathon I did a thirteen-mile training run. After four or five miles a young boy of seven or eight gave me water. He asked, "Sir, will you be able to make it?" Such sympathy he was showing me after four or five miles!

RB 246. *Shray Chumchum*

At another point during my thirteen-mile run one man said, "Shray Chumchum!" as I ran by.

RB 247. *Encouragement*

At about seven and a half miles into my run one lady shouted, "You will be able to make it! You will be able to make it!"

RB 248. *The fidgety number*

My number was jumping up to my chin. Finally I said, "I have enough problems," and I gave it to Jahnabi, who was standing on the side of the course, cheering on the runners.

RB 249. *The irate man*

At about eight and a half miles one man was insulting Bhashwar and Guy like anything because they had stopped their car at the end of his driveway so that Bhashwar could take pictures. Fortunately, Guy does not understand English. Sometimes it is better not to understand English.

RB 250. *The funeral song*

At one point, when some of you were singing running songs to encourage the runners, you were singing so slowly that it sounded like a funeral song. One man asked, "Is that our funeral dirge that is playing?"

I said to myself, "That is what I always say about my disciples' singing when they sing too slowly."

I felt sorry that I could not acknowledge you people when you were singing and encouraging me, but I was dying. Sometimes I couldn't even see your faces.

RB 251. *God wants us to surrender*

The Prevention Marathon course was very difficult. Some of the hills were 800 metres long. What can you do? You surrender. God wants us to surrender in every way. Just philosophising won't do. Surrender has to be practised.

RB 252. *Running friends*

A husband and wife were running together for several miles. Then the wife got permission from the husband to go ahead. I ran with her for a mile and a half. Then I surrendered, and she went ahead of me.

When I went back to watch some of the disciples finish the marathon, I didn't see any of my running friends that I had met during my thirteen-mile training run.

RB 253. *Running in the other world*

At one point I saw Bill Flowers running. We were waving at him, but he was in the other world, running with his eyes closed. He was using his third eye to see where he was going.

RB 254. *Our Indian Pope*

This morning when I was running, I passed three black boys going to school. The tallest was telling the younger ones: "Our Indian Pope is running around the block."

I said, "Thank you, thank you!"

I am also known for my monkeys. Three or four times I have heard school children talking about them. The children stand in the street and watch them on my porch.

RB 255. *Lost time*

Databir always loses so much time whenever he sees me during a race. He is usually so far ahead of me that he turns around to come back before I do. Then when he sees me coming from the other direction, he comes to talk to me and encourage me. In this way he loses precious minutes from his own marathon time.

RB 256. *Meeting up with Joe Henderson*

Before the start of the Chico Marathon I was talking with Joe Henderson, the running author. When they called for the runners who were going to run thirteen miles, he ran to the starting line. He told our boys that he would come and greet me when I finished 26.2 miles.

RB 257. *The mayonnaise cup*

At the one-mile point in the Chico Marathon I heard the time: 7:46. I said to myself, "It's too fast." Then it went on, went on. At every mile when I heard my time, I felt it was too fast.

I had told Sharon and Una to give me water and ERG every second mile, but twice it happened that I didn't get it from them. At the two-mile mark the cup was very small. It was like the cups with mayonnaise or something that they give in restaurants. Instead of entering into my mouth, the water entered into my nose.

At the fourth mile Sharon didn't come at all. Finally she came at four and a half miles to give me a tiny cup of water, but it didn't quench my thirst. At the fifth mile I began screaming that I was dying of thirst. Then they brought the thermos cup, which is bigger. So I was satisfied. From then on I was drinking like anything, but for the first five or six miles I was quite thirsty.

ERG powder I took many times. It helped, but the best was water. As soon as I drank water, I got energy. Before the race I didn't have to drink tea or coffee; water was enough.

RB 258. *Guru, you are doing well*

Around six miles somebody far behind me shouted: "Guru, you are doing well, quite well."

Now, I had requested the disciples not to run this particular marathon since I was running, so I was wondering who this could be. Finally I saw that it was somebody who had "Reno" written on his T-shirt. His wife is our disciple, and he has been planning for the last three years to become a disciple. Still he is in the planning stage. He is a lawyer.

Another gentleman runner recognised me and said I was doing extremely well. He also called me "Guru."

RB 259. *The hand-shaker*

At the seven-mile mark a young man came up to me and grabbed my hands, saying, "My name is Mike. You don't know me, but I know you."

He wanted to shake hands.

RB 260. *Your races are terrific*

Just before thirteen miles an old man was running faster than me. Whether he was encouraging me or discouraging me, God alone knows. Then he recognised me and said: "Sri Chinmoy, all your races are terrific. I am going to run your marathon in Davis, California, next month."

RB 261. *Longing for a half-marathon*

After thirteen miles those who were only running a half-marathon were finishing, but the rest had to go two more rounds. At that time my entire being was longing for a half-marathon.

RB 262. *It is good to be beside you*

Later, there were two or three runners who recognised me and started encouraging me to run faster. Saumitra was taking movies. One of them wanted to be with me in the picture, so he slowed down. He said, "You are a great man. It is good to be beside you." Saumitra took our picture.

RB 263. *A chat with Jay Helgerson*

Around fourteen, fifteen or sixteen miles, a young man was running ahead of me. All of a sudden he turned around and asked, "Do you recognise me? Last year I was at your place."

Immediately I recognised him. It was the great runner Jay Helgerson, who ran a marathon every week for one year in 1979. He was on his last loop, but he stopped to chat with me. At first he didn't smile, but then he started smiling at me.

RB 264. *An encounter with Joan Ullyot*

A few minutes after I saw Jay Helgerson, Joan Ullyot passed me. She said, "Keep on going."

Then she turned around just for a fleeting second, and Una and Sharon recognised her. She is the famous running doctor from California, an excellent runner.

RB 265. *My friends, cramps*

At around seventeen miles my friends, cramps, came. At the end of seventeen miles my left calf cramped up. Then later my right leg cramped, and then again my left. At least two or three times every mile Nirvik had to massage me. So what kind of time could I expect? Nirvik and Doug were behind me on bicycles. I would run a few hundred metres, and then Nirvik would massage me. When I ran, it was a nine-minute pace, but I would lose three or four minutes each mile when he massaged me.

A little boy ten or eleven years old also had cramp problems. His hamstrings were bothering him. He felt miserable. He finally said to me, "How I wish somebody could massage me."

Then he and I became good friends. When I ran, he walked. When he ran, I walked. When I was getting massaged, at that time he would run two or three hundred metres ahead of me. Then he would stop and walk. In this way we were together until twenty-three miles. Then my dying spirit got new inspiration and the poor boy fell behind. I didn't see him anymore.

RB 266. *The steep hill*

The course was excellent, and the weather was really ideal. Only in two or three places they hadn't swept the course and there were big stones and pebbles. And there was one extremely steep hill, three or four metres long. It was so difficult after the third loop to go down it.

On the third loop Garima was running ahead of me to inspire me. When she ran down that very steep, short hill, I said, "How am I going to make it?" I didn't dare to even walk down it, it was so steep. But that was the course. In at least four places it could have been a little more flat.

RB 267. *The soul returns home*

Altogether there were four loops. It seemed that every time I came near the finish line, they played my flute music over the loudspeaker. When I was finishing, at least three hundred metres before I crossed the finish line, they were playing "Phire Chalo." It was absolutely the correct song to play: the soul was going back to its heavenly home. The last three hundred metres I ran hearing only my "Phire Chalo" on the flute.

RB 268. *Nice of you to run*

The race directors were very nice people. After I finished, one of the officials came up to me and said, "It was very nice of you to run."

RB 269. *Mutual faith*

I have the same fate as my disciples. Once my disciples descend in their aspiration, they find it very difficult to ascend. Similarly, since I have descended in my running, I haven't been able to ascend again. Still I am staying at the foot of the tree.

As I have not given up hope that any disciples who have descended will once again go up in their spiritual life, my disciples should not give up faith that I will again go up in my running. There has to be mutual faith.

RB 270. *A race for the military*

In California we held a race especially for the military. Unfortunately, they heard about it only at the eleventh hour, so there were hardly ten runners. Our runners joined them.

The race began at seven o'clock in the morning. Around five-thirty I got inspiration to compose a song on the military. I didn't know that there were women in the military. Later I saw that four or five women soldiers were there.

One of the high-ranking officers came over to me and said, "This time we have very few people, but next time it won't be like this. We deeply admire your races." He took off his jacket and showed me one of our T-shirts. He said, "I run all of your races."

RB 271. *Restaurant experiences*

The first night in Fort Lauderdale I went out to run around ten o'clock. After I had run about two and a half miles, I became quite hungry. I had some money, so I went into a restaurant. But they said to me, "No, you can't eat here. You are not properly dressed." I was wearing tennis shorts which came right to my knees. They were quite modest — not the thin, Bill Rodgers running shorts.

So I left and went to another place. There was a guard sitting at the door. He said to me, "Do you want to eat?"

I said, "Yes, I am very hungry."

He said, "You can go inside and eat."

I went in, but here also, one of the waiters saw how I was dressed and said to me, "This is not the place for you. Here you can't eat." They also asked me to leave.

There was a place beside the main restaurant, like an adjacent dining hall. Nobody was there. I asked, "Can I not eat there?"

They said, "No, you are not properly dressed. You have no tie, no suit, nothing."

Two places had thrown me out. Now it was like a challenge to find a restaurant. Otherwise, I wouldn't care. But since I live in America, American blood has entered into me, and Americans love challenges. So I was running and running. Finally, around eleven o'clock, I came to an Italian restaurant. I saw a menu on the window, and I was reading it with the hope that I would be able to go inside. Somebody came out and looked at me. I said to that person, "I want to speak to the manager."

The man said, "I'm the manager."

I asked, "Can I go inside and eat?"

The manager asked, "What is wrong with you? You have no money?"

I said, "I have money, but I am not properly dressed."

So I went inside. Except for one table, all the tables were occupied. I ordered eggplant, as usual. Beside me there was a group of people at a big table: an airline pilot and his wife, the co-pilot and his wife and their parents. The wives were sitting on the right side of the husbands and next to them were the parents. It was one of the fathers' birthday and they were all very happy. They had ordered a cake, which one of the waiters brought, and they were about to sing "Happy Birthday."

Quite unexpectedly, a middle-aged couple came over to them. The couple had been sitting at another table. The co-pilot stood up and shook hands with the man and kissed the woman. O God, the co-pilot's wife became furious. She stood up and walked out of the restaurant. Her husband's father and some others went to bring her back. At the table, some were laughing, some were serious, some were shocked. Even people from other tables came over to see what the commotion was. But the co-pilot just said, "Let us sing 'Happy Birthday'."

My bill was for seven dollars and something. So I put a ten-dollar bill on the table and left. I was not enjoying my eggplant. "Next," I thought, "will come a fight. Before bottles fly in the air — bottle-bullets — let me leave this place."

RB 272. *The police chase*

It was around midnight and I was going back home. There were some grocery stores that were open twenty-four hours, so I went into one and bought a Tab, some fruit and juice — no candy at that hour. Two or three other people were also inside the store.

A middle-aged lady was behind the counter. Each time a person wanted to come in, she would open the door from the inside and then bolt it again. She was very nice.

O God, suddenly three young men tried to open the door forcefully, but the lady would not let them in. The three young men were being chased by the police. While the other two were still banging on the door, trying to escape, one fellow hid under a car. There were three or four cars in front of the grocery store. The police were having such trouble getting this man, because they were too fat to get under the car. They were screaming at the fellow, but he continued to stay under the car. The other two had already been arrested, and they were laughing at the police. I said, "O God, O God, I don't want to know the remainder of this story." So I bought four or five dollars' worth of things and I left.

RB 273. *Looking for Sally*

I was coming back home around twelve-thirty. About three hundred metres from my apartment was a small hospital, with windows facing the street. One fellow was standing on the street drinking and calling for his girl-friend: "Sally! Open the window. I want to see you. I have not seen you for a long time." He was screaming up to the second or third floor for the patient, Sally, to open the window and talk to him.

But she was not opening the window. Another man from upstairs started screaming at the drunk fellow: "What are you doing at this hour?" He used all American slang, screaming at him from the third floor.

RB 274. *A young running companion*

Another time in Fort Lauderdale I was out running. A beautiful six or seven-year-old child, wearing a necklace, came up to me and asked, "Master, can I run with you?"

I said, "Why not?"

I had been running at an eight or eight and a half minute pace. Now, very slowly I ran with her. We covered three blocks, and then she stopped near her house. She came from a respectable family. She was so happy and proud that I ran with her. She thanked me and gave me a broad smile.

RB 275. *Mister, will you help me?*

Two days later, a little child, even younger than the other little girl, was on her way to school when I ran by quite fast. All of a sudden she said, "Mister!" There were no cars, but she wanted me to help her cross the street. So very slowly I walked across the street with her. I didn't even need to hold her hand, because there was no traffic. As soon as we had crossed the street, she thanked me and entered into a little school.

RB 276. *Lost and found*

Another day I went out to run for two hours. After I ran for about an hour and forty minutes, I got totally lost. It was raining. I said, "O God, where do I go? I don't have any money." Luckily, I remembered the apartment number and, with greatest difficulty, I even remembered the name of the street — Las Olas. I said, "This is the time for me to look for a taxi."

I asked a lady where Las Olas Street was. I had to listen for at least five minutes while she explained which road to take and where I should turn. I didn't understand her in spite of her five-minute explanation. I said, "All right, let me take this street."

Then whom did I see running down the street? Savyasachi! I said, "How can it be?" I had run six or seven miles. He was staying only one mile away from where I had stopped running. He had just gone out for a short run, and he got great joy when he saw me. Then we ran together.

When I play tennis with Savyasachi, his standard always makes me laugh — not only inwardly but also outwardly. But when he runs with me, I feel that inwardly he is laughing at my standard.

RB 277. *The braggart*

As I was running the next day, a young man went ahead of me. Four men saw him run past. They said to me, "He is bragging. Don't pay any attention." The runner went four or five hundred metres ahead, while I continued slowly running. Then he stopped and began to walk. His bragging was over. I passed him. When I was returning from my run, he was still walking.

RB 278. *Competition-blood will never leave me*

Another day I saw an old man running. I said, "If my speed has really increased, I will be able to pass him." I came nearer, only to discover that the runner was a lady. I said, "Let me run according to my speed." After two hundred metres, I turned around. O God, she was so far behind! I tell the disciples to have no competitive feeling, to compete only with themselves. Here I was competing with an old lady! Competition-blood will never leave me.

RB 279. *Dog problems*

While running in Fort Lauderdale, as usual, I had dog problems. A dog started barking at me and didn't allow me to go by. When I returned home, I told Alo about the dog.

The following day she went to look for it, so that she could insult the owner. As it turned out, she found a different dog, so everything went peacefully.

RB 280. *The lost running companion*

Another day I was running about seven miles. At one point I was about to make a right turn, but something within told me to make a left turn. Alo was there looking for me!

Another day I was running and she was following me. I would go ahead two hundred metres and then come back, go ahead and come back. Once, after running two hundred metres and coming back, she was not there. I said, "Where can she be?" But she was not to be found.

What happened was that she had gone across the street to look at a clothing store. I didn't see her standing across the street, so I kept going up and down the block — three or four times.

When I came back home, she was there, worrying about what had happened to me. She had gone out two times to look for me. But she didn't find me because she just went in front of the building, and I was somewhere else.

RB 281. *Psychological competition*

In the beginning of the Brooklyn Half-Marathon, I was competing with three old ladies. At two miles one surrendered and the other two were still running with me. I saw how hard they were breathing, how much noise they were making through their mouths. So I didn't make any noise, even though I was tired. Psychologically, they felt that they were more tired than I was. But they didn't know what was going on inside me — how tired I was. Then, at five miles, I went ahead of them.

RB 282. *Competition without animosity*

The kind of competition that I tell about in my running stories
is not serious; there is no animosity in it. For example, there was
one girl with whom I was having this kind of joking competition
during the half-marathon, and at around nine miles she was
four or five metres ahead of me. At one point she started going
straight ahead, following Ashrita and somebody else on the road
crew who were running back to the car. She didn't see the long
white mark on the road indicating the correct course. I screamed
at her to make a left turn. So she came back to the course and
was very happy that I had told her. Otherwise, she would have
gone another two hundred metres out of her way. If I had really
been competing with her, I would have kept silent and just tried
to go as far ahead of her as possible.

RB 283. *The road crew*

I was running on the right side of the street all the time and my
road crew was also stationed on the right side. At the second
mile mark I was shouting at my road crew that I was coming,
but Sudhir was not seeing me. Peter and Databir were looking
right at me. I even passed by them, but still they didn't see me.

After I had crossed the ten-mile mark and had run hardly
three hundred metres, Databir was saying, "Almost eleven
miles!" It was false encouragement.

RB 284. *Canada bows to India*

During the Brooklyn Half-Marathon one Canadian boy, a new Quebec disciple, ran with me. Then after five miles he slowed down.

RB 285. *The fun run*

Around me, people who were running were enjoying the half-marathon like anything. They would go over to shake hands with people standing on the sidewalk. Or if their parents had come to watch, children would say hello to their parents as they ran by. One girl shouted, "I am running thirteen miles, Mom, Dad! What are you going to give me to eat, Mom?" The mother was telling the daughter what she was going to make for her to eat, and the father was begging her to run faster.

So many people were talking as they ran. Somebody said that once he had run five miles in Central Park and afterwards he lay down and wouldn't get up. His girl-friend said, "Yes, it took you five hours to get up."

There were young people who started walking; they didn't run all the way. After seven miles, during each and every mile I walked for several metres. I could have managed without walking, but walking was a great relief.

RB 286. *Don't lose to the girls!*

One black policeman was encouraging me like anything, telling me, "Don't lose to all the girls!"

RB 287. *False illusion*

While running, when I look at others who are ahead of me, it doesn't seem that their legs are going faster than mine. I am not at all impressed with their speed. Their leg speed seems absolutely slow. I feel that my legs are going faster, yet they are ahead of me. I have created an absolutely false illusion. Because I am making noise with my breathing, I make myself believe that I am going faster.

RB 288. *Downhill troubles*

Towards the end of the race I saw a man who was having trouble going downhill. When he was running uphill, he was doing well, but while going downhill he was absolutely in trouble. This meant that he was using all his energy going uphill.

RB 289. *Last-minute victory*

During the last mile and a half a very tall man was competing with me — running about a metre away from me. When we neared thirteen miles, I said, "All right, let him go ahead," and I started walking. The man was so happy that I had started walking, and he went thirty or forty metres ahead of me.

Then Databir, Gayatri and a few others started screaming and cheering, and I got such joy. I said, "Now is the time for me to go ahead of him." I got inspiration to run fast and I defeated him by six or eight metres.

RB 290. *The announcer-friend*

The announcer at the finish line was one of the officials of the New York Road Runners Club who likes me so much. He always comes and shakes hands with me. When I was two hundred metres from the finish line, he announced over the loudspeaker, "Sri Chinmoy is coming."

RB 236. *(p. 123)* 11 November 1980

RB 237. *(p. 124)* – 22 January 1981

RB 238. *(p. 124)* 24 January 1981

RB 239. *(p. 125)* 30 January 1981

RB 240. *(p. 125)* 30 January 1981

RB 241. *(p. 125)* 5 February 1981

RB 242. *(p. 125)* 5 February 1981

RB 243. *(p. 126)* 5 February 1981

RB 244. *(p. 126)* 1 March 1981

RB 245. *(p. 126)* 1 March 1981

RB 246. *(p. 127)* 1 March 1981

RB 247. *(p. 127)* 1 March 1981

RB 248. *(p. 127)* 1 March 1981

RB 249. *(p. 127)* 1 March 1981

RB 250. *(p. 127)* 1 March 1981

RB 251. *(p. 128)* 1 March 1981

RB 252. *(p. 128)* 1 March 1981

RB 253. *(p. 128)* 1 March 1981

RB 254. *(p. 129)* 2 March 1981

RB 255. *(p. 129)* 3 March 1981

RB 256. *(p. 129)* 8 March 1981

RB 257. *(p. 130)* 8 March 1981

RB 258. *(p. 130)* 8 March 1981

RB 259. *(p. 131)* 8 March 1981

RB 260. *(p. 131)* 8 March 1981

RB 261. *(p. 131)* 8 March 1981

RB 262. *(p. 131)* 8 March 1981

RB 263. *(p. 132)* 8 March 1981

RB 264. *(p. 132)* 8 March 1981

RB 265. *(p. 132)* 8 March 1981

RB 266. *(p. 133)* 8 March 1981
RB 267. *(p. 133)* 8 March 1981
RB 268. *(p. 134)* 8 March 1981
RB 269. *(p. 134)* 8 March 1981
RB 270. *(p. 134)* 8 March 1981
RB 271. *(p. 135)* 21 March 1981
RB 272. *(p. 136)* 21 March 1981
RB 273. *(p. 137)* 21 March 1981
RB 274. *(p. 137)* 21 March 1981
RB 275. *(p. 138)* 21 March 1981
RB 276. *(p. 138)* 21 March 1981
RB 277. *(p. 139)* 21 March 1981
RB 278. *(p. 139)* 21 March 1981
RB 279. *(p. 139)* 21 March 1981
RB 280. *(p. 140)* 21 March 1981
RB 281. *(p. 140)* 22 March 1981
RB 282. *(p. 141)* 22 March 1981
RB 283. *(p. 141)* 22 March 1981
RB 284. *(p. 142)* 22 March 1981
RB 285. *(p. 142)* 22 March 1981
RB 286. *(p. 142)* 22 March 1981
RB 287. *(p. 143)* 22 March 1981
RB 288. *(p. 143)* 22 March 1981
RB 289. *(p. 143)* 22 March 1981
RB 290. *(p. 144)* 22 March 1981

RUN AND BECOME, BECOME AND RUN

PART 6

When I was in Switzerland in June 1980, the Olympic gold medalist Emil Zatopek and his wife came to visit us.

On the second day of his visit we had a Sri Chinmoy Run. The disciples had found a very beautiful course around a lake with two or three small loops and one big loop. Zatopek was supposed to start the race. He was so enthusiastic, as if he were running himself. He called out, "Where is the gun?" He was screaming, "No gun? No gun?"

We said, "We don't use a gun."

Then his wife said, "You don't need a gun."

When his wife said that, Zatopek said, "All right, I will clap."

The race was to start on a small bridge. There were a little over two hundred people on the bridge. They were standing under a big banner saying "Sri Chinmoy Lauf." "Lauf" means race. Zatopek was standing on one side. He started the race by saying something in German, ending with a final clap. When he clapped, everybody clapped, and the race started.

All the London disciples — even elderly women — were running. Our very good runners were also there. Among the disciples, Sundar came in first and then Janaka. But they were defeated by local Swiss boys. I was not feeling well and was running last, behind everybody.

When I ran along the small loops, Zatopek was so excited. He was clapping like anything. His wife stood up also and was clapping and clapping, although I was running behind everybody.

Some of the girls who are useless runners kept taking short cuts at the places where the monitors where directing them around the loops. I told them later that they were all rogues. If they were supposed to run around someone who was standing in one place, instead they cut across. They saved fifty or seventy metres on four occasions. I was so disgusted. On one loop, at least two hundred metres they didn't run. They took a short cut. What were they doing? Just because they were third class runners, they felt nobody would pay any attention.

When it was over, Zatopek gave the prizes. I was so embarrassed. The first, second and third prize trophies were of the same size, with the same figure. Only it was mentioned on the trophy, "first" or "second" or "third." I said, "How can it be?"

John announced the winner's name and handed the trophy to Zatopek, who handed it to the person. To each person who came up for a trophy, Zatopek had something encouraging to say. He was very, very nice. There were also health food prizes — honey and other things — for the winners. Zatopek was so happy to see that we had health food for the winners. After he gave each person his trophy, he pointed to the health food so happily and said, "Take this. You select."

I thanked both Zatopek and his wife, and Zatopek spoke, appreciating us. Then he came up to me and grabbed my hand and said, "Our Guru, this is the best." That was his comment. The race and the atmosphere — everything — pleased him, so he said, "Our Guru, this is the best."

The Mayor of Zurich, who comes from Canada, sent his assistant to honour me. He came with a proclamation and he spoke so highly of me for about seven or eight minutes. All of a sudden, his wife, who was very tall — much taller than her husband — came and gave me a huge bouquet. She was smiling at me. The husband said, "She wants to offer you this bouquet." So I took it and I thanked her.

RB 292. *The rainy race*

At the Pan American Masters Games in September 1980 I was supposed to join in the 100-metre dash. Just before the race, it started raining. Many others didn't run because of the rain, but I wanted to show off. At the race they had starting blocks. During my 20 years of competing in India, I had never used starting blocks. I lost my balance at the start and I was last. God wanted me to have this experience.

Once upon a time I was first — for 16 years. But here, there was at least a 50-metre gap between the first runner and me. The audience was enjoying the fact that there was such a gap between us.

On the board it was mentioned, "Sri Chinmoy, Puerto Rico." The Puerto Rican disciples were so delighted. I had said that I was not going to run the 400-metre dash, but they didn't listen. My name still appeared on the board: "Sri Chinmoy, Puerto Rico."

RB 293. *Old friends*

After the race, a thin, tall black man came up to me and said, "Guru, don't you remember me? The other day I ran 800 metres with you."

Then I recognised him. He was in the Randall's Island race in New York City. I had told Danny to videotape him. I said, "Yes, you ran extremely well. I was far, far behind." He is national champion in his age category. He was so happy to see me. He couldn't believe that I was in Puerto Rico. At Randall's island he ran a 2:10 and my timing was three minutes. But in India in the 800 metres I had stood first.

In half an hour again he came up to me just to chat. In the Pan American Games he defeated everyone in the 800, but in the 100 he didn't get a place. So, he said nice things and I said nice things.

RB 294. *A Puerto Rican runner*

On the plane coming back from Puerto Rico I was sitting in the first seat of the front row. One of the stewardesses said, "Please let me take the bag that is in front of you until the plane is in the air. Then I will bring it back."

So I gave it to her. Then there was an announcement that the plane would be delayed for twenty minutes. When I went to the stewardess to get some books out of the bag, a tall man came and stood in front of me and said, "Master, Master, why didn't you run yesterday in the half-marathon?"

I said, "I couldn't do the 400-metre dash. How could I have done the half-marathon?"

He said, "Your races are so good because they are held early in the morning. I always enter your races. Early in the morning I run."

There the half-marathon was held at three-thirty in the afternoon, so he didn't run. And he is Puerto Rican! Puerto Ricans are accustomed to that kind of heat.

So you see, if you start races early in the morning, there will be at least one person who will be happy and grateful.

He said, "Your students, your disciples, are so good."

Another stewardess happened to be there and she said, "Because the Master is good, the disciples are good." Then she said, "Master, I have been to your meetings quite a few times, but now it is different. At the meditations you are very distant. It is good, but you are somewhere else. Now you are talking."

I said, "At that time I meditate."

She said, "Yes, that's why you are so distant."

RB 295. *The persevering runner*

Yesterday while playing tennis I saw a woman running very slowly. I am sure she was going at a twenty-minute pace, at least. She had to lose about forty pounds, but she was going on, going on. You should have seen how slowly she was running! I was admiring her patience and perseverance.

RB 296. *How can I complain to God anymore?*

This morning I was running twelve miles down Main Street to Northern Boulevard. Hundreds of people were waiting for the bus on Main Street; I could hardly run. Then I saw two lame men who were walking with canes, one after the other. I said, "God, I can't blame You anymore. I can't make complaints to You about my running anymore." How could I make complaints to God when I was running so many miles and these two men were walking with canes?

RB 297. *The clever runner*

Today I was playing tennis and Chetana was running at the Jamaica High School track. At times she was so clever. Whenever she came near me, she started running faster. Then, when she was on the other side of the track, she went so slowly that she looked like she was walking. I didn't envy her speed.

RB 298. *The blink of an eye*

Two days ago I saw Barada and Karabi running on the same block. When I saw them, they smiled. Then I just turned my head for a moment. When I turned back, they were seventy or eighty metres ahead of me!

RB 299. *Two-mile races*

Two-mile races are my favourites because I am always able to finish them. I enjoy running a two-mile race but for a one-mile race I don't have the speed. Out of fifty two-mile races we are having this year, at least thirty I will run.

In the last race, as I was approaching the turnaround point I saw Karabi and Cathy. They were only twenty metres ahead of me. It was tempting to try to catch them! But it's easy to forget that you have to run another twenty metres before you even reach the turnaround!

Then I was going back on one side and Hashi was coming on the other side. My ego went so high! I also saw Nayana and a few others behind me. Then I saw Chameli very far behind. I said, "You! In the 26-mile New York Marathon, you smiled at me and after 17 miles you went ahead of me." She was smiling in this race also.

For most of the race I was a little ahead of Gayatri. Because of my fever I never had any energy. When Gayatri went ahead of me, I didn't have any power left. I made a sincere surrender to her.

RB 300. *Instant recognition*

Today I was watching the Seven-Mile Reversible Race in Central Park. Two middle-aged men were running. I was standing at the side watching when they passed by me. I think their timing was better than my best timing for seven miles. Suddenly, both of them turned around and said, "Sri Chinmoy!" They did not ask me, "Are you Sri Chinmoy?" No! They were saying, "Sri Chinmoy!" They were so surprised to see me. When they first passed by me, they did not recognise me. Then, after three or four steps, they turned around and greeted me.

Then a black woman came up to me and said, "Sri Chinmoy, do you have the time?" I could not tell her the time. I was wearing my yellow stopwatch which does not have the regular time. So she smiled at me.

RB 301. *An old friend*

After the race a tall, thin gentleman came up to me and said, "Do you remember me, Sri Chinmoy?"

At first I thought, "How am I going to remember who he is, even though I am looking at him?" Then I remembered that his name was John Graham. He was formerly with the U.S. Mission to the United Nations. It was he who wrote a letter to the U.S. State Department arranging for my talk there last year, and I thanked him deeply.

He said, "I was glad to be of help to you." He told me his timing for the seven-mile race. It was about an eight-minute pace. My timing is better for seven miles, but I didn't tell him.

Before he left the U.S. Mission, I gave him an interview after one of our meetings at the United Nations. During the interview he had asked me how he could bring forward and utilise his power. So I had given him an answer and he had remembered it. He had even memorised some of my words and he quoted them to me.

After he left the U.N. he went to India to give lectures on "How to change the world." He was at Gandhi's ashram. For seventeen years he has been in politics. Now he has learned about spirituality and he is a real seeker. Still he is giving lectures. His theme is always "How to change the world."

RB 302. *A rare smile*

Tom Curtin did so well in the Seven-Mile Reversible Race. Out of 500 people he stood tenth, and he was sixth in his age category. He never smiles, but today he came up to me smiling and said, "Guru, I stood tenth."

I said, "I am so proud of you."

He said, "I am getting a trophy, but I have to wait an hour for it."

I told him, "You should wait for it."

RB 303. *Heartbreak hill*

Tony ran twenty miles in Central Park and then he ran with me for three miles. When we came to the hill, he said, "Guru, this is 'Heartbreak Hill.'" But he had already run twenty miles. Still, his speed was quite good. I ran five miles altogether.

RB 304. *The old runner*

The day before yesterday I was running back from a four-mile run. A fat old man stopped me and said, "You are still running! You don't want to grow old."

I wish to say that people who aspire will never become old. They will always remain children in the Heart of our Beloved Supreme.

RB 305. *Two short-striders*

I ran about nine miles of the Boston Marathon. While I was running, I saw three Japanese women runners. The two younger ones were running with the older one for a mile or so. When they went ahead of her I said, "I am the right person to run with the older lady, since her stride is shorter than the shortest."

Our competition was going on very nicely. After two miles I left the course and about four or five minutes later I came back. I didn't see the older Japanese lady running. I knew she had gone quite far ahead. I ran and ran very fast and finally I saw her again and started running with her. From time to time she gave me a good smile. She was very old and very short. She was the right person for me to run with! She was drinking after practically every mile, but I didn't drink at all.

RB 306. *Encouraging words*

While I was running in Boston two young men were behind me. Then they passed me and said, "Buddy, come on."

One gentleman said to me, "Friend, my friend, don't give up!"

At one point I was breathing heavily. A little boy came up to me with a few pieces of orange. Usually I don't take oranges, but the little boy was so kind, so I took a piece of orange from him. Then he said, "Don't die, don't die!"

RB 307. *The crazy girl*

After four miles I had absolutely the funniest experience. I saw a crazy girl about seventeen or eighteen years old running. She was very tall and had on a fancy dress. She came up to me and said, "I love your gloves." After four or five steps she added, "But I love you, too." Then she left the street and entered into the crowd and started dancing. After a while she again came back and started running. Whenever she saw elderly people she would go and shake hands with them or embrace them. She was really crazy, but she had good speed.

RB 308. *The non-conformist*

Today I watched the Long Island Marathon. Many disciples were running. As soon as the marathon started, after about a quarter-mile, Gayatri came running by on the lawn. Everyone else was running on the street, but she was running on the lawn.

RB 309. *The dying helper*

Nayana was helping Chetana. Chetana had already run thirteen miles before Nayana started running with her, but Nayana was dying to such an extent that she needed help herself. After eight hundred metres Chetana went ahead of Nayana. I told Nayana to try to catch up with Chetana and help her anyway. Nayana was very obedient. She ran and ran, but she could not catch up with Chetana — even near the finish line.

RB 310. *The wall of China*

Snigdha said to me at seventeen miles, "I am tired!" I told her to go on. Sunanda was running so well. We saw her at five miles and also at ten miles. She was taking such long strides. Who ever thought that at twenty miles she would see the Wall of China? She lives in America, but still she had to see the Wall of China.

RB 311. *A familiar old man*

At one point I saw somebody wearing one of our T-shirts. "Who is over sixty years old and running on our team?" I wondered. His whole body was twisted, and I couldn't recognise him. Then I saw it was Udayan. It seemed he had no hair; he looked practically bald. He was thirty metres away from me, but because of his bald head and totally twisted body, I thought to myself, "How could this old man have our T-shirt on?"

RB 312. *You make us stronger!*

While I was watching the race, seven or eight runners recognised me. One of them said, "Sri Chinmoy, you make us feel stronger!"

Then Gary Muhrcke, the winner of the first New York Marathon, came up to me and said, "I'm sure many people are running from your club."

I said, "Yes, many, many."

Then Norb Sanders came up. I didn't recognise him; he has grown a beard now. He was asking me about my knee pain.

RB 313. *Looking for the Ottawa Holiday Inn*

In Ottawa I went out to run early in the morning. I had been running for about an hour and fifteen minutes when I realised that I was lost. I asked a very nice and kind-hearted black lady where the Holiday Inn was. She said, "Oh dear, it is so far! Go straight down for at least twenty blocks and then ask people to show you where it is. You won't be able to understand how to get there from here, so after twenty blocks you ask someone where it is."

I ran about twenty blocks to a place that I later found out was only two or three blocks away from the hotel. Unfortunately, when I asked a young boy where the Holiday Inn was, he told me it was in exactly the opposite direction. Instead of telling me it was two blocks in one direction, he turned the other way and said, "Run that way. Go only a couple of blocks — two or three more — and then you will find it." He even pointed the way with his finger.

I ran two or three, then six or seven blocks and still I didn't see the hotel. Finally, I approached someone else and said, "Somebody told me that the Holiday Inn was only two blocks in this direction."

The man said, "Not this direction. It is in the other direction. Turn around and go the other way."

I said to myself, "Whom to believe?" The first time, when I was following the young boy's instructions, I was having no doubts. But by this time real doubt had started. O God, what could I do? When one is a stranger, one has to believe in these people. Finally I said, "All right." So I covered six or seven blocks in the other direction, and finally I found the Holiday Inn.

RB 314. *Practising what you preach*

In Toronto there was a two-mile race. I had already run a lot early in the morning before the race, so I was very tired and exhausted. Also, I didn't have any energy because I had not been eating solid food. But I started running anyway.

There were about twenty-five runners in the race. Four girls who were running started to pass me. I said, "I have no more strength to run. I preach all the time 'surrender, surrender, surrender' to my disciples. Now God wants me to practise it." O God, one, two, three, four — the girls all went ahead of me. Then, after one mile, one by one I caught three of them. But one girl was still ahead of me. After a mile and a half, I had absolutely no energy left. I started walking very nicely and the girls whom I had passed went ahead. I said, "Oh, now I am practising and practising. Not only do I preach surrender but I practise it also."

A young man, a new disciple who still had long hair and a moustache, came up to me near the end of the race and said, "Guru, I want to run with you because I want peace. I am getting so much peace from you."

I thought, "Oh, he is getting peace and I am dying."

So, near the finish line, when I started walking, he also started walking. Then about a hundred metres from the end I told him, "Now, please, you go and run. Finish it running." So he completed the two-mile race running.

RB 315. *The stranger from Texas*

In Brazil there was a seven-mile or ten-mile race. I was tired, exhausted, since I had run eight or nine miles that morning, so I didn't join.

I saw a man with a dog near the start of the race and I said to him, "Excuse me, can you tell me how many miles they are going to run? I see there is going to be a race."

The man said, "I don't understand your English!" in a very abrupt way.

Immediately I saw that he was an American. I asked, "Where do you come from?"

He answered, "I come from Texas. Where do you come from?"

I said, "I come from New York."

He said, "Now I understand your English. Ask me again."

When I asked him, he said, "I am also a stranger, like you."

RB 316. *The candy*

The other day we were riding in Databir's car after I had checked out a running route. I had five or six candies next to me that I was planning to give to the four or five people in the car. But Databir started falling asleep, so he ate all the candy to keep awake. Then, when I started looking for the candy to give to everyone, he said, "Oh, Guru, I finished it!" So the others didn't get any.

RB 317. *No more peace!*

The other day I was going down the 150th Street hill very peacefully when I saw Sunanda and Barada running quite fast. I was so jealous of their speed!

RB 318. *To see Chandika smiling!*

When I saw Chandika during my seven-mile run, she was so happy. To see Chandika smiling is really something! At that point I was walking — for me to run seven miles is no joke! I was running on the street around the track and Chandika was on the track itself. I saw her three times. I thought that secretly I was seeing her, but later she said that she had seen me.

RB 319. *Greetings*

Peter's course is by far the most difficult. As soon as you start, it is only up. With greatest difficulty you are running up the hills; you are killing yourself. And who greets you? Always there is a particular dog who greets you!

RB 320. *The deer*

Before the Westchester Half-Marathon we met with the excellent runner Gary Fanelli, and the singers sang the song that I had dedicated to him. In the song I had mentioned his deer-speed. He thanked me and said that quite often he thinks about a deer while he is running. He said, "It is a very beautiful song. I love you all very much. I hope you all have a good race today."

I told him, "You should come first, as you did last year. You show your deer-speed!"

"After this song I am charged, plugged in," he said.

163

Then I gave him a copy of the song and I returned the pictures of his two daughters, Laura and Celeste, that he had given me. He saw that I had written "Blessings and Love" on their foreheads. He said, "Nothing means more than your blessings in my life."

I am so happy that he won the half-marathon. Many years ago he had been interested in following our path when he was living in Los Angeles.

RB 321. *The slow runner*

During the Westchester Half-Marathon I walked eight or nine times. Shame! Sometimes when I was running, people who were walking were going faster than I was. Since they were walking faster than my running speed, I said, "The best thing is to walk."

Then Cahit Yeter came back after he had finished and ran the last mile and a half of the race with me.

RB 322. *Screaming for water*

At one point in the Westchester Half-Marathon I came near Edie only to hear her screaming: "Aahhh!" She was screaming and screaming. Later she told me that she had been screaming for water.

RB 323. *What can one do?*

The other day in the half-marathon, after one mile Sunanda went ahead of me. She was smiling and smiling as she went by. She and Arjava were running together. I said, "What can I do?"

RB 324. *The first goal*

In yesterday's two-mile race, Mitali was my first goal. She was ahead of me, but finally I transcended my first goal and passed her.

RB 325. *Good morning!*

Today Agraha's sister, Cathy, saw me while I was running down the 150th Street hill. She folded her hands in a very obvious way. Then when I came back up the hill, she still had her hands folded. These things only happen when I run after six o'clock in the morning. When I run at four or five o'clock, I never see any disciples.

The other morning at five o'clock, when I was running up 150th Street, Michael Berens started yelling from his window, "Good morning!" Since he lives in Sal's house, he could see me from his room. He was yelling, "Good morning, Guru!" out the window, but I was tired and I didn't have the strength to tell him, "Good morning!"

RB 326. *Mr. Hill*

I got a new name today. While I was running a middle-aged man was driving by in a small van. He was calling out, "Mr. Hill, Mr. Hill!" and looking at me. It seems that everybody has heard of our race on 150th Street, fifty times up and down the hill.

RB 327. *Enjoying the hill*

This morning, a little before four o'clock, I went on my first run for the day. The second time I ran it was around five o'clock. At that time two people saw me as I was running up the 150th Street hill. They started making fun of me. They said, "Now it is your turn to enjoy yourself. Before your 'deesciples' died, and you watched. Now you are enjoying the hill." They were referring to our 150th Street races.

So I said, "Yes, now I am enjoying it. You come every morning at five o'clock to enjoy running with me. You people come!"

They were very surprised. They had thought that I would remain like the silent Brahmin and wouldn't talk to them. I was on my fifth mile of hill work and I was dying. I was panting and making noise and they were mocking me.

After running five miles, I walked two miles up and down the hill. So I did seven miles of hill work. It is a little different when you run alone with nobody to cheer for you.

RB 328. *Friendly encounters*

Usually I go out running for the third time at about quarter to seven each morning. Starting at four or five o'clock, every hour I go and run. Many times at quarter to seven I see Harry's son, Bruce, who is so nice to us when we use P.S. 86 for functions. Bruce has a small van. Quite often when he drives by he says, "Guru, Guru! Hello, Guru!"

The bus drivers also are very nice to me. I can be on the other side of the street, but still they will honk and wave. Often I go out to run, so now they recognise me.

RB 329. *The sign of the cross*

During the five-mile race today a gentleman was ahead of me. All of a sudden he stopped and turned around and said, "Are you Sri Chinmoy?" I was panting and no words were coming out of me. So I gave him a smile.

He said, "You are Sri Chinmoy!" and he made a cross sign on his forehead — not on his chest. He was very happy to see me. Then he ran with me for about two hundred metres. But he felt that he was a better runner so he went ahead of me. I was just behind him.

RB 330. *Closed-mouthed*

At the two-mile point two women were running near me. When I was passing by, one of them was so excited to see me. She said to the other one, "Do you know who that is?"

The other one said, "Who?"

O God, the first woman who saw me wouldn't answer because I was coming very near them and she didn't want me to hear. Perhaps she was afraid of the pronunciation, afraid that she would be embarrassed.

Then, when I was about five metres ahead of them, the lady said, "Sri Chinmoy." But when I was running next to them, she wouldn't tell her friend who I was.

RB 331. *The five-mile race*

Mitali completed our five-mile race today. For Mitali to complete five miles is really something! Her better half, Boiragi, was so happy that she had finished. I also was so delighted! I was clapping and clapping. On other days when I smile at her, she smiles, but today she was dying, so she could not smile at the finish.

Mitali was my first competitor when I started running and the second was Nemi. Like that I competed with about ten girls. Pranavananda's assistant, Susan, gave me a very hard time. I ran and ran trying to pass her. At one point she went to drink water and I was very happy that she had stopped. I didn't go to take a drink. O God, after drinking water, she got extra energy! So my intuition was totally wrong. I didn't even dare to think of defeating her after that. But after covering a few hundred metres, she finally slowed down. Then, with Kritagyata, I had to struggle for at least four hundred metres to pass her.

After four miles I thought that all the worthless runners were behind me, so I didn't have to worry. My ego was quite satisfied. Then all of a sudden I saw Sarama. I couldn't lose to Sarama, so I was praying to my ego to come forward. Then my ego listened to my prayer and I defeated Sarama. It is a great achievement to beat Sarama. I didn't know she was so far ahead of me, but I passed her at the four-mile mark.

After four hundred metres, whom did I see? Ilona! She was making noises: "Eee, Eee!" I said to myself, "Wait, wait." Then during the fifth mile I ran so fast that I went two or three hundred metres ahead of her. She was nowhere near me at the finish.

RB 332. *If you don't eat*

Last night in Puerto Rico, Kamalakanta and I were running in the heavy rain. The streets were in very bad condition, and we passed two or three bars where the people were very undivine. But the rain gave us extra energy. Even though I hadn't eaten in days, we walked and ran over four miles. So if you don't eat, perhaps you get extra energy.

RB 333. *Running at random*

This morning in Puerto Rico I ran randomly. When I run randomly, God knows where I go. My aim was to run for one hour. Nowadays I only care for the time, not the miles. So I ran by Shubhra's house. In thirty-five minutes I was there.

O God, suddenly a police car came up quite fast and stopped abruptly. Two policemen came out of the car. They slammed the doors and entered into a small house nearby. A lady and her husband were in a panic about something. Something had happened. In ten minutes' time I followed the same route home. I said to myself, "Let me see what is happening." But there was no police car. There was absolutely nobody around.

RB 334. *The little dogs*

Once I was running in Puerto Rico and six dogs started barking at me. Fortunately, they were in a yard behind a gate. They were not out on the street. I counted. There were six little, little dogs!

RB 335. *The spectacular runner*

In the first one-mile race in Puerto Rico, Chetana went ahead of me and ahead of all the girls. After four hundred metres she screamed, "Eee!" Chetana's running was very spectacular — the way she screamed! Then she slowed down.

RB 336. *My best disciple*

Pratyaya is my best disciple. She stays behind me in all distances. When I collapsed after a few miles in the thirteen-mile race in Puerto Rico, she was still following me. So I gave her a ride in the car. But it seems that in the one-mile race I ran faster than she could run, so she could not run near me.

RB 337. *The hundred-metre challenge*

Ten years ago how fast I used to run the 100-metre dash! I used to challenge the three musketeers — Ranjana, Chetana and one other. I used to whistle and then go way ahead of them. In ten years how slow I have become!

RB 338. *Race organisers*

Many of the people who organise races have given up running themselves. Only in the evening they walk. They have all developed nice stomachs.

I am the only spiritual Master who runs. Others just hold meditations and become fat. I will definitely defeat all the spiritual Masters in running.

RB 339. *The dangerous intersection*

One of my running routes, my hilly course, was marked off by Vinaya. This course is where Sanatan had the bicycle accident several years ago. Each time I run on the hilly course and reach that particular intersection, automatically I think of Sanatan and his accident. Either I think of Sanatan or Sanatan's soul thinks of me. Then, after that I continue. I have run there so many times. It is a very dangerous intersection!

RB 340. *How can they be ahead of me?*

In our two-mile race in Flushing Meadow Park, after a mile and a quarter I saw Madhuri. I got really puzzled. How could Madhuri be ahead of me? Then I said to myself, "Perhaps she is still completing one mile." Then a little farther on I saw Tanima and Mitali, so I knew they were all still completing one mile.

RB 341. *To drink or not to drink*

Pragati was ahead of me in the two-mile race when we passed the water station. Somebody came to give her water. She didn't want it and waved the person away. Then she herself went to the table to take water. Perhaps she did not like that person.

When we run, at that time we forget everything. I will say I don't need water. Then one second later I realise that I am so thirsty!

RB 291. *(p. 149)* 20 June 1980
RB 292. *(p. 151)* September 1980
RB 293. *(p. 151)* September 1980
RB 294. *(p. 152)* September 1980
RB 295. *(p. 153)* 26 March 1981
RB 296. *(p. 153)* 27 March 1981
RB 297. *(p. 153)* 28 March 1981
RB 298. *(p. 154)* 28 March 1981
RB 299. *(p. 154)* April 1981
RB 300. *(p. 155)* April 1981
RB 301. *(p. 155)* 4 April 1981
RB 302. *(p. 156)* 4 April 1981
RB 303. *(p. 156)* 4 April 1981
RB 304. *(p. 156)* 7 April 1981
RB 305. *(p. 157)* 21 April 1981
RB 306. *(p. 157)* 21 April 1981
RB 307. *(p. 158)* 21 April 1981
RB 308. *(p. 158)* 3 May 1981
RB 309. *(p. 158)* 3 May 1981
RB 310. *(p. 159)* 3 May 1981
RB 311. *(p. 159)* 3 May 1981
RB 312. *(p. 159)* 3 May 1981
RB 313. *(p. 160)* 11 May 1981
RB 314. *(p. 161)* 11 May 1981
RB 315. *(p. 162)* 1 June 1981
RB 316. *(p. 162)* 14 June 1981
RB 317. *(p. 163)* 20 June 1981
RB 318. *(p. 163)* 23 June 1981
RB 319. *(p. 163)* 27 June 1981
RB 320. *(p. 163)* 28 June 1981

RB 321. *(p. 164)* 28 June 1981
RB 322. *(p. 164)* 28 June 1981
RB 323. *(p. 164)* 1 July 1981
RB 324. *(p. 165)* 1 July 1981
RB 325. *(p. 165)* 8 July 1981
RB 326. *(p. 165)* 8 July 1981
RB 327. *(p. 166)* 11 July 1981
RB 328. *(p. 166)* 11 July 1981
RB 329. *(p. 167)* 12 July 1981
RB 330. *(p. 167)* 12 July 1981
RB 331. *(p. 167)* 12 July 1981
RB 332. *(p. 168)* 18 July 1981
RB 333. *(p. 169)* 18 July 1981
RB 334. *(p. 169)* 18 July 1981
RB 335. *(p. 169)* 20 July 1981
RB 336. *(p. 170)* 20 July 1981
RB 337. *(p. 170)* 21 July 1981
RB 338. *(p. 170)* 21 July 1981
RB 339. *(p. 170)* 1 August 1981
RB 340. *(p. 171)* 1 August 1981
RB 341. *(p. 171)* 1 August 1981

RUN AND BECOME, BECOME AND RUN

PART 7

RB 342. *The noisy lady*

In the one-mile race today one lady was making such noise! You could tell from fifty metres, even from a hundred metres, that something was going on.

RB 343. *Accept my surrender*

I can never become as short or as thin as Barada is, so how can you expect me to run as fast as she does? I can't go back to her height and I can't go back to her weight, so she has to accept my surrender in the running world.

RB 344. *Peter's sauna*

At four o'clock in the morning I wanted to run for three miles, but the course I picked took fifty-two minutes. Then in the afternoon I asked Peter to take me along the same course. He measured it and found it was five miles and twelve hundred metres-practically six miles. How did I go so far? It is difficult to judge the distance if you don't know the route and you have to go just by time.

In the car I was wearing a running suit, a thick sweater and then a rubber suit on top of that. I even had on my hat and gloves. Peter turned on the heat as high as possible, and after checking the course, we continued driving in the car. All this to lose weight in Peter's "sauna"! After twenty minutes it was too much. We opened up the window. We drove another two miles and then I walked for two miles.

RB 345. *Starting too fast*

In today's three-mile race in Flushing Meadow Park I saw Snigdha after one hundred metres. I couldn't believe it, but she was falling behind me. For eight hundred metres she ran with me and then she finally went ahead.

After the first four hundred metres I was still with the boys. What was I doing there? Mukunda and others were behind me. My time for the first mile was 6:39. Had it been only a one-mile race, for the last three hundred metres I could have gone faster, and my time for the mile would have been better.

Nirjhari caught me when I started walking. She passed me and left a large gap between us. I said, "Go ahead, go ahead!" Then Subala passed me, then Linda. Nayana passed me after a mile and a half. I said, "Go!"

RB 346. *He has my job*

In the five-mile race today I couldn't imagine what happened to Adrian from Australia. He started walking after one mile. Then after running for 150 metres, again he started walking. As I was watching him, I said to myself, "He has got my job." He is such an excellent runner, but he was walking after only one mile.

RB 347. *Human encouragement*

In the five-mile race I was very bad. I was telling Gangadhar to defeat Snigdha, his wife's best friend. But Gangadhar just raised his arms and surrendered. Of course, it was the human in me that told him to defeat her; the divine in me always wants whoever deserves it to win.

Gangadhar is a man. What was he doing behind Snigdha? When I encouraged him, the distance between him and Snigdha became even wider. The moment I told him to defeat her, Snigdha started going faster.

Later I saw Snighdha in her car quite happy and cheerful. I thought that definitely she had defeated Gangadhar. Then I found out that he had defeated her by one second.

RB 348. *Looking for Prabhir*

Today when I went out on a short run, for at least two hundred metres I was following Prabhir. Then, after that I didn't see him at all. What happened to him I don't know. I was waiting for the light to change and I was looking forward. When I started running again, I didn't see Prabhir. At one point I turned around, but I saw only Dorothee from the Zurich Centre, who came out of the blue. Prabhir always reminds me of John Landy, the world champion runner.

RB 349. *Exhaustion*

As you know, I am a wonderful runner. I can inspire my children to run, but when it is a matter of me personally, from the beginning to the end running is sheer torture. I run. Why? The secret reason is so that I will not get fat and compete with Indian swamis in fatness. But the main reason is to inspire my disciples to run, so that they can become fit instruments of the Supreme.

This morning I got inspiration to run at six o'clock. Usually I go running much earlier, but today I went late. I ran one, two, three, four, five and then six miles, until I reached Dan's Supreme Supermarket. This is my usual turnaround point on that course. Then I became tired and started running and walking. Three hundred metres I would run and then fifty metres I would walk. In that way I covered another three miles. Finally,

I was totally exhausted. Totally is not an exaggeration; it is an understatement. I was seeing everything as white or black or brown. My eyes were not functioning at all!

I stood and rested for a while and then I started walking. While I was walking I saw a very old, crippled lady using a cane. I said, "O God, You are still kind to me. At least I don't belong to her group."

I was dying of thirst; I was so dehydrated! But I didn't have a cent with me. What could I do?

Now, begging is not in my line. God gave me stupid pride, which I still have. Three times I was about to beg individuals for a dime to make a phone call. But when I went near them, I said, "What will happen if they don't give me the dime?" That was my stupidity. I passed two gas stations and each time I was about to ask for water or for a dime, but again I was afraid of what would happen. At one point I saw a young boy. It seemed to me that he had money. I was about to tell him that if he gave me a dime, in fifteen minutes I would give him a ten dollar bill. Again I said, "What will happen if he does not give me the money?"

I was struggling and struggling. Perhaps I have never been so exhausted. I felt as if I had run fifty miles, which I have never done. Still I went on. At one place there was a sign that said "College Point." I stood there for five minutes and then I started walking. I had covered over two hundred metres when all of a sudden I saw a car stop near me. A gentleman came out of the car and asked me the way to College Point. As you know, I am not very good at giving directions. Most sympathetically I told him that I didn't know. Then I came back to my senses and realised that I had just seen the sign and had even been standing there. But by that time the car had passed by. That kind of tiredness I had!

When I was only six hundred metres away from my house, I was so exhausted that I said, "Let me wait here for ten minutes. Let me take rest for ten minutes." Then I finally walked home.

So running can make people very tired if they are useless runners like me. It is always advisable to carry some change or a dollar with you. For me it is always advisable to take someone with me when I run — preferably someone with a car, not a runner. Yesterday I took Peter with me. But when you take someone with you, at that time you are not exhausted. Yesterday I ran seven miles. I was showing off, running quite fast. When you take someone along with you, at that time you do not need help. And then when you don't take someone, at that time all the world's help you need.

RB 350. *No surrender*

During our marathon in New Jersey I ran thirteen miles. For the first seven miles I ran at an 8:10 pace. Kirsty was running just a little ahead of me. She wasn't looking over her shoulder, but each time I came near her, all of a sudden her speed would increase. Whenever I came only four or five metres behind her, she would hear my footsteps and go faster. But she never looked behind her.

I tell my disciples to surrender, but I myself don't know how to surrender, especially to my girl runner-disciples. Each time I am determined to defeat them badly.

RB 351. *The false finisher*

At the finish of our marathon, when I saw the runner that came
in third, I couldn't believe that he was such a good runner. Then
I came to know that he didn't run the entire race. He ran over
the finish line by mistake.

RB 352. *Running long distance*

During my thirteen-mile run today, only once did I walk a few
metres while drinking water. Otherwise, the rest of the way I
ran.

The first two years I ran in the New York City Marathon, I
had cramps in spite of my practising. This year, I have not been
able to practise. How will I be able to run the marathon?

When you run long distance, as opposed to short distance,
you sometimes feel that you won't be able to complete the race.
You are afraid that you will get cramps and won't be able to
finish the distance.

RB 353. *The birthday blessing*

At five o'clock this morning when I went out to run, inwardly
I blessed Robin's soul because today is his birthday. Then, a
little after six-thirty, I went out to run again and this time I saw
Robin in the physical. He was near Savyasachi's house. I was
running down the 150th Street hill when I saw him press his
wristwatch and start running with long strides. I thought that I
would turn around and meet him. But then I said to myself, "I
will never be able to catch him."

RB 354. *The inner and outer running*

As in the outer running I struggle and struggle and struggle in order to survive — while winning the race is far, far beyond my imagination — even so, most of my disciples struggle and struggle and struggle in the inner running. Unfortunately, the goal is still a far, far cry for them.

But who knows, in the near or distant future I may make satisfactory progress in my outer running, although I just completed half a century. Similarly, my disciples can and will make satisfactory progress in their inner running.

This is my fervent hope, and I do hope that my Beloved Supreme, out of His infinite Bounty, will fulfil my soulful and prayerful wish.

RB 355. *A good follower*

The day before yesterday was a wonderful day. Around six o'clock in the morning I was running in front of my house, doing my speed work — fifty metres slow and fifty metres fast. Then I saw the fat lady who is very fond of me, with her two dogs. Two or three years ago she had a fight with another lady while walking her dog, and I took the fat lady's side. So she always shows me her gratitude.

After each hundred metres, I was taking rest for a few seconds. At one particular moment I took rest and walked. The white dog was following me — not chasing me — and barking.

The lady said to me, "So you see, you see!"

I said, "Good morning, good morning!"

The lady said, "Like your other followers, my dog also is following you. He will be a very good follower."

So I thanked her.

RB 356. *Happiness and sadness*

When I was running thirteen miles during the marathon last weekend, I was feeling such sadness and happiness. I was feeling sadness when I thought of my limp, and I was feeling happiness because I was still going on.

RB 357. *A difficult exercise*

Two weeks ago Sunanda was practising speed work. She was running so fast! This morning she was taking exercise, bringing her leg forward to her chest. This very exercise I was trying to do at five o'clock this morning. After one try I got such pain in my toes! And this very exercise she did twenty or thirty times. I wanted to do ten, but I did only one.

RB 358. Sri Chinmoy Race *song*

Before the start of today's seven-mile race, I went to change my clothes in the men's room. One man was singing and chanting, *Sri Chinmoy Race, Sri Chinmoy Race,* to his own tune. Each time he was changing the tune. He didn't know I was there.

RB 359. *Are you all right?*

During the seven-mile race I stopped to drink some water and I walked a few metres at the four-mile point. One man was asking me, "Are you all right? Are you all right?" But I was just taking a drink of water.

RB 360. *Stopping for water*

At another point Ilona and I were running near each other. Once I stopped for water and walked for fifty or sixty metres. Then, finished! She took the lead. But then, near the end of the race, my ego came forward so powerfully, and I passed her.

The problem always starts when you drink. Good runners don't drink. If you drink, you are finished! You lose distance, and then for forty or fifty metres you feel miserable.

RB 361. *Surrender to the spiritual Master*

In today's race Kirsty very nicely surrendered. First she gave me a fight for one or two miles. Then I went ahead of her. I am so bad. Each time somebody was about to pass me, I looked around to see if Kirsty was coming. If I saw that Kirsty was not coming, I felt I was safe.

In the New Jersey marathon last week it was she who did not want to be behind me. She would increase her speed if I started to come up behind her. This time it was my turn to look around to see if she was coming.

RB 362. *Come on, legs!*

At the end of the race, as one man was finishing, he was shouting, "Come on, legs! Come on, legs!" It is on the videotape.

RB 363. *The past is gold*

I always say that the past is dust. In my case the past is gold. For inspiration I was watching a videotape of my best seven-mile race performance in Connecticut on 30 March 1980. That day I ran at a 7:19 pace. So the past for me is not dust; it is gold.

Five minutes before the race, Wally brought me a cup of coffee and I got strength from it in the beginning of the race. But later on it stopped working.

One man ran next to me. He was Mohan's brother-in-law. He gave me drinks along the way. Then he went ahead of me at the last moment. At the end, after finishing, he congratulated me.

RB 364. *Twenty-four-hour friends*

At least ten times Jim Roser spoke to me during our twenty-four-hour race. I have never seen a runner who encouraged me so much. He was so nice. He was always cheerful and always had something nice to say. Once he said that he wanted to pronounce my name correctly because so many people were pronouncing it incorrectly.

At one point Nathan Whiting — the one with the long hair — said to me, "You do so many things."

I said, "I can't run."

He said, "So what? So many other things you are doing."

When I stopped to take rest, he said, "Everybody needs rest." He is very kind-hearted.

Dave Peabody, the tall man, is also very nice. He shook my hand.

Norman Allen ran with Beverly Nolan the whole way. He was calling himself "Beverly's friend." He wouldn't say his real name to the counters. He is a real joker. He was asking the counters to count Beverly's mileage and his mileage together so they would come in first. Thomas is also a joker. At one point, he was also calling him "Beverly's friend," instead of using his real name.

RB 365. *Praying for leg cramps*

When I was running my last six miles during the twenty-four-hour race, I was going ahead of everyone, no matter which runner I came near. But I said to myself, "O God, some of them have run almost a hundred miles and I have run only twenty-two."

At one point I was behind Yasu. Poor fellow, he was holding his left leg, the hamstring. He was getting cramps. I prayed to God to give the cramp to me immediately, but God didn't listen to my prayer. My prayer was sincere. I said, "Let me suffer and let him go." He was only one metre ahead of me. I felt miserable, but God didn't listen to my prayer. So I went on.

RB 366. *World-class children*

I may not be a champion runner anymore, but my children are all world-class. I am so proud of my children who ran in the twenty-four-hour race. In a few years there will be no record that they cannot break in ultra-marathoning.

RB 367. *Marathon Tune-Up*

Today I ran the 25-kilometre Marathon Tune-Up in Central Park. Quite a few disciples also ran. At the start, Nayana was standing just ahead of me with her husband at the eight-minute pace marker. I said, "Go!" Then, after some time I saw that she fell behind me.

At one point both Peter and Tulasi were asking people at the water stations if they had water, but they had run out.

Kurt Steiner likes me so much because we help the New York Road Runners Club in so many ways. Two or three times during the race he mentioned my name over the loudspeaker. When I finished, he mentioned my time. Niriha was standing with him on the platform taking video. She says that she helped him practise saying my name.

RB 368. *I don't see anything in him*

Yesterday afternoon around three o'clock I asked Vinaya to watch me while I did hill work on 150th Street. He is a good guard, except that he sometimes falls asleep when he is on duty. But this time he was wide awake.

At the bottom of the hill I saw a boy about thirteen or fourteen years old waiting for the Q-44 bus. The boy looked right at me and said out loud, "I don't know why everybody makes such a fuss about him. I don't see anything in him."

There was absolutely nobody else there only he and I. So I looked at him and said, "I don't see anything in you either."

Then he was really embarrassed and he turned away. I smiled at him and started running back up the hill.

The boy was very brave to say what he did, and I was also brave. He didn't walk away; he just turned around and looked at the fence, still waiting for the bus. By the time I went down the hill a second time, the bus had arrived and he had gotten on it. So I didn't have to encounter him again.

RB 369. *Looking for Union Turnpike*

My oldest long-distance running route I discovered by myself. No one on my road crew found it. On this route I go down Union Turnpike to Springfield Boulevard and then to Northern Boulevard, and back. When I first used to take this route, instead of going back to Springfield and home along Union Turnpike, I would forget to turn and keep going straight along Northern Boulevard. Many times I would get lost.

I would be only one or two blocks away from Union Turnpike, and I would start asking people where Union Turnpike was. Sometimes I would have to go back on Northern Boulevard to Springfield because I couldn't find Union Turnpike.

Once I was actually standing on Union Turnpike and I asked someone where Union Turnpike was. My mind was so exhausted from my long run that day!

RB 370. *Keep going!*

Today Pahar and I ran while Peter drove alongside us. We went on Union Turnpike to Springfield Boulevard and then to Northern Boulevard. At around seven and a half miles there was a very steep hill. I was dying, but Pahar was dancing inwardly and outwardly.

An elderly couple saw us running. The lady, who was quite fat, looked at me and said, "Keep going, keep going!" because I was panting so hard. I should have invited her to join us. I was dying and she had to say, "Keep going, keep going!"

RB 371. *Losing weight*

When you have to lose weight, it is no joke. Today I took only four hundred calories and ran fifteen and a half miles — only to lose weight.

Usually I weigh more after I finish running than I did before I started. This time I decided to catch the culprit! Before I went out, I weighed my ERG bottle when it was full. It weighed one pound and three ounces. Then I subtracted the weight of the bottle — an ounce and a quarter. From now on after I run I will know how much I have gained from drinking.

RB 372. *The Toledo Marathon*

The Toledo Marathon in 1979 was my best marathon. I did it in 3:55. It was so cold that day! Sometimes I was running on the left side so I could pass people, but sometimes I ran in between people to keep warm. In the beginning, before the sun came out, it was twenty-four degrees, so I was running in between people. Even so, at one point my back was freezing.

RB 373. *What's wrong with it?*

Before our four-mile race at Breezy Point this morning one man looked at me and asked his friend, "Who is that man?"

His friend told him who I was. Then the first man said, "Why is he running?"

The friend said, "Why not? What's wrong with it?"

RB 374. *The hostile runner*

Just before the four-mile run started, I was unfortunately stand-ing beside a man who was very hostile. While Thomas was giving instructions to the runners, the man said, "Stop chirping!"

When Thomas asked for one minute of silence, the man said, "What nonsense!"

This same man finished far behind me in the race.

RB 375. *Pulin's last-minute victory*

In the four-mile race, Pulin was behind me most of the way. When we turned around to go back at the two-mile point, I saw that he was behind me and I was very happy. Then after three and a half miles, he increased his speed and passed me. Then he went ahead of Hangsa. I said, "Good!" Then he went ahead of some other people. He was showing off.

RB 376. *Competing with the girls*

When I reached the turnaround point in our four-mile race, I saw that Kumuda was behind me. My ego became so big and my chest expanded. But Karabi, her sister-in-law, was no good. After eight hundred metres she and Savita went ahead of me. At least I was ahead of Sunanda and Nilima for five hundred metres.

Barada was so nice to so many people. She started the race five minutes late, so she did not defeat me or any of the others who were ahead of me.

RB 377. *Susan's friend*

During the race Susan was so nice! She was running with a small child. When I passed them on my way back from the turnaround point, Susan pointed at me and said, "That is Sri Chinmoy." She had been telling the child all about me as they were running together.

RB 378. *Over-fifty competition*

As one man was passing me, he asked, "How old are you, Sri?"

When I said, "Fifty," he said, "Oh, you are great!" Then he went ahead of me.

At the awards ceremony I gave him the second prize in the over-fifty category. He was so happy to have defeated me! Perhaps I was third in that category.

RB 379. *The admirer*

After the four-mile race, a man came up to me and told me that he had attended one of my disciples' courses. He was very moved by the course, so he came to one of our Wednesday night public meditations. I was not there, but he is planning to come again.

RB 380. *The foliage run*

After running our four-mile race, I ran the ten-kilometre or 6.2-mile Foliage Run in New Jersey. The course had good mile markers and it was very beautiful. The trees on both sides of the road gave shade and created a soothing atmosphere. These kinds of races are really good. Sometimes in the races with thousands of people you get lost.

The only problem was that at times the course was dangerous because of the cars. Even near the finish line two cars were driving in front of me and not allowing me to go by them. At another place there was a parked car and the runners couldn't make a turn properly. Of course, this is because of the speed we were maintaining. The race officials were very careful that the front runners were unobstructed.

Also, there were many hills on the course — practically mountains. At one point, I walked about fifty metres up a very steep hill. I didn't dare run up it. Everybody else was also walking.

RB 381. *Give me his cramps*

In the Foliage Run a young man had given up after five miles. He was massaging his hamstring. Whenever I see a young runner getting cramps during a race, I pray to God, "O God, give me his cramps." But God doesn't listen to my prayers.

RB 382. *Young competition*

From the start to the finish, I passed about thirty or forty people in the New Jersey race. Whenever I saw that someone was no more than ten metres ahead of me, I would run faster to catch him. Then, again I would see new people ahead of me and I would try to catch them.

One child about ten years old was competing with me mile after mile. He was not running; he was dancing and jumping. I didn't see his feet touching the ground!

Then he saw a little girl who was younger than he was go ahead of us and his ego came forward. He could not bear it. He ran very fast to go ahead of me and catch her. Then he saw that she had stopped; she had surrendered. After five miles the little boy himself surrendered and I didn't see him anymore.

RB 383. *Old runners*

When I am running and old people go ahead of me, I say, "How can they do that?" I forget that I too am old.

One old man finished the race and then he went back to run with his wife. His wife was only five metres ahead of me when he came to join her at about the five-and-a-half-mile point. I finished a little ahead of her. When she finished, she was breathing so hard that she was practicably screaming. She sounded as if she were dying.

RB 384. *Victory to Sarama*

Like me, Sarama should have come to the Foliage Run after running our four-mile race this morning. She would have got another prize in her age group. This morning she was lucky because Ilona did not come; she was dreaming — fast asleep. Or perhaps Ilona had some bad injury or she had to go to work. Otherwise, she can defeat Sarama.

RB 385. *The missing place card*

After the Foliage Run the officials were making announcements for runners to turn in their place cards. My card was just sitting on the grass near me. Finally Pahar saw it and went to return it. So I was one of the culprits in that respect. But they were not waiting for the place card of finisher number 236 — me. They were waiting for the cards of some of the top runners.

RB 386. *My pacer-coach*

My coach, Pahar, ran with me today to pace me during the ten-kilometre race. I was running and he was jogging. Pahar is often my pacer for distances from one mile to twenty-six miles. But when I was his age I could definitely have defeated him. He is not an eleven-second sprinter. His timing for one hundred metres is fourteen seconds. In my entire athletic career I never ran the hundred so slowly! I started with twelve seconds and then improved. Of course, I was running without shoes — farmer's feet — on a cinder track. Otherwise, my timing would have been better.

RB 387. *The shopkeeper's tip*

After the Foliage Run I went into a bakery to buy prasad for all my helpers. The shopkeeper had a good soul. I asked her to put four pastries in one box and six in another. She said, "Yes, I will do it. I am pretty good in counting."

I said, "Only last week when I was in Woodstock a lady gave me less than what I had paid for."

The shopkeeper laughed and laughed. Then she gave me seventy-six cents change. I gave it back to her and said, "This is for you."

She said, "This is awfully kind of you. I have been working here for five years, and I have never gotten any tips. You are such a nice man."

RB 388. *Bad luck in losing weight*

Before I ran this morning, I weighed 136 1/2 pounds. Then, after running both our four-mile race and the ten-kilometre New Jersey race, how much did I weigh? 138! I gained almost two pounds. And what did I have to eat all day? Only ERG and one piece of pizza. Bad luck!

RB 389. *Unrecognised*

In the beginning of the Schaeffer five-mile run in Flushing Meadow this morning, I was standing right beside a man who was wearing one of our T-shirts, but he didn't know who I was.

RB 390. *The lone runner*

This morning when I was running, after about four miles I saw Nishtha and Savita. They were standing with folded hands. After I had completed five miles, I saw Lucy and Nilima coming up the hill from Union Turnpike. But today I was not planning to run with anybody because I wanted to run ten miles.

RB 342. *(p. 177)* 2 August 1981
RB 343. *(p. 177)* 2 August 1981
RB 344. *(p. 177)* 3 August 1981
RB 345. *(p. 178)* 4 August 1981
RB 346. *(p. 178)* 15 August 1981
RB 347. *(p. 178)* 15 August 1981
RB 348. *(p. 179)* 15 August 1981
RB 349. *(p. 179)* 1 September 1981
RB 350. *(p. 181)* 13 September 1981
RB 351. *(p. 182)* 13 September 1981
RB 352. *(p. 182)* 13 September 1981
RB 353. *(p. 182)* 15 September 1981
RB 354. *(p. 183)* 16 September 1981
RB 355. *(p. 183)* 17 September 1981
RB 356. *(p. 184)* 18 September 1981
RB 357. *(p. 184)* 18 September 1981
RB 358. *(p. 184)* 20 September 1981
RB 359. *(p. 184)* 20 September 1981
RB 360. *(p. 185)* 20 September 1981
RB 361. *(p. 185)* 20 September 1981
RB 362. *(p. 185)* 20 September 1981
RB 363. *(p. 186)* 20 September 1981
RB 365. *(p. 187)* 27 September 1981
RB 366. *(p. 187)* 27 September 1981
RB 367. *(p. 188)* 4 October 1981
RB 368. *(p. 188)* 8 October 1981
RB 369. *(p. 189)* 8 October 1981
RB 370. *(p. 189)* 8 October 1981
RB 371. *(p. 190)* 8 October 1981
RB 372. *(p. 190)* 8 October 1981

RB 373. *(p. 190)* 10 October 1981
RB 374. *(p. 191)* 10 October 1981
RB 375. *(p. 191)* 10 October 1981
RB 376. *(p. 191)* 10 October 1981
RB 377. *(p. 192)* 10 October 1981
RB 378. *(p. 192)* 10 October 1981
RB 379. *(p. 192)* 10 October 1981
RB 380. *(p. 192)* 10 October 1981
RB 381. *(p. 193)* 10 October 1981
RB 382. *(p. 193)* 10 October 1981
RB 383. *(p. 194)* 10 October 1981
RB 384. *(p. 194)* 10 October 1981
RB 385. *(p. 194)* 10 October 1981
RB 386. *(p. 195)* 10 October 1981
RB 387. *(p. 195)* 10 October 1981
RB 388. *(p. 196)* 10 October 1981
RB 389. *(p. 196)* 11 October 1981
RB 390. *(p. 196)* 15 October 1981

RUN AND BECOME, BECOME AND RUN

PART 8

RB 391. *Street celebrity*

The other day I was doing hill work on 150th Street. Whom did I see? The great Australian runner Robert de Castella. He was planning to eat at Annam Brahma and he was doing some running before he went there.

RB 392. *The boxer*

This afternoon I walked five miles and then I ran another three.

My five-mile walk was real fun! Databir was sleeping like anything in the car. But Vinaya was so good; he watched me every step of the way with his eyes wide open.

Baoul was driving. I was walking at random, looking for two-way streets so Baoul could drive alongside me. I had to always think of Baoul. I could walk anywhere, but driving was the problem.

We didn't follow any of my regular running routes, so I didn't know where the roads would lead us. It turned out to be uphill most of the way. As you know, I hate hill work. I was wearing six-pound weights on each leg. This is the kind of thing that boxers do to build up their legs. So I am another boxer.

The other day I used two-pound weights on my legs, then three. Gradually I will make progress and go up to seven and a half pounds.

RB 393. *The three-mile run*

After my walk, we drove to Flushing Meadow Park. I was going to run another three miles with the great runners Sushobhan, Databir, Pahar and Vinaya.

As we were driving to Flushing Meadow, the four boys ran while I watched from the car. Three of them were running at under a six-minute pace.

Databir has the tendency to race, and his first mile was a 5:42. Then, how he suffered! It was too much for him, so he entered into the car with me and did not get out again.

Vinaya was running even slower than a nine-minute pace. We were waiting for him to reach Flushing Meadow Park, but he was too slow. We had to go back to get him.

During our run together in Flushing Meadow, only Vinaya ran slower than I did. One person, at least, surrendered to me!

RB 394. *The truck drivers*

Today I ran five miles with the boys and then two miles on my own. When I was running with the boys on Main Street, some truck drivers started cutting jokes with us. They were standing next to their truck. As soon as they saw us running by at an eight-minute pace, they started jogging in place. Then they asked us, "Getting ready for the New York Marathon?"

RB 395. *The jokers*

When the boys go jogging with me, I know they can run much faster. But the way they make noise, panting and breathing hard — "Hah, hah," — they sound as if they are dying. They are all jokers!

RB 396. *The fun run*

Today I ran three short races in New Jersey. At the beginning of the first race, a mile-and-a-half fun run, some children were in front of me. Children don't run; they dance. One child absolutely wouldn't move out of my way. Very politely I touched his shoulder and passed him.

Then, one black man and I were fighting and fighting to go ahead of each other. Finally I went three or four metres ahead of him. That was the time I had to make a wrong turn. Three girls who were just ahead of me made a wrong turn, and I followed them. These three girls and others who took the "short cut" didn't go back the right way. But the race director happened to come at the very moment that I made the wrong turn. So he shouted at me that I had gone the wrong way. I was the only one who went back the right way. By that time the black man was four or five metres ahead of me. After some time I caught him again. But in the end he finally defeated me. We had a very good competition. The girls who took the short cut also defeated me.

RB 397. *False encouragement*

At one point in the first race Pratyaya made me feel that the goal was very near. She told me to go straight, but actually I had to make another turn. Then, in the last race, she screamed, "Just cross the road and you can see the end!" But the end was not in sight.

Databir also gives me false encouragement. In the second race today he was saying, "The end is very near." O God, I had to run about two hundred metres, and only then I saw the finish line way ahead of me.

Of course, these two and all those who cheer for me are only trying to encourage me. In a sense they do the right thing when they say these kinds of things. Encouragement comes and makes me feel that the goal is just in front of my nose.

RB 398. *The policeman's wrong turn*

In the race that Rejean ran, just before my third fun run, the policeman in the lead car took a wrong turn. So the race ended up being two hundred metres short. What could Rejean do? He was the first runner and he was just following the lead car.

RB 399. *Time splits*

Third-class runners like me should not think of their timing. Even when you hear the timing, usually it is so slow that you do not get inspiration to go further. Sometimes in a two-mile race when you hear the time for the first mile you have the capacity to go faster. But in a marathon, at ten miles frustration starts because you are running so slowly. You are killing yourself, and then when you hear the time, you see it is so slow.

RB 400. *Toledo Marathon splits*

When I ran my best marathon in Toledo, Gayatri would tell me one timing and Peter would say something totally different. The funniest thing is that Peter was standing two or three metres farther along than Gayatri, but the timing he gave me was less than hers. Then I started getting annoyed — who was giving the right splits? It turned out that Peter was giving the official timing and Gayatri had her self-chosen time. For four or five miles how I suffered because of the timing!

RB 401. *A hard time*

In the third race today, one girl gave me a very hard time. Finally, I went ahead of her. For twenty metres she really died to keep up with me, but then she fell behind.

RB 402. *The basketball player*

At the last race one man was so nice. He was a basketball player. After the race he came over to thank us for coming. The man was saying how young I looked and how unusual it was for someone my age to have such good speed. Niriha interviewed him. She became both a reporter and a camerawoman. Trishul missed his opportunity! He would have asked the basketball player so many questions.

RB 403. *The competitive curse*

Sometimes when we run, we try to pass the runners who are ahead of us. But when they fall behind us, at that time pride does not come. We only feel miserable that we wanted to pass them in the first place. We wonder why we are killing ourselves. First we try to beat others. Then, when we go ahead of them, we curse ourselves for wanting to pass them. We feel it was better just to run behind them.

In one of today's races, at least six or seven runners passed me. Then, one by one, I passed them and went ahead again.

RB 404. *Guru's gratitude*

Today I ran three good races. It is all due to my disciples' encouragement. All those who were in the bus and others who accompanied me to New Jersey deserve my absolutely most powerful gratitude. Because of their silver inspiration, gold aspiration and diamond sacrifice, I was able to accomplish what I have done today.

So these people deserve gratitude — G-R-A-T-I-T-U-D-E — in the purest sense of the term.

RB 405. *The dog's message*

Today I was doing hill work on 150th Street. I was about to complete two miles when I saw the fat lady who used to have two dogs. Now she has only one dog; the other one died. The dog started following me. I knew the dog wouldn't bite me; she was only trying to lick my left knee. I stopped running and the lady said, "Don't be afraid of my dog. She is saying 'Good luck' to you!"

RB 406. *Songs from running*

Quite often when I run, many songs appear inside my brain. This afternoon when I was running, two or three new songs came to my mind. Then, after I finished running, I had to sit down and notate the songs.

I will die, but I know my songs will live on. Indians, especially Bengalis, in every nook and cranny will sing my songs.

RB 407. *The embarrassing run*

Today I ran four miles with Pahar in Flushing Meadow Park. So many silly and embarrassing things happened! Before I started, I put on heavy clothes — shorts, trousers, plus the thick rubber belt I use to support my back. The first mile, as usual, was at my bullock-cart speed: 9:25. My timing for the next two miles was 8:18 and 7:40.

After the third mile I said, "Now I want to run a fast mile — seven minutes or under." I took off the rubber belt so that I could breathe more deeply. After two hundred metres, what happened? My trousers began falling off on my right side.

First I tried holding them up with my right hand, while I was still pumping with my left hand. Then they started falling down on my left side also. So I had to hold my trousers up with both hands. Whenever I let go, for a few seconds they would stay up and then they would fall down again. Because of this I could not run fast, so my timing was 7:50. Easily I could have gone faster! I forgot that I had on shorts underneath. I should have stopped and taken off my trousers.

RB 408. *Two divine beings*

The day before yesterday I ran seven and a half miles. After five and a half miles I came to the intersection where the Kew Motor Inn is.

It was about a quarter to eight in the morning. I was not in the middle of the street, but all of a sudden someone started honking. I looked around and saw a policeman on a motor bike. He was Puerto Rican. Since nobody else was around, I thought that perhaps I had done something wrong.

The policeman raised both hands and started screaming with joy, "Sri, Sri, Sri!"

I said to myself, "So, I have not committed any crime."

When I reached Main Street, I was about to make a left turn. Then I saw that a car had made a right turn and was waiting across the street. The driver — a fat, black man — was signalling me to come across. When I came near him, he said, "You are a very nice guy. I love you."

So, within eight hundred metres, I met two nice human beings, two really divine beings.

RB 409. *First New York Marathon*

The first year I ran the New York Marathon in 1979, I became so tired after fourteen miles. Then I saw Lucy. She was doing stretching exercises, but I didn't have the capacity even to bend. Then she went ahead.

As soon as I would come near Radha, she would take off. Then she would relax. When I would catch her again, she would run faster.

RB 410. *Two Long Island Marathons*

At the start of the 1979 Long Island Marathon I was taking such long strides because I was running with Bhashwar, Bhima and a few others. The first thirteen miles I ran so fast! If I had not walked the last three miles, I would have finished in under four hours.

The following year I ran only thirteen miles, and Lucy skated the full twenty-six miles. I thought I was running behind Shephali and Savita, but afterwards I found out it was Shephali and Amy. All the time I was hiding and keeping behind them. Shephali didn't recognise me at all.

RB 411. *The oath*

About four years ago Barada defeated me at one of our races in Connecticut. At that time I took a solemn oath to defeat her. Three years have very nicely passed by and my oath still remains in Heaven. Barada has improved like anything!

RB 412. *Running the New York Marathon*

During the New York Marathon at least five people recognised me, although I was not wearing a Sri Chinmoy Marathon Team uniform. Some of them called out, "Keep going, keep going! Don't give up, Sri!" Some people were saying, "Go, Sri Chinmoy!" because Sushobhan, who was running with me, had on a Centre jacket.

Some of the 24-hour-race participants saw me and thanked me for the race. They are very nice people.

It is so funny! You pass people at fifteen or sixteen miles, smiling and smiling. Then, without any warning, cramps come later — at about twenty miles. Then you have to stop and walk.

One policeman said to me, "You can't walk, you have to run." He was encouraging me to run, but I was dying.

RB 413. *The first competition*

I started my life of competition in Santa Barbara on 5 June 1979 with a three-mile race. My pace was 7:43. For the first four hundred metres I was running with excellent runners at a six-minute pace. Then everything went blank; I couldn't see anything. After that I started walking for a while.

RB 414. *The post-marathon one-mile race*

In the one-mile race this morning, at the last moment, coming around the last turn, I defeated Nemi. I said, "This is the time!" I got such innocent pleasure by defeating her. First I had to defeat Tanima, then Mitali and so on. Each time I went ahead of someone I got such joy!

RB 415. *California races*

I was in California for two and a half days. We had several races. In the two-mile race, I did nine seconds over my best two-mile timing: 13:51. In San Diego we had a four-hundred-metre race. My timing there was seven seconds more than my best four-hundred-metre timing. One of our Seattle disciples bragged that he was going to win the two-mile race. Then Astika defeated him badly. But he did come in second or third — to everybody's surprise.

RB 416. *The private conversation*

During our seventy-mile race the young son of George Gardiner, the American record-holder for one hundred miles on a track, came up to me and said he wanted to talk to me privately. Then he told me, "You are a good person," and he congratulated me on the sixth anniversary of my writing *Transcendence-Perfection*. He had his arm around my shoulder. Then, when Bhashwar took our picture, I put my arm around him. His name is John.

RB 417. *The massage*

Later, when I completed thirteen miles during the seventy-mile race, this little boy, John, came up to me and started massaging my calf muscles. He said, "You are tight!"

RB 418. *Meditating on George Gardiner*

When George Gardiner finished the race, he folded his hands when he saw me. But he was feeling very sick, so he went into the medical tent. His son John begged me to please come see his father. So I went into the tent and meditated on him. Then he was all right.

George couldn't believe I was meditating on him in the tent. He sat up and said, "Thank you for everything." Before he got his prize, over the microphone he thanked me for saving his life.

RB 419. *The big hand*

After the race I gave John a special prize for the way he encouraged the runners right from the beginning of the race. I told him that he was a very good boy. Many times over the microphone he had asked the spectators to give the runners a big hand. So then I asked everyone to give him a big hand.

RB 420. *Running equals*

Today while I was running I saw Boiragi running. Then later I saw his wife Mitali running. Boiragi can defeat me badly, but I can defeat his wife badly. So we are equal.

RB 421. *Birthday hill work*

Today was Nancy Barr's birthday. I saw her when I was doing hill work on 150th Street. She was also doing hill work. She ran and ran with me. I was going up when she was going down, and she was going up when I was going down. I didn't know it was her birthday at the time, but later I found out.

RB 422. *Two-mile rivals*

In the two-mile race at the park where Cahit's running club practices, I will never forget that my first rival was Mitali. Next came Melissa and third was Amita. Then at the end it was Lucy. I was telling her to go and she was telling me to go. In this way we finished the race. After the race the singers sang the song about Cahit.

RB 423. *The guard-runner*

Today at the United Nations the guard saluted me as I came in. He said, "I was the only runner last time in your race for the Security and Safety Service." Sal ran with him so he would have competition, but towards the end Sal stopped. That's why this guard got first prize.

RB 424. *Gary Fanelli in Philadelphia*

Gary Fanelli is now growing long hair and a beard and moustache. So at first I could not recognise him when he started running with me in the Philadelphia Marathon. He ran alongside me for at least three hundred metres. He said to me, "Guruji, I didn't know that you would be here. Otherwise, I might have run."

I told him, "Outwardly I could not contact you on your birthday, but I meditated on you inwardly." His birthday was the day before the New York Marathon. He said, "I thought of you on my birthday."

He said he was going to Honolulu to run the marathon on December 13th.

RB 425. *Practice marathons*

The first mile of the Philadelphia Marathon was no good. The road went up into the sky. After two or three hundred metres it went up, up, up — like a building! As soon as I started the race, I had no life energy.

I am very tricky. I just run the course and if I don't complete it, I call it practice. Otherwise, if I take it too seriously, I suffer. I think, "Oh, I have to complete it." But this way I don't have to worry. I just start and do as many miles as I can.

RB 426. *Pace problems*

Pahar has given me a schedule for seventy miles a week. Up to Saturday, it is possible for me to follow the schedule. With greatest difficulty I do it. But when Sunday comes, I am totally lost. How can I do twenty more miles in one day? I am not able to fulfil Pahar's desire. I stop at seven or ten miles, so it doesn't add up to seventy miles.

I feel that if I run very slowly, I will be able to run a higher mileage during the week. Sometimes before I start out, I am determined to run at a twelve-minute pace. Since it is an Indian bullock-cart pace, I think I will be able to run farther. But what happens is that I start at about a 10:15 pace. Then it becomes 9:50 and then 8:15. Each mile that I do in a good time gives me such joy. But by the time I reach five miles, I am finished.

The problem is that when I run at a ten-minute pace, it is boring. An eleven or twelve-minute pace is out of the question. It is not even running! But a nine-minute pace becomes too difficult. So I can't figure out what to do. One moment it is too slow, but if I speed up, the next moment I am completely exhausted.

RB 427. *The record-breaker*

In our half-marathon in Flushing Meadow Park today over six hundred people ran. One man from the Millrose Athletic Association broke his own national record for the half-marathon in the over-forty age group. After the race he started congratulating me and saying, "Everything was so good!"

RB 428. *Two firsts*

Cahit Yeter stood first is his age group in the half-marathon. After he finished, he came back to run with me. Usually Rejean comes back to run with me. Perhaps today, after standing first overall out of so many people, he was dead, so he did not come.

RB 429. *Guruji is dying*

When I was running, at one point two Indians were passing me. One of them said, "Namaste, Guruji. Namaste, Guruji."
Then the other one said, "Oh, Guruji is running."
I said, "No, Guruji is dying."
They said, "Don't die, don't die!"
They were both wearing T-shirts with my picture on the front, which they had gotten at some other race.

RB 430. *Everything is proper*

Another man running by me looked at me while he was passing me. He practically stopped and turned around. Then, looking at me face to face, he said to me, "Everything in your group is proper, proper!"

RB 431. *Here is Sri!*

There were four or five young black boys watching the race. When they saw me, they started jumping up and down and shouting, "Here is Sri, here is Sri!"

RB 432. *Our Rosie Ruiz*

Today we had a "Rosie Ruiz." She started walking at one point during the race. Then she cut across the course and came out near the end. She didn't run six or eight hundred metres of the course, and then she said that she had won. Fortunately, two other runners told Thomas what had happened and he disqualified her.

RB 433. *Do you want a cigar?*

The first day in Florida while I was running, I saw a young man smoking a cigar. He said to me, "Do you want to have a cigar?"

I waved my hand and said, "No, thank you."

The man ran after me and said, "You thank me and you are not taking one."

This time I just ignored him, so he stopped bothering me.

RB 434. *Strengthening the chest*

The same day, after fifteen minutes I saw a very nice old man running with his hands behind his head. He said to me, "Good morning."

I asked him, "Is there any reason why you are doing that?"

He answered, "To strengthen my chest."

In silence I said, "You don't need to strengthen your chest, but I need to strengthen mine."

RB 435. *Freezing in Florida*

Another time I was running on a very cold day around five o'clock in the morning. Florida also can be quite cold in the winter. A newspaper boy saw me. He said to me, "Don't keep running. Go home! You will be frozen up." He advised me not to run, but on that day I ran thirteen miles.

RB 436. *Waiting for the bus*

On that cold day when I was running, I ran by a girl waiting for the bus. Half an hour later, when I was returning, she was still waiting in that cold weather.

RB 437. *The twenty-four-hour-race friend*

Before the start of the Jersey Shore Marathon, Dave Peabody, who had run in our twenty-four-hour race, came up to me. I asked him, "Your wife is allowing you to run? She doesn't mind this time?"

He answered, "Oh no, she is very happy. She is here supporting me and helping me. Today she is smiling."

Quite often his wife used to object when he ran races. When he ran our twenty-four-hour race, he didn't tell his wife beforehand that he was going to do it. He just left her a note. But then she came to the race and watched him.

RB 438. *The windy marathon*

When I ran ten miles in the Jersey Shore Marathon today, the wind was so bad. The trees were half bent. Three or four times I had to stop.

RB 439. *Slow calculations*

Fortunately, today I took an oath that I would not get angry with my road crew, no matter what happened. At the second mile Sundar was supposed to give my split, but he couldn't calculate it fast enough. So as I ran by, he said, "Eight...." and then there was a big pause. After I had gone twenty metres he said, "Forty."

RB 440. *The crowded start*

Just after we crossed the starting line, it was very crowded. At one point a lady and I were stepping on each other's toes. I was trying to take off my jacket. A man right behind me said, "Come on, get out of the way."

Ranjana said to him, "Take it easy. You've got three hours!"

RB 441. *Do it quickly*

While I was watching the Long Island Marathon, Ranjana was sitting in the car waiting for me when a policeman started bothering her. He asked her for her license and registration and took them into his car. When I came back I went up to the police car and acted disheartened and disgusted. I said, "Do anything you want to do, but do it quickly! You can fine us, but do it quickly!"

When I said that, he threw away the ticket. When I spoke to him, he calmed down and we didn't pay anything.

RB 442. *The food of champions*

The second-best marathoner in the world now is our great friend, Robert de Castella. Yesterday he ran the famous Fukuoka Marathon in two hours, eight minutes and eighteen seconds — only five seconds behind Alberto Salazar's world record.

While his wife was away in Canberra, he had to cook for himself. So he consulted our Sri Chinmoy Cookbook. He liked the recipe he used very much. So the world's second-best marathon champion eats our food. His father also likes us very much and reads my books.

RB 391. *(p. 201)* 15 October 1981
RB 392. *(p. 201)* 15 October 1981
RB 393. *(p. 201)* 15 October 1981
RB 394. *(p. 202)* 17 October 1981
RB 395. *(p. 202)* 17 October 1981
RB 396. *(p. 203)* 18 October 1981
RB 397. *(p. 203)* 18 October 1981
RB 398. *(p. 204)* 18 October 1981
RB 399. *(p. 204)* 18 October 1981
RB 400. *(p. 204)* 18 October 1981
RB 401. *(p. 205)* 18 October 1981
RB 402. *(p. 205)* 18 October 1981
RB 403. *(p. 205)* 18 October 1981
RB 404. *(p. 206)* 18 October 1981
RB 405. *(p. 206)* 20 October 1981
RB 406. *(p. 206)* 20 October 1981
RB 407. *(p. 207)* 20 October 1981
RB 408. *(p. 207)* 24 October 1981
RB 409. *(p. 208)* 24 October 1981
RB 410. *(p. 208)* 24 October 1981
RB 411. *(p. 209)* 24 October 1981
RB 412. *(p. 209)* 25 October 1981
RB 413. *(p. 209)* 29 October 1981
RB 414. *(p. 210)* 29 October 1981
RB 415. *(p. 210)* 1 November 1981
RB 416. *(p. 210)* 1 November 1981
RB 417. *(p. 211)* 1 November 1981
RB 418. *(p. 211)* 1 November 1981
RB 419. *(p. 211)* 1 November 1981
RB 420. *(p. 211)* 2 November 1981

RB 421. *(p. 212)* 2 November 1981
RB 422. *(p. 212)* 6 November 1981
RB 423. *(p. 212)* 7 November 1981
RB 424. *(p. 212)* 8 November 1981
RB 425. *(p. 213)* 12 November 1981
RB 426. *(p. 213)* 12 November 1981
RB 427. *(p. 214)* 15 November 1981
RB 428. *(p. 214)* 15 November 1981
RB 429. *(p. 214)* 15 November 1981
RB 430. *(p. 215)* 15 November 1981
RB 431. *(p. 215)* 15 November 1981
RB 432. *(p. 215)* 15 November 1981
RB 433. *(p. 215)* 29 November 1981
RB 434. *(p. 216)* 29 November 1981
RB 435. *(p. 216)* 29 November 1981
RB 436. *(p. 216)* 29 November 1981
RB 437. *(p. 216)* 6 December 1981
RB 438. *(p. 217)* 6 December 1981
RB 439. *(p. 217)* 6 December 1981
RB 440. *(p. 217)* 6 December 1981
RB 441. *(p. 218)* 6 December 1981
RB 442. *(p. 218)* 6 December 1981

RUN AND BECOME, BECOME AND RUN

PART 9

RB 443. *Running and losing weight*

Quite recently I weighed myself, and I literally cried! Then I ran and walked eleven miles, without taking any food. In a day or two I took off nine pounds. Tomorrow also I will take off another one or two pounds. If I can do it, others can also do it.

There are many, many things which I do to encourage and inspire others. I run and keep my weight down because what I preach, I also want to practise in my life. Many Masters don't do this kind of thing — losing weight and taking exercise. Their God-realisation will not disappear if they become exorbitantly fat.

RB 444. *The watch stopper*

I saw Snigdha running this morning. She was on one side of the street and I was on the other side. She stops her watch when she stops running, even when she pauses for a minute at a side street.

RB 445. *More bad runners*

Today in Mexico City we went to watch a three-mile race. There were many good runners and many bad runners. But the bad runners were many, many more in number.

RB 446. *A soul's message*

This morning while I was running seven and a half miles, Garima's soul sent me a message. Then two seconds later I saw Garima running. I was running on one side of the street and she was running on the other side.

RB 447. *A divine twenty-seven miles*

I still can't believe that in Puerto Rico I recently walked and ran a divine twenty-seven miles!

The first five miles I ran and the second five miles I walked and ran. Like this I continued, and finally it became twenty-seven miles.

Even from the first mile I was literally dying. My whole body was swimming in perspiration.

RB 448. *The show-off*

The other day Anupadi was showing off. For a while she was running near me, and then she went off ahead. Her strides have become longer now. Previously, her strides were so short.

RB 449. *Dog attacks*

None of the disciples were attacked by dogs this morning during the race. That was because they were running in a group.

I ran seven miles by myself, and at least four times I was attacked by dogs. Perhaps the reason they attacked me was because I was wearing a red shirt. When they came at me, I stood there very bravely until they stopped barking at me. In one case a dog crossed the street to where I was running, but it didn't bite me.

Especially when you are running fast, you get alarmed when you suddenly see a dog. If you are running slowly, it is not such a shock. In my case, I was going so slowly — at bullock-cart speed.

RB 450. *Watching the races*

I usually finish my running before our races start so that I can enjoy them. Abadh is always far ahead; he does not die. But second is always Abarita, and he always dies while he runs. Kailash and others struggle, but they don't actually die. Jason never even struggles. I don't see him even getting properly tired during a race.

When Kalatit runs, he looks like he has some bitter thing in his mouth. His whole face is miserable.

Gayatri is also miserable, absolutely miserable, when she runs. She does not have the misery of tiredness; she is just miserable.

In every race Nilima gives her life-breath at the end. Today she and Karabi were sprinting so fast at the end. They were chasing Nirjhari. Then, in the last two metres, Nilima gave up.

Whenever Nayana sees me, she smiles. Hashi tries to smile, but Chetana does not even try. She surrenders.

Today Garima was very good. When she saw me, she folded her hands and bowed to me. The other day I made complaints that she did not even seem to recognise me while she was running. So this time when she saw me, she bowed.

RB 451. *Observations*

If Khudita can run fast, what is wrong with me? I may be fifty years old, but I am not as "thin" as she is. Again, she carries all her extra weight so powerfully. She has physical strength. She is so strong! Such determination she has to carry her body. I am proud of her.

Each disciple-runner has some peculiarity. When I see "tall man" — Adhiratha — how he is struggling! His strides are quite long, but there is no speed inside them. He looks like he is going so fast, but what actually happens? Why is he behind so many people?

RB 452. *The best style*

I have to be very frank. In long distances Bill Rodgers' style impresses me most. It is a very good style. He literally flies.

RB 453. *The run in the dark*

This morning I ran seven miles while it was still very dark. When it is dark, you forget about speed. You feel that as long as you continue running, it is enough. The first mile I did in nine minutes and the last was at an eight-thirty pace. Altogether I averaged only a nine-minute pace, so God knows how slowly I ran the other five miles. A nine-minute pace is very bad. Of course, I was not racing. But if it had not been dark, I would have taken off at least fifteen seconds per mile.

RB 454. *Thanks a lot*

The day before we left Mazatlan I was running early in the morning. At one point a small car that was going quite fast came near me and stopped. A little boy five or six years old got out and asked me for directions in Spanish. He said three lines of Spanish, and I could not understand anything. I had been running fast, doing speed work, and I was exhausted. I don't know Spanish, and I was so tired that I was helpless.

When the boy saw that I didn't understand him and also that I was too tired to talk, he said very soulfully, "Thanks a lot." There was no sarcasm involved. Then he ran back and entered into his father's car.

Another day while I was running in Mazatlan very early in the morning, I saw an American running. This man I had previously seen playing tennis. He was bearded and not very nice looking. He asked me the time, and I said, "Five fifty-six."

Then he said, "Damn you! Why can't you say four minutes of six!"

I never use the expression "Thanks a lot," but I told him, "Thanks a lot," and continued running.

RB 455. *Long legs*

Recently in Bermuda I went out to run at five o'clock in the morning. I was running right in front of the hotel. Seventy or eighty metres I ran. Then I stopped, and then again I ran. I did this seven times. The weather in Bermuda was like Chicago: very windy! At times you couldn't even walk, so how was I going to run?

There were about seven or eight taxis in front of the hotel. One taxi driver, an old man, was joking with me. He came very near me and was watching me. Then he said to me, "Champ, you have two long legs. Champ, you have long legs, long legs!" I was wearing shorts, although it was quite chilly. He was a gentleman, so he was wearing trousers.

It was so dangerous there. There was no proper sidewalk. I saw so many scooters. How fast they went! It reminded me of our vacation in Bermuda a few years ago.

RB 456. *400-metre standard*

When I first ran the 400-metre dash in 1944, I did it in one minute. In 1945 my time was 56 seconds and in 1946 it was 54 seconds. From then on, I always did it in under 54 seconds — 53.6 or less. Even in 1961 or 1962 it was still under 54 seconds.

RB 457. *Running in P.S. 86*

This evening at nine o'clock I went to P.S. 86, and I jogged there for an hour. The witnesses were Databir, Nirvik and Kanan. We went to the large room, and by going from one side to another we found a course that was over three hundred metres long. I passed through the room where the disciples sit at functions and then entered into the big hall.

In this world people can be good or bad. The principal there says that I will be able to run there in the morning or evening for free, without having to rent the building. So he is proving to be a very good man.

RB 458. *Starting again*

The first day I started running again after being injured, I could only run one block. Then I would have to stop and walk. Yesterday I ran eight hundred metres, and then I walked a little. Today it was better. When you stop running, your stamina goes away totally. It is not like tennis, where you retain your ability to a certain extent. Also, tennis always gives such joy; even if you miss the ball, at least you are playing a game.

Many years ago the Supreme gave me the capacity to run, but He didn't give me enough time. I was acting like a slave to so many people — every day serving five masters at my various jobs in the ashram. What could I do? I just didn't have time to practise running, although I had the capacity. Of course, now I have eight or nine hundred masters to please!

In addition to the disciples, I have two more masters: my two dogs, Sona and Kanu. For the last two weeks my little three-month-old Kanu has been blessing me so that I get no peace at night. He just cries and cries. When I finally bring him upstairs, he is so restless. He won't stay in one place for more than two minutes. Sometimes around seven o'clock he rests a little, but usually until eight-thirty in the morning when the disciples come to work, I am a perfect slave to my little dog.

RB 459. *The unspoken invitation*

When I was running this morning, I passed by a very fat man about my age waiting for the bus. He was wearing a heavy coat and scarf. God knows how long he had been waiting, and I felt sorry for him.

I was making loud noises while I was running, huffing and puffing. The fat man said to me, "How old are you?"

I said, "Fifty."

"You are running like a hundred-year-old man," he said.

After I covered thirty metres more, a thought entered into my mind: "Let me invite him to run with me." But this was all in the mental world, not in the practical world, and I kept on running.

RB 460. *The two rivals*

Kirsty and I are two rivals. God is not satisfied with punishing me alone; He has to punish Kirsty also. I can't run; God has blessed me. Now I see that Kirsty can't run either. Usually one rival wins. In our case God has demolished both of us. For the last few weeks neither one of us has been running.

One day we shall be able to fight against our fate. This year in the New York Marathon we have to do well.

RB 461. *The mountain and the Lilliputian*

In our marathon today I was watching Sarita run. I thought, "If you have will-power and strength, who cares about extra body weight?" She has tremendous strength from practising for five or six years. Five or six years ago she would sometimes faint when she ran. Now she is so strong!

Sarita and Snigdha were running together. Sarita looked like a mountain and Snigdha looked like a Lilliputian next to her.

RB 462. *The dangers of the sauna*

Last week a very famous boxer fainted after coming out of a sauna. Last year Vinaya's "sauna" almost made me faint on the street.

Vinaya's car-sauna is hotter than the hottest. It can kill the strongest man on earth. On that day we drove about ten miles in his car-sauna along my running course on Union Turnpike. After ten miles I got out. When I opened the door and stepped out onto somebody's lawn, I almost fainted. I told him that the owners wouldn't appreciate it if I fainted on the lawn, and I got back into the car.

Once I entered the car, I asked him to drive as fast as possible back to my house and not to worry about the police. On Union Turnpike we were going seventy, seventy-five, eighty miles per hour. I am a fool and he is a fool. We didn't think of lowering the heat or opening the windows. We just went on driving as fast as possible. He said, "Guru, before I joined the path, I did this kind of thing. Now you are asking me again to drive eighty-five miles per hour." He was so delighted to go back to his old life!

When we reached my house, some boys had to carry me out of the car onto the lawn. One was massaging my head, one my feet. They put ice all over my body, and there were two fans. I couldn't recognise anyone, and I couldn't even get up.

My next door neighbour Mrs. Chino came out of her house in a panic. She said that she didn't want to lose me. "I recently lost my husband and I don't want to lose you," she said.

Finally the boys took me upstairs. I closed the door — only to have a more serious attack. I couldn't keep my eyes open.

I always used to advocate that Amita and others ride in Vinaya's sauna. Amita says she enjoys it like anything. But for me, Vinaya puts it on the hottest. He wants to show off — to show me how powerful his sauna is. Before I enter into the car, he runs the motor for ten or fifteen minutes. When he shows off and when I show off, where do we stand?

You may ask why my inner beings didn't warn me that this would happen. They could have, but they knew I was not going to die, and they wanted to give me an experience. This suffering that I went through was necessary; otherwise, I would not have learned the needed lesson and taken the message seriously. Now this message I am giving to all my disciples.

The sauna can be very dangerous if you try to lose five or six pounds all at once. The sauna should be used only for ten or fifteen minutes — not for an hour or two. Eat less and run more: this is the only cure for weight problems. The only answer is to run and then to not eat, to not eat and then to run. In my case I also put weights on my legs and get very good exercise when I walk.

Those who say they don't eat and still gain weight have to pray to the goddess of air: "Please don't come near me." As the Indians traditionally pray to Saturn, "Saturn, please don't come near me," they have to pray to the air goddess or the wind god, "Please don't come near me, because if you come, I gain weight."

Recently I took some pills which Dhananjaya bought in Mexico. If you take these Mexican pills, you may lose nine pounds but you get unbearable cramps. The other day I took them, only to die. When I got the cramps, I screamed from upstairs for help. Baoul and Databir were outside. They heard me calling, but because of the birds' screaming, nobody in the house could hear me. Now Dhanu has installed a buzzer system in the house so that I can be heard from upstairs. It rings in every room of the house.

The Mexican pills were not as dangerous as the sauna, but they were still quite dangerous. From now on I have decided, "No pills, no sauna!"

RB 463. *Wishful thinking*

I am just starting to run again, but still I cherish wishful thinking! Before I start running, I am hoping to run my fastest. Then, after 400 metres, I stop. I can't run even one mile! For 400 metres I walk and for 400 metres I run. Then 800 metres I walk and 800 I run.

Today I ran three miles. For the first two miles I walked for 400 metres and I ran for 400 metres. This is what happens when you don't practise for a month. In Puerto Rico I had a tooth problem and a very high fever, so I couldn't run. So many other things as well have prevented me from training.

RB 464. *A confusing race*

Today we went to run five miles in the marathon held in Eisenhower Park. It was all confusion! The police car made a wrong turn, so the first ten runners who were following it had to run a half mile more.

The course was five loops, so it was very confusing. Pahar and Nirvik could not follow the signs. After running five miles, we ran 400 or 500 metres extra!

Cahit Yeter was running, and he was very happy to see me. Among the disciples, Christopher ran for twelve or thirteen miles. Trishul was exhausted because he had already run two other races recently. This was his third race in three weeks.

Ketan was with us in the back seat while we were driving. Databir kept asking Ketan for directions, and Ketan immediately gave readymade answers.

There were about thirty disciples, mostly Canadians, who went to see our performance and cheer us while we ran.

RB 465. *They don't run*

All the girl disciples say that they don't run very much. But then I go to my four-mile point and see somebody like Kirsty running. In this way I catch them.

Today, at my three-and-a-half-mile point, I saw Nirjhari running. So I know she ran at least seven miles.

RB 466. *Walking shorts*

Chayanika made me some very warm shorts, and I went race-walking in them this afternoon. She has proved that spring is here, at least for today.

RB 467. *How is your business?*

When I was race-walking, Dhanu's car was following me. There were some distinguished people in the car: Nirvik, Ila, Garima, plus Trishul. I covered many miles.

When I had covered only 500 metres, a young boy smiled at me and said to me, "How is your business going on?" Now, what is my business?

Later, a young man offered me a can of beer. I smiled at him. He said afterwards to the people in the car that there was much protein in beer.

RB 468. *Old man, keep going!*

After I finished race-walking, I was doing speed work in front of my house. Three very nice black men said to me, "Old man, keep going, keep going! Some day you will do well."

RB 469. *Abhipsa's light*

While I was walking, I saw Abhipsa at a distance. He had on a Bill Rodgers running suit, and the back of it was shining.

Once a seeker was misusing his occult power by showing light, so Sri Ramakrishna took away the light. Ramakrishna did the man a big favour. But Abhipsa was not misusing his light, so I didn't take it away.

RB 470. *Hillwork*

I do so much hill work! Today I did two miles in this area, and then I went to Yonkers and ran another two and a half miles. In Yonkers there are frightening hills.

Dhanu was driving, and Databir, Ila and Nirvik were in the car. They are all witnesses.

RB 471. *The blind runner*

This afternoon I went to Yonkers to run. The marks for the Westchester Half-Marathon have now become nearly invisible, so Dhanu couldn't follow the proper course while driving near me in his car. I saw the marks, but I had more faith in him than in myself, so I followed the car.

After half a mile, I realised that he had made a wrong turn. Then we retraced our steps until we came to a particular side street. I remembered from our previous training runs that it was the correct street, so I was looking over my shoulder at the car and signalling for Dhanu to come. He was ahead of me forty or fifty metres. While I was still looking backwards, I started running in the street.

Two young boys were passing by — one was running and the other was cycling. The boy who was cycling went right onto the sidewalk to avoid me and said to the other boy, "Can't you see this blind man? He is looking in one direction and running in the other direction."

The other boy said, "He can't do a thing." He didn't listen to the other one and kept running on the street.

RB 472. *Dobbs Ferry Hills*

When I run near Dobbs Ferry, I start near the Hudson River and run for three miles. The first mile is all uphill. At one point I run fifty metres straight to the top of a hill. Right at the top I am always attacked by dogs.

Once Nathan was bragging that the hills he runs in Arizona are very steep. So I told him, "You come with me." At first he didn't want to admit that the hills I ran were steeper. But when I started barking at him, he confessed that these were steeper and more difficult.

RB 473. *The runners club*

The other day, when I was in the car on my way to do hill work, I saw four girls at the one-mile mark — Tina, Christine, Diane and Irene. Instead of running, they were standing around in a circle.

Later, I heard that they have a club. They run together every morning. After one mile they meditate before going back.

RB 474. *The snakes*

Children have no sense. In the beginning of the three-mile race in Long Island, they criss-crossed back and forth like snakes.

RB 475. *"Ultra, ultra!"*

While I was running the three-mile race, a man was looking at me out of curiosity. He said, "Ultra, ultra!"

Then, just as I was crossing the finish line, they made an announcement that I was finishing.

After the race a photographer from a Long Island newspaper came to take my picture.

RB 476. *Mantra from Heaven*

During a two-mile race in Alley Pond Park, I saw a husband and wife who were also running. After twelve hundred metres the wife was unable to keep pace with the husband, and she wanted to give up. But the husband was encouraging her to continue. He was saying, "This is discipline. If you don't have discipline, you can't accomplish anything."

I thought, "This mantra that he is saying is absolutely descending from Heaven. God is speaking to her through her husband." I was so moved.

RB 477. *Tanima's descent*

This morning I was running up 150th Street. At one point I saw Tanima the great going down the hill — driving.

RB 478. *Rejean's handshake*

Rejean won the two-mile race in Cunningham Park today, and they gave him only a handshake. If the organisers of the race did not plan to give the winners anything, why did they charge a dollar fee to enter?

Since Rejean was the best runner, he should have shook their hands as hard as possible. Then they would have remembered his handshake. They might have forgotten his running, but they would never have forgotten his handshake.

So victory today went to Rejean. Abadh was second. Then just a little behind was Utpal. Nirvik also did well. He has broken his previous record.

RB 479. *Great master and great disciple*

Nirvik and I are great. First we ran a one-mile race in Eisenhower Park, and then we went to Central Park and ran five miles of hills, all up and down. Then we ran in the Green Leaves and Ripe Fruits race. A great Master and a great disciple! The only difference is, the disciple massages the Master after running, even while he himself is dying.

RB 480. *Good morning, sir!*

I started my running-journey this morning at three-thirty. Then I ran again at five o'clock, doing hill work. A lady who was out with her dog said, "Good morning, good morning, Sir!"

Early in the morning is the best time for running. There is no car problem. You can run in the middle of the street.

RB 481. *Starve unto death*

If you want to lose weight, there is no middle path. Buddha spoke of the middle path. But if you want to lose weight, you have to go to the extreme — starve unto death. Then you can fly when you run.

Saturday I was under a hundred and forty pounds. Then I ran in a two-mile race. During the race I felt that I had conquered the world, but after the race I felt tired and exhausted. Then relaxation started, and I gained four pounds.

RB 482. *Baoul's trance*

Today Baoul meditated so well. He was waiting in the car to take me running. I entered into the car and called his name. Still he did not come out of his trance. He remained fast asleep.

RB 483. *Compensation*

Today I was running very fast, taking long strides. Each stride was at least fifty inches, going up to sixty-two.

The man who lives across from me was out with his dog. He was on the sidewalk and I was on the street. He always greets me first. But this time we just looked at each other. I did not recognise him, and he did not recognise me.

When I saw him enter into his house, I came to know who it was. Then I felt miserable. I said, "Every day he greets me, but today he did not greet me. "Baoul went to speak to him. He was very sad that he had not recognised me. So we both felt sad. I went home and felt sad, and he went home and felt sad.

Later I was playing the esraj on the porch, and he happened to be outside. I raised my hand, and he smiled. In this way we compensated.

RB 484. *Mistaken identity*

Today when I was riding in the car, I saw someone running. I said, "Look at this girl. Definitely it is one of our people."

O God, when the runner turned around, I saw that it was Kanan. Luckily he didn't hear what I had said. I did not want to disturb him because he was going for a long run. Therefore I deliberately did not call him to come join us in the car.

RB 485. *The laggard*

Today for the first time Chidananda followed me in the car when I was running on my loop. Twice I looked around but I didn't see the car there. Then I saw that his car was a hundred metres behind me. Usually people driving with me stay only twenty or thirty metres behind me, but he was a hundred metres behind.

RB 486. *Resolutions*

Even in the face of injuries or poor health, I will not give up running so easily. Now running is unbearable. So first I have to make it bearable, then enjoyable. It is my wish every day to run at least five miles at a stretch and ten or twelve miles altogether. And once a week I will do at least three miles of hill work.

RB 487. *The taxi driver*

The day before yesterday, around three-thirty in the morning, I was running by my one-mile mark, near the place where you make a turn on Main Street to go to Flushing Meadow Park. A black man was driving by in a taxi — at that hour! He stopped the taxi and said, "Excuse me, can you give me a can of beer?" I said, "Thank you." Then I just kept running. That was the only man I saw there. I ran two or three more miles, but I saw only one more car.

RB 488. *No bite, no bark!*

This morning I ran two miles. The wind was killing me. As soon as I started, I met my old lady friend with her dog. First she said with tremendous anger and frustration, "Why are you running in this weather? It is freezing!" She was speaking with her German accent.

Then she said to me, "No bite, no bark, my Pauly!"

At that moment her dog started barking. I said, "As long as there is no bite, I don't have to worry."

But she got mad at her dog for barking.

RB 489. *The green light*

This morning I covered fourteen miles. After I had run eleven miles, I was running slowly while crossing the street at a green light. A very old, fat cab driver wanted to go against the red light. He said, "Mister, can you run a bit faster?" I showed him that I had the green light. He said again, "What, you can't run faster?"

He was so fat and old! I don't think he could have run eleven miles.

RB 490. *All in a week's work*

On Monday I ran twenty miles. First I ran twelve miles in the morning. Later I ran another mile. Then, coming back from the dentist, I ran two and a half miles, and at night I ran another four and a half miles.

On Tuesday the snow was killing me. I could not run in that kind of blizzard.

On Wednesday I ran four miles.

On Thursday in the morning I ran seven miles, then half a mile and then three miles. I was showing off. Bansidhar was running with me on Union Turnpike. He is a good runner. During the three-mile run I was taking such long strides! Then, when we came to the last four hundred metres, my strides were sixty-five inches. Later Bansidhar said it was difficult to keep up with me. So yesterday I completed ten and a half miles.

Then today, fourteen miles! Altogether I walked only sixty metres. After seven miles I walked twenty metres. Then, after ten miles, I walked forty metres. If I had done only thirteen miles, the pace would have been 9:23. But the fourteenth mile brought the average down.

RB 491. *Short girl, long strides*

Yesterday I was enjoying Pragati. She is such a short girl. How can she take such long strides? As I ran by her, she looked down at my feet. She did not realise that I was also looking at her feet, watching her strides.

RB 492. *The soul's blessing*

This morning when I was returning home after running five miles, all of a sudden somebody's soul came to me and asked for special blessings. I said, "All right. I am dying now, but you need blessings." So I blessed the person. Then I said, "I hope you do really well in the 12-hour walk."

Two seconds later I just raise my eyes, and I saw that same person right in front of me. It was Sunanda the great. She is the only one whom I saw while I was running today. Her soul had come to me one second earlier.

RB 443. *(p. 223)* 4 December 1981
RB 444. *(p. 223)* 20 December 1981
RB 445. *(p. 223)* 20 December 1981
RB 446. *(p. 223)* 21 December 1981
RB 447. *(p. 224)* 21 December 1981
RB 448. *(p. 224)* 29 December 1981
RB 449. *(p. 224)* 31 December 1981
RB 450. *(p. 225)* 31 December 1981
RB 451. *(p. 225)* 31 December 1981
RB 452. *(p. 226)* 31 December 1981
RB 453. *(p. 226)* 4 January 1982
RB 454. *(p. 226)* 9 January 1982
RB 455. *(p. 227)* 11 January 1982
RB 456. *(p. 228)* 17 January 1982
RB 457. *(p. 228)* 26 January 1982
RB 458. *(p. 228)* 31 January 1982
RB 459. *(p. 229)* 31 January 1982
RB 460. *(p. 229)* 31 January 1982
RB 461. *(p. 230)* 31 January 1982
RB 462. *(p. 230)* 3 February 1982
RB 463. *(p. 232)* 13 February 1982
RB 464. *(p. 233)* 14 February 1982
RB 465. *(p. 233)* 15 February 1982
RB 466. *(p. 234)* 15 February 1982
RB 467. *(p. 234)* 15 February 1982
RB 468. *(p. 234)* 15 February 1982
RB 469. *(p. 234)* 15 February 1982
RB 470. *(p. 235)* 18 February 1982
RB 471. *(p. 235)* 18 February 1982
RB 472. *(p. 236)* 18 February 1982

RB 473. *(p. 236)* 18 February 1982
RB 474. *(p. 236)* 20 February 1982
RB 475. *(p. 236)* 20 February 1982
RB 476. *(p. 237)* 21 February 1982
RB 477. *(p. 237)* 24 February 1982
RB 478. *(p. 237)* 27 February 1982
RB 479. *(p. 238)* 28 February 1982
RB 480. *(p. 238)* 2 March 1982
RB 481. *(p. 238)* 2 March 1982
RB 482. *(p. 239)* 2 March 1982
RB 483. *(p. 239)* 6 March 1982
RB 484. *(p. 239)* 7 March 1982
RB 485. *(p. 240)* 7 March 1982
RB 486. *(p. 240)* 9 March 1982
RB 487. *(p. 240)* 31 March 1982
RB 488. *(p. 241)* 7 April 1982
RB 489. *(p. 241)* 9 April 1982
RB 491. *(p. 242)* 9 April 1982
RB 492. *(p. 242)* 10 April 1982

RUN AND BECOME, BECOME AND RUN

PART 10

RB 493. *The starting line*

Today I ran fifteen miles in the Boston Marathon. Among the disciples, Abadh was the first one I saw. He was standing at the six-minute-pace section. I was tempted to join him, but I was afraid people would run over me. When you think of your capacity, you start in the back. When you forget about your capacity, you go forward.

RB 494. *Encouragement in Boston*

People who encourage the runners in the Boston Marathon are much more divine than people who encourage runners in many other races. How they cheered us on!

Even before I covered the first mile, I was totally exhausted. You can call it tiredness or hunger or thirst — God knows. After seven miles a little boy stood right in front of me and gave me a glass of water, literally forcing me to drink it.

I said, "How old are you?"

He said, "Four."

So many runners patted me on the back, saying, "Come along, friend, you can make it. Don't give up. Go on, go on, go on!" They were going ahead of me and encouraging me as they passed by. They were very nice people.

RB 495. *Kim*

One thin girl who had run in our twenty-four-hour race was running the marathon. She is very thin, like Kusumita. Her name is Kim. She had been behind me, but around the ten-mile point she passed me. As she went by she shouted, "Hello, Guru. I am happy to see you." While she was saying this, she was taking off her long-sleeved shirt. It was like our purple shirt. It had my picture on the back and said "Sri Chinmoy Marathon." Underneath she was wearing a short-sleeved T-shirt. I thought she would throw the long-sleeved shirt on the street, but she held it as she ran.

I saw two or three more non-disciples wearing different shirts of ours. But Kim was the only one who recognised me.

RB 496. *The hoses*

The children watching the Boston Marathon were so nice. Little, little children were offering us ice. The people who were spraying us with hoses were my best friends. But some runners didn't like it; they got annoyed. Some runners were for water and some were not. I was for water.

An elderly black man and I were running together, and two or three times people got so much joy from drenching us. We were two runners who were getting new life from the hoses. But other runners were cursing them. They had to go to the other side of the street to avoid the hoses.

RB 497. *Looking good!*

Even if you are dying, people always say, "Looking good!" At one point one girl said, "Looking good," to encourage me, and another girl corrected her. She said, "Doing good."

RB 498. *The boy from London*

There was a little boy seven or eight years old who was bragging that this was his fourth marathon. Somebody asked him where he was from. He said, "From London."

The man said, "From England?"

The boy said, "Where else?"

RB 499. *Blind runners*

In two or three places I saw blind men running. Each of them was holding a small cane and being guided by a person who could see.

RB 500. *Alaska Eskimo*

One elderly man came from the Alaska Eskimo Track Club. Two runners who were running behind him were repeating the mantra — "Alaska Eskimo." One would say "Alaska." The other would say "Eskimo." The elderly man was running in silence.

RB 501. *Some ripe fruits*

In today's eight-hundred-metre Green Leaves and Ripe Fruits race for men and women over fifty, Vince and I were going slowly and only keeping pace with Ilona during the first four hundred metres. But we knew that we would end up going ahead of her. After four hundred metres we started widening the gap, and Ilona fell behind us by a big margin. Whenever I increased my speed, Vince would increase his speed. In the last hundred metres we had a wonderful fight. I won by only one second.

I was planning to walk the whole race, but then Vince would have had no other competitor, except for a few ladies. His fate would have been like Senani's in the sixty-and-over race.

RB 502. *To smile or not to smile*

Yesterday, after running four miles, all of a sudden I thought of Dhrubha and Nayana. I had been cutting jokes with Dhrubha the previous night, telling him that his wife had a horrible running style, like Pulak. Then I said to myself, "Pulak is a little better."

Nayana and Dhrubha have exactly the same style, but Nayana twists her face and smiles while she runs. Dhrubha never smiles.

RB 503. *Blind disciples*

The day before yesterday I ran seven miles, yesterday I ran seven miles and this morning also I ran seven miles. When I was returning this morning, first I saw Jyotsna. She greeted me and smiled at me.

Then I saw Sanatan. For thirty or forty metres I was smiling at him, but he was blind; he could not see me. Then, when he came near me, he folded his hands.

Then I saw Sudhir on the other side of the street. Only when I started shouting his name did he recognise me. Then I saw Shephali. By that time I was dying.

RB 504. *Familiar faces*

Today as soon as I started running, I saw Gitika, and then on the other side of the street I saw Pidgeon. Then I saw Bob Barrett. I said to myself, "Since Bob is there, perhaps his wife is running behind him." I was right. O God, she was so far behind! Then I greeted her. As Bob was coming back to where I was, he shouted, "O Guru, it is so nice to see you!"

Then, after about two miles, somebody right behind me said, "Very good pace, very good pace!

I said to myself, "A joker!" and looked around. Whom did I see? It was the young black man who had stood third in our race on Sunday. He said, "You put on a very good race, and I enjoyed it very much." So I smiled at him. After two minutes he was still running ahead of me. Then, after three minutes, he was nowhere to be seen.

After about three miles I saw Karabi. As I continued running, I saw the young man returning. When he saw me, he raised his arms over his head, greeting me.

RB 505. *Take it easy!*

After I had run three and a half miles, I started returning. At the point where Parsons Boulevard meets Union Turnpike, usually I stop for a minute. This time I was running slowly and getting the inner courage to go faster. A young man drinking coffee or tea said to me, "I see you are tired. Take it easy, take it easy!" He was smiling at me.

RB 506. *The braggart*

Today Databir and I were buying running shoes. The young man who was selling the shoes was saying that all the shoes were very good, just because he wanted to sell them. When he brought out one particular shoe, he said that he had used this one to run a 4:46 mile. Then he said he had run 800 metres in 1:30. His best time of all was in the quarter-mile, he said. He was bragging that he had done a quarter-mile in 55 seconds — not only once, but twice.

I couldn't help laughing. I said, "I am an Indian. I did it in 54 and 53.6. Under 54 I did it many times before you were born."

Then he said, "I am so honoured that you have come."

Then Databir told him that I had done it without shoes, on a cinder track.

The first time, in 1945, I did the quarter-mile in one minute. Then in 1946 from one minute it came down to 56 seconds, then 55 and then always under 55–54, 53.9 and so on.

RB 507. *A seven-mile run*

At four o'clock this morning we vagabonds went to run. We had planned to run fifteen miles, but in the end we had to be satisfied with seven.

Seven miles a day I ran for five days. Is it a joke? And Union Turnpike has hills!

I have maintained my weight at 138 pounds for so many days! Today I have come down to 136. I have a chart of good runners. Out of twelve runners, only one runner is fat. Eleven are thin.

RB 508. *The bald-headed friend*

Before the start of the Long Island Marathon, an old bald-headed man came up to me. He didn't fold his hands, but he was full of reverential awe. He said, "Are you Sri Chinmoy?"

I said I was.

He said, "I am so happy and honoured to be here and speak to you. This is my first marathon."

So I congratulated him. He said, "I have run quite a few races of yours."

Then the funniest thing happened. After fourteen miles, I got the shock of my life. He was passing me coming from the other direction. I asked myself, "How could he be so far ahead of me if this is his first marathon?"

I waved to him. I usually don't wave to anybody, but he had been so nice to me. Later I realised that I was actually ahead of him. He finished far behind me.

RB 509. *Nice to see you*

Right before the marathon another man came up to me and said, "So nice to see you." He was a young man, very nice. He said, "It is getting warm, so I won't be able to do well."

RB 510. *The handshake*

Many runners greeted me during the Long Island Marathon. At least six or seven people recognised me and came up to me. One man was at least twenty metres ahead of me. All of a sudden he got the inspiration to stop. I said to myself, "Why did he stop?" He stopped only to shake hands with me.

RB 511. *All right*

At one point during the marathon I was walking for a few metres. There was one man who asked me if I was all right. He kept asking, "Are you really all right?"

I said, "I am all right."

Then he was telling the people who were helping me, "He is all right, don't worry."

Then I started running, but he was still walking.

RB 512. *Thundering legs*

Today, first I saw Nishtha the great, then Vidagdha the great. After I passed Vidagdha, I heard someone running towards me very fast. I said, "How can Vidagdha run so fast?" Then when I turned around, I saw it was Yasu.

After Yasu I saw Sundar. He was running so fast and making such noise with his legs; they were thundering!

RB 513. *The bee*

At one point while I was running a young boy was behind me. All of a sudden he got inspired to go ahead of me. He crossed the street only to be stung by a bee or some insect near a tree. He started screaming and holding his right eye. When I passed by that tree, I was praying I wouldn't get stung, and I didn't.

RB 514. *Late night encounter*

Last night a little after twelve-thirty I went running. After five and a half miles or so, when I was on my way back, I saw a car that was making absolutely unthinkable, unbearable noises. Luckily, I was on the other side of the street, so I was quite safe. Then that same car went ahead, made a U-turn and came to my side. It was still making such noise! So I jumped onto the sidewalk, and continued running quite peacefully.

Suddenly the car stopped right alongside of me. It was a red car with a black hood. Two young girls were inside. One of them said, "Excuse me, excuse me, are you Sri Chinmoy? Are you Sri Chinmoy?"

I said, "Yes."

She said, "We are so happy to see you. We saw you on television two days ago." They were so excited to see me at that hour. So I thanked them.

They were very, very nice girls, but what were they doing in that car at that hour?

RB 515. *The police chase*

While I was running, I saw a police car chasing another car. Both the cars were going so fast — at least eighty or ninety miles per hour. But the police car was not able to catch the culprit.

RB 516. *The neighbourhood run*

I was out running at three-thirty this morning near the old Bohack Supermarket. Now it is a Sunset Electric store. There is a bar across the street. Outside the bar I saw eight or ten undivine people. I said, "O God, let me go another way." So I had to retrace my steps and take another street in order to avoid them.

Then I was near Divine Robe Supreme. I wanted to go to the playground, so I took a side street, again only to meet four or five undivine people — near Chidananda's house. They were very bad people. So I went back and started running on another road. After I got to the track there was no problem. Then I ran alone on the beautiful track.

While coming back near Annam Brahma, I saw somebody trying to start his motorbike. The noise was unbearable. His girlfriend didn't want to go with him on the motorbike. With one hand he was holding the bike and with the other hand he was holding her.

RB 517. *The running nose*

Karabi is wonderful. Yesterday she saw me while I was running, but I didn't see her. She was in her car, coming back from the Queens College track. She gave a full description of what I was wearing.

After running five miles I was returning, near Main Street. According to my standard, I was going fast. But a middle-aged lady said to her friend, "His nose is running faster than his legs!"

It was true that my nose was running.

So the other lady said, "Yes, you go and join him and try to run."

Inwardly I thanked the second lady.

In the morning what kind of appreciation I get! These people's souls want to talk to me.

RB 518. *The secret run*

This morning before the ten-mile race, I ran to the three-and-a-half-mile mark in Flushing Meadow Park, and then I ran home.

Yasu saw me, then Kalatit and then Edythe. She was in a car, driving to Flushing Meadow to set up. But once I got home I pretended that I had not yet run so I could surprise everyone later.

During the race I was afraid Yasu would say, "I saw you running this morning," but fortunately he didn't say anything, so I kept my secret.

I was running so slowly during the ten-mile race that I didn't feel tired at all, even after nine miles. Then I waved to Lucy and Chetana, saying that I was going to go faster for the last mile.

So this morning altogether I ran seventeen miles.

RB 519. *How do you keep so fit?*

Before today's ten-mile race a black girl came up to me and said, "Sri Chinmoy?"
I said, "Yes."
She said, "How old are you?"
I said, "Fifty."
She said, "How do you keep your body so fit?"

RB 520. *Competitors*

In the ten-mile race an old man with a green shirt was in front of me for a while. Then he fell behind. Another runner, a girl in yellow, was getting cramp after cramp. These were some of my competitors.

RB 521. *9 May 1982*

After the awards ceremony a man came up to me and asked me, "How do you like the shoes you are wearing?"
I told him, "They are very comfortable."

RB 522. *Running in Scotland*

While I was in Scotland recently, Janaka, Janani and I went running. David was following us in his car. After each mile David would honk. After three or four miles Janani surrendered. She started going very slowly.
I was proud that Janani was far behind us, because I still remember how she defeated me in Antigua. Altogether Janaka and I ran seven miles. Then we drove back to get Janani. She was so happy to stop running!

Afterwards, we went to an Indian restaurant, but unfortunately the food was very bad.

RB 523. *The hill*

On another day in Scotland I wanted to run my seven miles for the day. I ran with Janaka for three and a half miles. Two and a half miles were all hills that we had to really climb. Janani and David were watching us run.

Then we came to such a steep hill! It went straight up. We saw one man run about a hundred metres up the hill and we were admiring him. I also wanted to run up that hill, but the Scottish disciples were saying that the road was not good enough to run on.

RB 524. *The beautiful course*

The Scottish disciples showed me a place where they had taken Nemi a few years ago to show her the scenery, but Nemi hadn't liked it. It is a place where they run, near the water, and it is very beautiful. I liked it very much. I went running there along the water.

RB 525. *The hilly course*

In Scotland they have a thirteen-mile course which has five hills. Once a year they have a race there. Some of the runners there are so strong and they do so well. Other people just deceive everyone because it is easy to take a short cut or to start somewhere along the course.

RB 526. *Such a difference!*

Another day in Scotland there was a two-and-a-half-mile race. At the finish, the boy who stood first was at least five hundred metres ahead of the person who was second. The second one was about a hundred metres ahead of the third. Such a difference!

RB 527. *The clever man*

I am a clever man. I ran seven miles before our five-mile race started so that I could enjoy watching the race. While I was running, a huge dog was following me. Then another dog was bothering me. A videotape was made, and it shows the dogs bothering me.

RB 528. *The five-mile race*

Over two hundred people ran in our five-mile race. Many were excellent runners. How fast they ran! One had been in the Commonwealth Games. He did a 4:22 pace and came in first. The second runner was far behind him and the third was far behind the second.

Abarita was the fifth over-all. For the first mile Abarita ran with the top runners. I was so happy. Then, at the second mile, he fell behind. He could not keep up with them. Among the disciples Abarita was the first boy and Indu was the first girl. The girl who stood first over-all was far ahead of Indu. She was quite fat, but she was such a fast runner!

RB 529. *The children runners*

Devashishu is going to be an excellent runner. He ran a seven-minute pace in the five-mile race, and a six-thirteen in a two-mile race. His father was so far behind him!

Everybody thought that Devashishu's little brother, Aaron, had got lost, but he was running at an eleven or twelve-minute pace. When the father finished, he ran back to find Aaron, and then he started running with him. They were coming towards the finish line together so I said, "Now let us have the physical father and the spiritual father run together with the son." So I was on one side and his father was on the other. Aaron was killing himself to beat us. I stopped deliberately to let him go ahead, and he was so delighted that he could defeat me. But his father didn't stop.

RB 530. *Two unforgivable things*

Hashi has done two unforgivable things. In the Long Island Marathon I got such a leg cramp and mental cramp at nineteen miles, and she went ahead of me.

Then, in the ten-mile race a week later, I was about to catch her, but then she disappeared and defeated me.

RB 531. *The long strides*

Once I was running in Flushing Meadow Park in such a relaxed way. I thought that my strides were no more than forty inches, but they were actually fifty. Savyasachi was watching. Then, in order to prove it to the others on the road crew, again I started running in a relaxed way. They all saw that my strides were actually fifty inches.

RB 532. *Too cold!*

This morning around six-thirty I was doing interval work. At one point I had stopped running at the end of my block and I was walking. The German lady who lives nearby came up to me, grabbed my shoulder with her left hand and massaged my arm down to my elbow. Then she shook hands with me — her left hand and my left hand. She said, "Too cold, too cold!"

Then she said, "You have two dogs."

I said, "Yes."

She said, "Good, very good."

I asked her, "What is your dog's name?"

She said, "Vila."

This lady is always walking her dog. So its name is Vila, like the tennis champion Vilas.

RB 533. *The jogging policeman*

This morning I ran four miles and then walked one mile. I wanted to do seven miles, but I didn't have the time.

When I was coming back from my run around four-thirty, at the thousand-metre mark what did I see? A policeman jogging. He had no car and he was not running to catch any thief. He had a radio with earphones and he was in his police uniform. He was a real policeman, with a badge and a gun. He was not someone joking or pretending.

As soon as I saw him, I smiled at him. Then he said to me either, "Sri" or "Shrai" — I could not hear very well — "Good morning!"

When I said to him, "Sir, good morning," he stopped and shook hands with me. He was very fat and very tall at the same time.

This was the first time I had seen a policeman jogging. He was going very, very slowly. What he was doing jogging at that hour, God alone knows.

RB 534. *My coach*

My coach is Pahar. He is so good. I always tell him how fast I want to run, and then he runs with me and keeps the pace. Every 100 metres he adjusts the pace and it is always very close.

RB 535. *The show-off*

One day Kalatit and Pahar ran ahead of me. They wanted to run ten miles. Pahar said Kalatit was showing off. On that day Pahar didn't want to show off. But Kalatit kept going ahead.

RB 536. *The San Francisco Marathon*

I ran ten and a half miles before the San Francisco Marathon started. Then I was in the car while Gayatri and others started running the actual race. I watched them run for several miles. Then I ran six and a half miles in the marathon.

At the seventeen-mile point, Sharon said to me, "Gayatri is coming up behind you."

I said, "Let me enter into the car. Take me at least two miles ahead of her."

So Sharon took me about two miles in the car, but she couldn't go any farther because of the beach. Then I started running very peacefully. After that, I saw Gangadhar running in the other direction. Then I saw Gayatri coming from a different direction and she was shouting to Gangadhar.

RB 537. *Is your heart all right?*

After about four or five miles, I was breathing heavily as usual. A middle-aged man said to me, "Did you have a checkup with your doctor for your chest? Is your heart all right?"

I said, "Yes, yes!"

Then I said to myself, "O God, I am not going to run with the runners. I don't want to show people how tired I am." From then on I ran on the left side of the street. Most of the runners were running on the right side. There were still some runners on the left side, but very few in comparison.

There were many people who were breathing louder than I was. In the Athens Marathon that I ran a few years ago, there was one person breathing so heavily that you could hear him a hundred meters away.

After about seven or eight miles, I saw a man lying down by the side of the road. Two people were helping him. Then the ambulance came.

RB 538. *Bad memories*

As I passed one point in the marathon, I remembered that at that same place two years ago I had got cramps. At that time I was practically lying down on the street while Pradhan and Nirvik were massaging me. After they massaged me, I could barely walk for three or four miles. I was absolutely miserable.

Before the marathon that year, a Chinese doctor had given a talk about how he had cured so many patients who had come to him. In spite of my cramps this doctor was two or three miles behind me.

This time nothing happened — no cramps or anything. I was absolutely flying. This is the difference between two years ago and now!

RB 539. *Brakes*

At one point during the marathon I saw a man who was in such pain and agony that he was walking. When you get cramps, you forget even your parents' names. When you use the car brake, you don't feel the car's pain. But when cramps put on the brakes, you feel the pain in your entire body.

RB 540. *Two Indians*

While I was running, six or seven people recognised me. Two or three stopped and shook hands with me.

Just before the twelve-mile point, there was an Indian ahead of me. He turned around and shouted, "Are you an Indian?"

I said, "Yes."

Then the man he was running with, an American, said, "He is the big boss."

That Indian lives only three houses away from Sharon. She knows him.

RB 541. *11 June 1982*

While running the marathon, Chetana and Chandika were talking and smiling the whole time. They were not only running a marathon, they were enjoying a marathon talk.

RB 542. *Thanking God*

I thank God from the bottom of my heart when I see some people's strides. During the California race I was watching the strides of an old man. I said, "God, I should thank You for one thing: that I don't have that kind of stride."

There was one old man whose style I will never forget. His right leg had one kind of position, his left leg another, and his shoulder had a completely different position. O God, how did he run? His entire body was twisted in three different places.

RB 543. *Nice to see you this morning!*

This morning around six-thirty I was walking down the 150th Street hill after running seven miles. At the bottom of the hill there was a big bus stopped at a red light. Behind the bus was a car with two very tall and stout black men in it. The driver had a beard and moustache. When I was about to go back up the hill, the driver got out of the car and took two steps towards me. "How nice to see you this morning!" he said.

I didn't know what to say. So I smiled at him soulfully. Then he went back into his car.

RB 544. *Look, Sri Chinmoy is running!*

Yesterday at about five-fifteen in the morning I was running near my two-and-a-half-mile point on Union Turnpike. A young man was talking on the phone in a telephone booth as I passed by. All of a sudden he started screaming, "Look, look! Sri Chinmoy is running!" He was so excited. He was telling the person he was talking to on the phone that he was seeing me run by.

I stopped and gave the young man a smile. He was in the seventh heaven of delight. He was tall and clean-shaven, with curly hair, and he had a pack on his back.

These people who greet me in the morning are in some ways my first-class disciples. They get up early in the morning, and they are so happy to see me.

RB 545. *Two crazies*

The other day when I was running up the 150th Street Hill, a lady on the street caught me. She stopped me and asked, "Can I speak to you?"

I called Databir and he came running. I told him, "Please talk to her." So Databir talked to her. Later, he said she was crazy. But she didn't seem to me to be crazy. Perhaps she also thought that Databir was crazy.

RB 493. *(p. 247)* 19 April 1982
RB 494. *(p. 247)* 19 April 1982
RB 495. *(p. 247)* 19 April 1982
RB 496. *(p. 248)* 19 April 1982
RB 497. *(p. 248)* 19 April 1982
RB 498. *(p. 248)* 19 April 1982
RB 499. *(p. 249)* 19 April 1982
RB 500. *(p. 249)* 19 April 1982
RB 501. *(p. 249)* 25 April 1982
RB 502. *(p. 250)* 27 April 1982
RB 503. *(p. 250)* 27 April 1982
RB 504. *(p. 250)* 27 April 1982
RB 505. *(p. 251)* 27 April 1982
RB 506. *(p. 251)* 28 April 1982
RB 507. *(p. 252)* 29 April 1982
RB 508. *(p. 252)* 1 May 1982
RB 509. *(p. 253)* 1 May 1982
RB 510. *(p. 253)* 1 May 1982
RB 511. *(p. 253)* 1 May 1982
RB 512. *(p. 254)* 4 May 1982
RB 513. *(p. 254)* 4 May 1982
RB 514. *(p. 254)* 6 May 1982
RB 515. *(p. 255)* 6 May 1982
RB 516. *(p. 255)* 8 May 1982
RB 517. *(p. 256)* 8 May 1982
RB 518. *(p. 256)* 9 May 1982
RB 519. *(p. 257)* 9 May 1982
RB 520. *(p. 257)* 9 May 1982
RB 521. *(p. 257)* 9 May 1982
RB 522. *(p. 257)* 20 May 1982

SRI CHINMOY

RB 523. *(p. 258)* 20 May 1982
RB 524. *(p. 258)* 20 May 1982
RB 525. *(p. 258)* 20 May 1982
RB 526. *(p. 259)* 20 May 1982
RB 527. *(p. 259)* 20 May 1982
RB 528. *(p. 259)* 20 May 1982
RB 529. *(p. 260)* 20 May 1982
RB 530. *(p. 260)* 20 May 1982
RB 531. *(p. 260)* 20 May 1982
RB 532. *(p. 261)* 27 May 1982
RB 533. *(p. 261)* 3 June 1982
RB 534. *(p. 262)* 5 June 1982
RB 535. *(p. 262)* 5 June 1982
RB 536. *(p. 262)* 11 June 1982
RB 537. *(p. 263)* 11 June 1982
RB 538. *(p. 263)* 11 June 1982
RB 539. *(p. 264)* 11 June 1982
RB 540. *(p. 264)* 11 June 1982
RB 541. *(p. 264)* 11 June 1982
RB 542. *(p. 264)* 11 June 1982
RB 543. *(p. 265)* 11 June 1982
RB 544. *(p. 265)* 11 June 1982
RB 545. *(p. 266)* 11 June 1982

RUN AND BECOME, BECOME AND RUN

PART 11

RB 546. *Why are you running?*

Early this morning it was raining so heavily! When I came back from running, the lady with the dog on 150th Street saw me. She said, "Why are you running?"

RB 547. *Eating before racing*

Before every long-distance race, I deliberately eat enough for four or five persons. This is supposed to be my carbo-loading. But then I have to carry this extra weight when I run!

RB 548. *The disco*

On the day of the Westchester Half-Marathon, I secretly ran eight and a half miles early in the morning before the race. When I came near the subway station on Queens Boulevard, I saw hundreds of people coming out of a large building. The building had pictures of movie stars on it. I was thinking to myself, "How can they show a movie at five-thirty in the morning?" But you can't drink in a movie theatre and all these people were absolutely drunk. Disciples told me later that it was probably a disco.

RB 549. *Lost time*

It took me almost a minute to get to the starting line of the half-marathon. Often when you start a race, you lose at least one or two minutes at the beginning. Then it is hard to run; there are so many people ahead of you blocking your way. There are always some poor runners who have to run right in front of you. Once I saw Kirsty, but I could not go in front of her because there were so many people blocking me. At one point there were three runners running together, and I couldn't pass them.

RB 550. *Passing*

Previously when I would start a race, hundreds of people used to go ahead of me. I would just run at my own pace and let everyone pass me. Now I can't believe it — when I run, I go ahead of others. That means my speed has increased. So many people I pass — ten here, two or three farther on. In silence I ask them, "What are you doing? You are doing what I used to do — falling back." Those people are having the same experience that I used to have.

RB 551. *The ERG stop*

At the three-mile point of the half-marathon, Vince was supposed to give me ERG, but he didn't see me run by. I saw him, but I didn't know that he was helping my road crew. Then Lucy saw him and told him that I was about a hundred metres ahead of her. Vince had to run to catch me. Then, once he caught up with me, he had to run another 100 metres because I still didn't know he was the person meeting me and I kept on going. I thought that he was running to inform somebody else that I was coming.

RB 552. *The quick change*

I would like to have T-shirts with zippers in the front. Then I could change in the middle of a race very quickly. This time, after five miles when I took off my nylon running suit, I felt so cold because my shirt was wet, but I didn't stop to change it. If I could have changed, I would have felt fresher and run faster.

RB 553. *Muscular power*

Sometimes I see that after only four miles or so, strong young men start walking. They are very strong and muscular; their chests, arms and legs are so developed. Perhaps they think that their muscular power alone will carry them through the race. But if that were the case, then weight-lifters would all be excellent runners.

RB 554. *Delay*

In the half-marathon I lost over a minute because of Databir. First I was screaming because he didn't see me. Then, he delayed me because he didn't have the ERG ready for me. He had put the ERG on one side of the road, near his car, and was standing on the other side of the road. He said, "Do you need ERG?" Then he had to run across the street to get it.

When you stop to drink ERG or water, for two hundred metres or so you lose your rhythm and your strides become short. Then you start getting back to your normal pace.

RB 555. *Cramps*

After running five miles in the half-marathon, I was finished; I had absolutely no strength. Then, at nine miles, I got such a painful cramp. By eleven miles my cramps were so painful that I had to walk. I couldn't run 800 metres at a time without walking. I stood on the sidewalk, trying to stretch my legs, but the cramps were so powerful that I couldn't do it. No matter what stretching exercises you take for cramps, they are so painful. What can you do? I had such pain that I could barely stand up. At that time I saw Nemi going ahead of me. I said, "Go!" I had to surrender to her speed.

RB 556. *Walking and running*

After about five miles I walked so many times. Before I would start running, I would decide how far I would go before I would start walking again. When I reached that particular place, I would walk for 50 or 100 metres. Afterwards, it came to the point where I was walking 20 metres and running 20 metres. Such pain I had! Two young black boys were joking with me and telling me to run. Of course, they themselves were not running in the race. They were only watching.

RB 557. *New disciples*

When I was dying around eight or nine miles, I saw some new disciples from Connecticut. There were two girls and one boy. They passed me with folded hands. I could see from their faces that they were disciples, but I didn't know their names. Then one girl said, "Guru!"

While I was walking, she went ahead of me 30, 40, 200 metres. She never stopped; she only ran. Then, when I started running again, I caught up with her. Later, when I started walking again, she continued running and passed me.

RB 558. *Virendra and his blanket*

When I had finished nine miles of the half-marathon, I saw Virendra with a big blanket wrapped around him. The nine-mile point was near the finish, so he came to watch after he had completed the race.

RB 559. *Going ahead*

At one point on the road it said one and a half miles to go. But even before that, people giving water were saying, "Only a mile and a half to go."

Right near the finish of the half-marathon, a man wearing a Citibank T-shirt came up to me and said, "Are you Sri Chinmoy?"

I said I was. Then he said, "Please don't mind if I go a little ahead of you. I won't be able to go very far ahead of you."

I said, "Please go."

He finished not even 50 metres ahead of me.

RB 560. *Running like a pig*

Yesterday's 21 miles were not enough. Today greed took me another 11 miles. If you eat like a pig, you suffer. If you run like a pig, you also suffer.

I have goat-speed climbing up hills. Now I need deer-speed.

RB 561. *Greetings*

This morning I ran eleven miles in the Father's Day Marathon around the Jamaica High School Track. When the race started, I waited until the last person was 30 metres ahead and then I started. The first person I passed was Chameli. As I passed her, I greeted her. Like that, I greeted many. I was getting such joy by competing with Anupadi. I passed her and greeted her seven or eight times. Many times I was looking at Anupadi's strides.

RB 562. *Watching strides*

When I see any runner, I don't look at any part of him — not at his head, not at his face, not at his feet. Even in the car if I see somebody running, I don't see the runner. Immediately I look only at his strides. I have that wonderful disease; I can see only the strides.

RB 563. *Age is laughing*

What a difference between the days when I ran in India and now! I don't know whether I should laugh or cry. The best thing is to laugh at age, but perhaps age is laughing at me.

When I ran the 100 metres in India, I used to run much, much faster. Now, nothing moves.

My left leg moves as if it were carrying a dead elephant — it is lifeless.

RB 564. *The 100-yard saviour*

I am so glad that we had the 100-yard race today so that at least in one event I could defeat Dipali. Otherwise, for me to defeat her in long-distance is impossible!

RB 565. *Two smiling rivals*

I smile when I play tennis with Sunanda, and Sunanda smiles when she runs with me. When we run, we know what happens — she always defeats me. When we play tennis, we also know what happens — she has to surrender to me.

RB 566. *The car crash*

Today I had absolutely my best experience running! One of the disciples was following me in his car while I was running in Flushing Meadow Park. I had covered three miles and I was starting my fourth mile, when all of a sudden I heard a big crash, as if two cars had collided.

I turned around to see that the car that was following only 40 metres behind me had crashed into a lamppost. It was a really frightening experience. Then the disciple came out of the car only to tell me that he had been drinking Coke and eating peanuts to stay awake, but in spite of that he fell asleep.

Can you guess the name of the driver? Databir!

Now I ask anyone who follows me while I am running to drive 100 metres either ahead of me or behind me.

RB 567. *The soulful monkeys*

Yesterday around noon, I was walking down the 150th Street hill with my weighted shoes on. When I was coming back up, I saw four little boys — three black and one white. One of the black boys stood in front of me, practically blocking me, with folded hands. There was no joke involved. So I looked at him very soulfully. I couldn't believe my eyes: the other three monkeys were silent. For them to even remain silent was something. Three of them just looked at me, but the other one folded his hands.

When I passed by them, I didn't hear anything, so I knew that they were not cutting jokes. This kind of experience I very seldom get. I was very, very deeply moved to get that kind of treatment from those monkeys.

RB 568. *The Rabbi's birthday present*

Today in our races for the boys, Sanatan — whom I always call my rabbi — lost to me in the 50, 60 and 100-yard races. But then he got extra energy because it was his birthday, and he defeated me in the 1,500-metre race.

RB 569. *Birds of a feather*

Yesterday I saw Shraddha running. I was so delighted to see him running. He had just finished and he was near Annam Brahma. Today I saw Dhananjaya running. So these two photographers have started flocking together. They have become good boys.

RB 570. *I am smart!*

Today Pahar and I were running near the 300-metre mark on 150th Street when we saw a middle-aged lady crossing the street. When she saw us, she said, "I am smart! I walk!"

RB 571. *The drum player*

Once while running in Flushing Meadow Park, I passed by a fellow who was beating a drum. The park authorities were asking him to play more softly. When I ran by, the young man said to me, "You run so fast, so fast!"

RB 572. *The uphill course*

On the Boston "Fifty Oneness-State-Songs" running course, the fifth and sixth miles were all uphill. In the beginning it was all downhill. But what benefit was it, since in the beginning I was fresh? Then coming back it was all uphill. Just when I was tired and exhausted, at that time I had to go up.

RB 573. *The Heartbreak Hill run*

After I ran my seven miles in Boston, I watched the disciples run two miles up "Heartbreak Hill" on the official Boston Marathon course. Nothing gives me so much joy as to watch others running. I really sympathised with them.

Chikur was the first boy. He was far ahead of the second boy, Pahar. Pahar was panting "Hah, hah!" while he was running, but he could not catch up.

RB 574. *The lady with the dogs*

This morning I was walking down the 150th Street hill at about 6:15. After about 100 metres I saw an elderly lady. This is the lady that I always see whenever I run there, even when I go out at three or four in the morning. She always has her two dogs with her and says hello. She is very nice to me. This morning she smiled at me and said, "My dogs will never bite."

RB 575. *The big shot*

Later, on my way to the tennis court, I was walking quickly in the street and four or five black children were walking lifelessly towards me. They looked right at me and said, "Oh, he thinks he is a big shot!"

I was in an absolutely soulful consciousness. What could I do or say?

RB 576. *Getting ahead*

Now when I run races, I see many people who start out ahead of me fall behind me after one mile. Of course, the really excellent runners have gone far, far ahead — God knows where. I can't even see their backs.

In today's five-mile race, towards the end I passed ten or twelve people. Then one girl went ahead of me. She looked at me to see if I was going to try to catch her, and in silence I said, "Go ahead." Later I caught her.

Another girl went ahead of me after four miles. She was taller than I am and so strong and muscular. Again in silence I said, "All right, go ahead."

RB 577. *Mistaken identity*

At one point in the race I passed Gayatri. She was wearing white. Then later, out of the corner of my eye, I saw someone in white coming along my side to pass me. I said, "How can Gayatri be running so fast?" Then I turned a little and saw that the person who was passing me had short hair. I said, "This can't be Gayatri." Finally I turned all the way around and saw that it was a man. Gayatri could not keep pace with me.

RB 578. *Appreciative competitors*

After the race, a white man and two black men came up to me and congratulated me for going ahead of them in the last 800 metres. All three came up to me and said, "We were struggling like anything."

RB 579. *Recognised in London*

During one of the times that I went to London secretly, without telling the disciples that I was going, I went out running. Suddenly I heard someone call, "Guru!"

I said, "Who could that be?" Then I saw Shankara. I said, "What are you doing?"

She said, "I am going to school."

Another time when I went there secretly, a car started following me while I was running. I started to get annoyed because the car was following me. I didn't know there were disciples inside. Finally, the driver came out and said, "Are you Guru?" It was Devashishu's parents, Kaivalya and Bhavani, who live in London. At that time they had just joined our path.

RB 580. *The traffic people*

In North Carolina the "Fifty Oneness-State-Songs" course was very hilly, and it was on a major highway. At one point I had to make a left turn from the right side of the road. If the disciples had told me ahead of time, I would have crossed the highway long before the actual turn. But they did not tell me. They just suddenly said, "Go left!" Chetana and Begabati were supposed to stop the traffic at the turn. But Chetana was only telling me a car was coming. She was not stopping the cars at all. She was only informing me that they were coming. There I lost so much time. I had to come to a total standstill and wait. Then Begabati was standing with her back to the cars and her arms spread, just looking at me. I lost so much time because of these two.

RB 581. *The 300-metre hill*

At one point in the sixth mile of the North Carolina course, there was a 300-metre hill. What could I do? Perhaps when the boys were measuring the course, they were half asleep, so they did not even notice the hill.

The San Francisco course was absolutely the best, so far, of all the "Fifty Oneness-State-Songs" courses. It was totally flat.

RB 582. *The dead elephant*

While I was watching the videotape of my run in North Carolina, I couldn't believe my eyes. I know that I am not a strong runner, but the videotape showed that I looked very strong — like another Bholanath. In the chest, back and thighs, there appeared to be so much strength!

At the same time, I was seeing the speed of a dead elephant and I was feeling and identifying with the dead elephant-runner in myself. I said, "If I really have that much strength, why am I going so slowly?"

RB 583. *Blind disciples*

Sunanda is a first-class blind disciple. Today I was running behind her for 200 metres down the 150th Street hill, with only a 50-metre gap between us. I saw her, but she didn't see me.

Later I saw her again near Jamaica High School. Databir was screaming her name from the car, but still she didn't see me.

I have so many blind disciples. I saw Saroja running, but she was so discouraged that she didn't see me. Sunanda had been running quite fast, but Saroja was running slowly. Perhaps she was disappointed in her running.

Then I saw Pratibha. She was looking at my car, but she didn't recognise it.

RB 584. *Screaming and beaming with joy*

I have never seen any disciple as happy, delighted and excited to see me while running as Mitali. Two days ago I was at my 400-metre mark and she was at the 500-metre mark. When she saw me, she started screaming with joy. I said, "Who can be screaming?" Then I saw her screaming and beaming with joy.

RB 585. *Three-mile record*

This evening in Flushing Meadow Park I ran a 3.1-mile race. For three years my three-mile record has remained the same. Now today I have finally broken my record by one second. Long live Sushoban! He went and got me a number at the last minute. My coach Pahar has also set a personal record.

Dipali ran extremely well. She was tenth among all the women runners.

RB 586. *Kick it in!*

Yesterday, when I was finishing the 3.1-mile race, over the loudspeaker the man was screaming at me to run faster. He was saying, "Kick it in, Sri Chinmoy!" So I kicked and defeated a girl. But in the chute she went ahead of me.

Then while people were receiving prizes, they announced my name and said that I had run. When Dipali got a prize, they said that she was from the Sri Chinmoy team. Then they said, "Sri Chinmoy also ran."

RB 587. *Why does Sri Chinmoy have to run?*

This morning I ran a four-mile race in Central Park. At the start I saw a middle-aged man talking to his wife and a friend. I was only ten metres away from them, by the side of the road. The man pointed to me and said, "I don't know why he has to run. Of all people he has to run."

His wife asked him, "Why are you saying that?"

The man said, "He is Sri Chinmoy, and his disciples run all over the world." Then he mentioned Thomas's name — no surname, just Thomas. "His disciple Thomas is going all over the country, running thousands and thousands of miles. Now why does Sri Chinmoy have to run?" he said.

His wife asked, "What is wrong with it?"

I was filled with pride and gratitude for what Thomas was doing. Then the man said, "He and his disciples are doing a very good job."

At that time I wanted to change my shoes, so Bipin ran and got another pair of running shoes from Dhanu's car. The man was looking at me with such appreciation, and I smiled at him. I was so embarrassed that everyone was helping me with my shoes while I was sitting there like a king. I tried to take one shoe and put it on myself, but unconsciously Nirvik pulled it away from me. I didn't want these people to see Nirvik put on my shoes. If it had been after the race, they could have thought that I was dying, but the race had not even started yet.

RB 588. *Shrai, you are going ahead*

At the halfway point of the four-mile race, I saw two men running — a fat man and his friend. As I was passing them, one said, "Hi, Shrai, how are you?" I said, "Fine, thank you."

Then the man said, "Shrai, you are going ahead of me!"

RB 589. *Dogs and snakes*

At the four-mile race there was a dog that was very bad. What was he doing in the race? The owner was there, taking the dog to this side and that side. Sometimes the dog wouldn't listen to him.

Children should be forbidden in these kinds of races. They should have their own races. It is so hard to run with them! They never, never stay in a straight line. While I take one step, they take three steps. And during these three steps they move like snakes — all serpentine winding!

RB 590. *The president has come*

In today's race I didn't know that Fred Lebow was ahead of me. They were announcing that Mary Decker Tabb would run there in September. Then they said, "The President has come." Karabi heard it over the loudspeaker as she was finishing.

Dipali, out of her infinite kindness, stayed behind me so that she could follow me to the end. But Karabi went ahead at the very beginning. Husiar was twentieth out of thousands.

RB 591. *Like a light*

A lady told Shephali that she saw me running once a few years ago before she knew anything about meditation. She said, "I saw a man running at a distance. He was like a light. I was so curious that I followed him in my car." The lady pointed to her third eye and told Shephali, "He was just like a light."

Then Shephali showed her one of my *Run and become* books, and the lady was laughing while reading the stories.

RB 592. *The 100-metre dash*

When I ran the 100-metre dash in India, after 60 metres, out of the blue I used to get such speed. But here on Sports Day, after 70 metres everything went blank. I was about to collapse.

Next year I will keep the same people in my heat: Pulin, Sandhani, Pulak and Sanatan. My time was 15.2 seconds. Now I am crying, but twenty or thirty years ago I would have laughed at this timing. Now I have to cry and cry and cry. When in my life did I ever run 100 metres even as slow as 15 seconds? I started at 12 seconds and then went to 11. Now, if I can run under 14, I will be so happy. Next year I have to aim at under 15.

RB 593. *I should commit suicide*

In India I used to do 200 metres in 23.4 seconds. But today it became 36.9. I should commit suicide. One or two years in India I stood second. Then after that, every year I was first.

In 400 metres I was always first. One year there was a tie with someone who was in another heat. If we had been in the same heat, God knows, I would have gone faster.

RB 594. *The false start*

Once in India I was using the starting blocks in a race. When you use the blocks your foot has to touch the ground. You cannot put your foot on the block unless it is also touching the ground. I was 100 percent sure that my foot was touching the ground, so I was surprised when the official gave me a false start. He said my left foot was not touching the ground.

The official felt sorry for me but he couldn't tell me what I was supposed to do. He could tell by looking that my left foot was not touching the ground, but he couldn't say anything to correct it. So I took a standing start, which is useless. Even then I won the 200-metre dash. Then afterwards he saw me on the street and said, "I feel very sorry about your timing."

I said, "I was first."

He said, "That is true, but if you had started from the crouching position, your timing would have been better."

RB 595. *Running during the parade*

Yesterday's parade route was seven miles long. From one end to the other, the marchers and floats spread out over 700 metres, practically half a mile. I would run one mile and wait for the parade to go by. Then again I would run one mile and watch the parade.

I told one of my attendants, Tejiyan, to be careful. Next year I will run at a seven-minute pace. He said he has started practising running so he will be able to keep up with me while accompanying me.

RB 596. *A real man*

I was running near my 500-metre mark on 150th Street when a young student with a tape recorder in his hand came out of his house. He was listening to music. When he saw me he said, "Happy birthday!"

I said, "Thank you!"

Then he said, "You are a real man. There are very few real men on this earth."

"Real" means that I am a good man.

RB 597. *Your birthday is over*

When I was out on a four-mile run, four or five children approached me and said, "Your birthday is over."

I said, "Not yet."

They had seen the parade, so they thought that my birthday was over.

RB 598. *How do you do?*

While I was running, a man said to me, "Hi, Sri Chinmoy! How do you do?"

He used my full name. He was very nice, and I waved to him. So there are good people in this world.

RB 599. *The Rabbi versus the Master*

I beat Sanatan in the 100-metre dash on Sports Day. As you know, I always call him my Rabbi. That means that this Indian spiritual Master is better than that Rabbi. Last spring the same Rabbi also lost to the Indian Master. And then a few days ago, again the Rabbi lost. Three times the Rabbi lost, so don't be a disciple of that Rabbi.

RB 600. *Compelled to run*

The two English brothers, Devashishu and Sahadeva, write to me quite often. One time the little one, Sahadeva, lodged a complaint against the older one. He said that sometimes he doesn't want to run, but his brother compels him. That's why he hates his brother.

But Sahadeva also loves his brother because his brother is kind in other ways. Now Sahadeva has to love his brother because Devashishu was able to run seven miles. That's why he got a special prize from me.

RB 601. *The surprise blessing*

Today I was practising speed work on the street in front of my house. I would run a hundred metres, stop for a short time and then run another hundred metres. After finishing one 100-metre sprint, I turned around only to see a white dog in front of my house. I didn't see the owner at all.

All of a sudden a fat lady with white hair came from behind me and put her hand on my left shoulder. She said, "You look so beautiful today!" I smiled at her. What could I do? She was blessing me.

This lady also has a granddaughter. Both of them sometimes sweep their backyard. Her dog's name is Pauly. Some years ago she had a fight with another lady on my street, and I took her side. So she and I became friends.

RB 602. *Smart guy*

This year I started the 47-mile run in the evening before the disciples started. While I was running around Jamaica High School, a boy who was observing me said, "You are showing off."

I said, "You are right."

Then the other fellow with him said, "He is a smart guy."

RB 603. *Can I help you?*

While I was running 47 miles, one person came up to me and said, "You do such nice things for people. Sir, can I be of any help to you?"

I said, "Thank you, I do not need any help right now."

RB 604. *What tennis has done*

During the 47-mile run, I was limping. Mahiyan, our tennis champion, passed me and said, "This is what tennis has done to you."

RB 605. *Observations*

I was observing all the disciples during the ultramarathon. Pranika sometimes found it difficult to smile at me because she was dying. Shephali dies inside when she runs, but she always smiles at me. Such a peculiar style Shephali has! She runs as if she is boxing. Her elbows stick out.

Heinz was the rabbit of the day. He is such a good sprinter. He was ahead for so long. Then all of a sudden, he slowed down and disappeared. He sells tofu for Abarita's factory, so he should have kept some tofu inside his pocket to give him energy.

Databir's goal was to defeat Khudita, but what could he do? At one point she was 16 laps ahead of him.

RB 606. *The curse*

While the race was going on, at one point a black lady was standing on the other side of the street, near Apeksha's old store, cursing us. She was screaming that I have brainwashed all of my disciples. She went on screaming and screaming so loudly!

RB 607. *Descent of an oath*

I was born on a Thursday, so I recently made an oath to run 27 miles every Thursday, starting any time after midnight.

After running thirty-four miles in the 47-mile run, my oath descended to 13 miles. Soon it may descend to 10 miles.

RB 546. *(p. 271)* 13 June 1982
RB 547. *(p. 271)* 13 June 1982
RB 548. *(p. 271)* 13 June 1982
RB 549. *(p. 271)* 13 June 1982
RB 550. *(p. 272)* 13 June 1982
RB 551. *(p. 272)* 13 June 1982
RB 552. *(p. 272)* 13 June 1982
RB 553. *(p. 273)* 13 June 1982
RB 554. *(p. 273)* 13 June 1982
RB 555. *(p. 273)* 13 June 1982
RB 556. *(p. 274)* 13 June 1982
RB 557. *(p. 274)* 13 June 1982
RB 558. *(p. 274)* 13 June 1982
RB 559. *(p. 275)* 13 June 1982
RB 560. *(p. 275)* 14 June 1982
RB 561. *(p. 275)* 20 June 1982
RB 562. *(p. 276)* 20 June 1982
RB 563. *(p. 276)* 20 June 1982
RB 564. *(p. 276)* 21 June 1982
RB 565. *(p. 276)* 21 June 1982
RB 566. *(p. 277)* 21 June 1982
RB 567. *(p. 277)* 26 June 1982
RB 568. *(p. 278)* 27 June 1982
RB 569. *(p. 278)* 2 July 1982
RB 570. *(p. 278)* 8 July 1982
RB 571. *(p. 278)* 9 July 1982
RB 572. *(p. 279)* 10 July 1982
RB 573. *(p. 279)* 10 July 1982
RB 574. *(p. 279)* 11 July 1982
RB 575. *(p. 280)* 11 July 1982

RB 576. *(p. 280)* 11 July 1982
RB 577. *(p. 280)* 11 July 1982
RB 578. *(p. 281)* 11 July 1982
RB 579. *(p. 281)* 11 July 1982
RB 580. *(p. 281)* 21 July 1982
RB 581. *(p. 282)* 21 July 1982
RB 582. *(p. 282)* 21 July 1982
RB 583. *(p. 282)* 21 July 1982
RB 584. *(p. 283)* 21 July 1982
RB 585. *(p. 283)* 6 August 1982
RB 586. *(p. 283)* 7 August 1982
RB 587. *(p. 284)* 7 August 1982
RB 588. *(p. 285)* 7 August 1982
RB 589. *(p. 285)* 7 August 1982
RB 590. *(p. 285)* 7 August 1982
RB 591. *(p. 286)* 7 August 1982
RB 592. *(p. 286)* 21 August 1982
RB 593. *(p. 286)* 22 August 1982
RB 594. *(p. 287)* 22 August 1982
RB 595. *(p. 287)* 22 August 1982
RB 596. *(p. 288)* 23 August 1982
RB 597. *(p. 288)* 23 August 1982
RB 598. *(p. 288)* 23 August 1982
RB 599. *(p. 288)* 25 August 1982
RB 600. *(p. 289)* 25 August 1982
RB 601. *(p. 289)* 26 August 1982
RB 602. *(p. 290)* 27 August 1982
RB 603. *(p. 290)* 27 August 1982
RB 604. *(p. 290)* 27 August 1982
RB 605. *(p. 290)* 27 August 1982
RB 606. *(p. 291)* 27 August 1982
RB 607. *(p. 291)* 27 August 1982

RUN AND BECOME, BECOME AND RUN

PART 12

RB 608. *Problems going up*

The other day while I was running in Flushing Meadow Park, a gentleman came up to me and inquired whether our marathon would be held in Flushing Meadow.

I said, "Yes."

Then he said, "In October?"

I said, "On the third of October."

He was very happy. So there are people like me who like to run on a flat course. We have problems going up. Of course, in the inner world if you have problems going up, then you are lost.

RB 609. *Ultra-marathoner*

If you look at Cahit Yeter after he has run a marathon, he looks as if he has just warmed up. Yes, some other runners defeated him in our Plainsboro marathon, but nobody looked as fresh as he did. Everybody else was out of breath, dying. Because of his ultra-marathoning, 26 miles was nothing for him. But then, if one says to him, "You are an ultra-marathoner," he will say, "Oh, I am not an ultra-marathoner. So and so is a real ultra-marathoner."

RB 610. *Dying for a picture*

When I was giving out the prizes for our Plainsboro marathon, the girl who came in third came up to me with such devotedness! Then, she was dying to have her picture taken with me. She came up with such respect and then she was waiting for a picture. Bhashwar took one, so I will send it to her with my autograph.

RB 611. *A champion in walking*

One day I saw Nemi running so fast. I knew that I could not keep up with her, so I surrendered. I said, "Let me walk so that I can say I was just walking and not trying to keep up with her."

Recently I have started practising walking. I sincerely want to become a champion in walking.

RB 612. *The kidnappers*

This morning I left to go running and walking at about 4:30 a.m. As usual, my road crew was following me in a car. Around 5 a.m. a newspaper delivery truck pulled up next to me, and the driver asked, "Tell me, are the people who are following you your friends?"

I said, "Yes."

He said, "I was worrying because the car was following you." He thought they were going to kidnap me.

RB 613. *Encounter in the dark*

After going six and a half miles I saw a gentleman riding a bicycle. At that time I was absolutely dying because I was trying to walk the fastest for that mile.

When he saw me, he started shouting, "Sri Chinmoy, Sri Chinmoy!" Can you imagine? Even in the dark, people recognise me. Now so many people know us when we run.

Later in the day he came into Annam Brahma and spoke to Dhanu. He said to him, "It was still quite dark. What was Sri Chinmoy doing out there so early?"

RB 614. *Not a runner*

At one point in today's run, there was an old man standing by the side of the street with his dog. I was running quite fast, but perhaps I had a tortured look on my face because of my injury. Anyway, when he saw me he said, "You don't look like a runner!"

I said, "You are right. I am not a runner."

God was speaking through that man. The man should have told me, "You should give up running and be a non-runner like me."

RB 615. *An annoying runner*

Today as I was running back to my starting point on 150th Street, for a mile another runner was bothering me. As soon as she saw me approaching, she began running faster, always staying just a little ahead of me. At first I thought it was Kirsty, but then I saw that she had black hair, whereas Kirsty's hair is golden.

Every time I came near her, she would go faster, so I couldn't pass her. Then I stopped running for a while and said, "I don't want to see her face." Finally she made a left turn onto a side street.

RB 616. *Greeting from the street*

During a recent run I saw a middle-aged lady running towards me. I was running on the street and she was running on the sidewalk. In order to draw my attention, she left the sidewalk and started running on the street. Then she smiled, raised her hand and said, "Hi!" When men greet me, I say "Hi!" back, but when women greet me, I only smile.

After she passed by me, I turned around and saw that she was again running on the sidewalk. It seems that she went into the street only because there were some parked cars in between us, and she thought that perhaps she would not see me if she remained on the sidewalk.

RB 617. *Crazy man*

While I was race-walking in Flushing Meadow Park, two black men saw me. One of them said, "Crazy man, as if you are going to do a full marathon!"

RB 618. *The rainbow*

As I was finishing a seven-mile walk from my house to Flushing Meadow Park, I was passing by the fountain in the park. An elderly man said to me, "Great walker, can't you appreciate the rainbow?"

So I turned around and saw that there was an extremely beautiful rainbow in the fountain. For at least fifty metres I was walking very slowly, watching the rainbow. Then immediately I remembered, "O God, my timing!"

RB 619. *The bag lady*

About three or four days ago I was walking and running on 150th Street. When I was only three hundred metres away from my starting point, a bus stopped and an elderly lady with two shopping bags got off. The shopping bags were full of groceries. With greatest difficulty she lifted up one bag and walked towards her house on a side street.

I looked at her and said, "May I help you?"

She said to me very abruptly, "Of course not!" She spoke so sharply that she practically took my soul out of my body. Then she looked at me again and said, "You are such a great man! Are you not Sri Chinmoy?"

So I gave her a smile and I picked up the other bag and walked with her. When we got to her house, I put the bag on her steps. Again she looked at me in utter amazement.

RB 620. *Amazingly beautiful*

The following afternoon Dhanu, Databir and quite a few visitors were watching me walk along Main Street. There we have a very accurate course marked off every hundred metres. All the marks on my courses are now accurate because Nirvik has done them. He has done a most careful and accurate job, measuring everything while walking with the wheel.

Since I didn't know where some of the new marks were, Databir went ahead of me to show me. At one point an old, very fat black lady — twice my size, but very short — saw us as we were crossing the street. She had two shopping bags, one in each hand. I think that Databir may have said something to her — God knows. But as I came closer, she was so kind. When I was two metres away, she took the bag from her left hand, put it in her right hand and gave me the right of way. I said, "Thank you so much."

Then she looked into my eyes and said, "Amazingly beautiful!"

Again I thanked her. Then she walked away.

RB 621. *Crazy Nathan*

In our 24-hour race this weekend, Kim was the nicest runner; she was nice all the time. Next was crazy Nathan. Every time he passed me, he had to say some crazy thing. But he was also very nice.

Once Nathan said to me, "Do you have a moment?" At that point I was walking and he was running. He continued, "I want to sing song for you."

I said, "That is fine."

His song was, "Oh, what a wonderful sponsor you are. I will owe it all to you." Then he sang it again. He had set a very nice tune to it, so I thanked him.

The funniest thing Nathan said was about meditation and contemplation. He asked me, "Do you meditate while you are walking and running?"

I said, "Yes."

He said, "I thought so. I can't meditate, but I contemplate." I said, "That is the highest state. That means you are higher than I am."

He looked at me and said, "It can't be higher than meditation." His wife is also very nice, but she does not act so crazy.

RB 622. *Immortal picture*

During the 24-hour race, Bhashwar had taken a nice picture of Cahit and me. I signed it and gave it to Cahit, along with another picture of him running. Cahit wrote me a letter saying, "Nothing is as immortal, as valuable as this."

RB 623. *Running in the street*

Before the marathon in Flushing Meadow Park, I ran about 14 miles on Union Turnpike. I was running in the outside lane and Pahar was running in the middle lane, next to me. My road crew was following me in the car. A policeman came and said, "Run on the sidewalk!"

So I ran a little bit on the sidewalk, but the sidewalk is much harder than the street and it hurt my legs. Finally I said, "Let the police come again," and we went back to the street. Then an old man and woman saw us running. The old man was barking, "Can't you see you are running in the street?" The old lady told her husband not to bother us.

RB 624. *Cheering Gary Fanelli*

In the first part of our marathon in Flushing Meadow Park, I saw Gary Fanelli running behind some other runners. I said to him, "Gary, go faster." In two minutes, as he came back in the other direction, he said, "Guru, thank you." Then from his pocket he put something in his mouth.

He ran another half mile before making a turn. When he came back from the small loop, he was in first place — a hundred metres ahead of the runner behind him.

RB 625. *The short cut*

Vince was helping at the nine-mile point, but I didn't see him. That was the place where I took a short cut. What could I do? Gary Fanelli was finishing and I wanted to see him.

Altogether I ran 14 miles before the marathon and then walked seven or eight miles during the marathon.

RB 626. *Without your blessings*

After Gary Fanelli won the marathon, I went to crown him with the laurel wreath at the finish line. He bowed to me and said, "Guru, without your blessings I could not have done it." Later he told me, "I am so honoured that you invited me."

RB 627. *Namaste*

The tall, thin man who won fourth place in our marathon belongs to the Prospect Park Track Club. When he came to get his prize, he said, "Namaste."

At one point during the marathon, while he was running he turned around to greet me. Many other people also turned around to greet me.

RB 628. *The mistaken invitation*

Pulin was the race director for today's marathon. After the race I said to him, "Pulin, that man with the moustache definitely ran in our 24-hour race. Please invite him to run in our next ultramarathon."

Pulin is so divine! He went to a different man, who also had a moustache, and invited him to come to our next 24-hour race.

RB 629. *The four-minute miler*

Today I ran on the course for our four-mile race at Breezy Point before the other runners. While I was running, I passed an elderly couple, and the husband started joking with me, saying, "Oh, a four-minute miler?"

I said, "Yes, a four-minute miler."

When I was coming back from the turnaround point, the wife was asking Savita about me. The lady said, "That's that older runner."

RB 630. *A certain attitude*

When I was giving the prizes for the four-mile race, the third-place girl said to me, "I am your disciple. Yesterday you accepted me."

When disciples come to receive prizes from me, they have a certain attitude of devotion. Her name is Vicki.

RB 631. *The street is all yours*

Towards the end of today's 20-kilometre race in Eisenhower Park, a little boy said to me, "The street is yours."

He was telling me that I could run on the street, but I went onto the sidewalk and continued my running there.

At one point we took a wrong turn, but Niriha saved us and told us the correct way. She was there videotaping my running.

RB 632. *The barking dog*

Some dogs on our block are so bad. This morning when I was running at about 6:20, I saw a man walking his dog. The dog was barking. The owner was calling the dog Russell.

A delivery man wanted to put a newspaper in the mailbox of a particular house, but the dog was blocking his way. He was afraid of the dog. Then, when the dog passed by him, he put the newspaper inside the mailbox.

RB 633. *Gary Muhrcke's advice*

Databir went to the Super Runner store to buy me new running shoes. The owner, Gary Muhrcke, is an excellent runner who was the winner of the first New York Marathon. He knows me well. When he found out the shoes were for me, immediately he took off 20 percent.

Then Databir told him that I wanted to bring my weight down to 131 pounds to run the New York Marathon. Gary is five feet eight and a half inches tall and weighs 125 or 126 pounds. He said I should come down to 125 and then, to get strength, eat before the marathon and come up to 131. He also said I should not run more than 40 miles a week before the marathon. So I am listening to Gary Muhrcke's advice. I am trying to come down in my weight, and I will not run more than 40 miles a week.

RB 634. *Short strides*

Once I was at Gary Muhrcke's store, and I asked him to show me how to run with long strides. He took me outside the store and showed me, instead, how to take short, quick strides. He suggested that I run with children because they take very short, quick strides.

RB 635. *Morning greetings*

Around 7:30 this morning an old man saw me running. He said, "Guru, why do you have to run?"

He was older than I am.

Then after five or six miles, somebody riding on a bicycle shouted, "Good morning, Sri Chinmoy!"

RB 636. *The crazy lady*

Today the funniest thing happened when I was race-walking on 150th Street. On my way back, at about the 300-metre mark, a gentleman grabbed my elbow and said, "I have got to talk to you."

I thought, "O God, he is going to complain about the 300-metre mark on the street." That is the famous mark that a German lady has given us so much trouble about.

But the gentleman didn't mention the mark. He told me that his wife had gone crazy. He said, "You see the bus stop over there? She does not want to stand there. She wants the bus to stop for her about 40 metres away, not where the bus is supposed to stop. Three times the bus passed her but the drivers didn't stop, although she waved her hand and screamed."

He told me that the fourth time a bus was coming, to draw the bus driver's attention he stood in the street in front of the bus. The bus driver stopped and insulted and scolded him. While the bus was stopped, his wife entered into the bus.

I asked, "Now where is she going?"

He said, "She is going shopping."

I said, "How do you know she will not do some crazy thing while she is away? How do you know she will not stand at some place and expect the bus driver to stop for her?"

I gave him my very sympathetic ear, and he felt that I really was sorry for him. But he had faith in her and felt she would come back.

RB 637. *Like father, like daughter*

A few months ago I was running three miles in a park near Union Turnpike. At one point I threw off my hat, and Robin ran and picked it up. Today when I was running a one-mile race in Eisenhower Park, my hat fell off. Like father, like daughter: Joanna immediately ran and picked it up.

RB 638. *Familiar T-shirts*

In today's five-mile race in Central Park I saw a black man running right beside me, wearing a white T-shirt with my picture on it. He did not recognise me, and I did not know him. I also saw somebody wearing our triathlon T-shirt.

RB 639. *Politics in the park*

After the five-mile race in Central Park, when our prasad was over, the Republican candidate for Governor, Lewis Lehrman, walked in front of me. Fred Lebow was talking to him as we were leaving the park.

RB 640. *Craig Virgin's question*

For such a long time I have had many famous runners' questions to answer for our newspaper column. Finally, today I answered a question from Craig Virgin. I did not know outwardly that today Niriha had taken a videotape of my running to show Craig Virgin at the New York Marathon clinic so that he could analyse my style. I was answering his question, and he was solving my problems! This is how things go together in the soul's world.

RB 641. *Creating a sensation*

For one week before the race, the New York Marathon creates such a sensation in New York City. Everybody knows that sixteen thousand people will run. There will be a sea of people flooding the streets.

Of course, since we are not the organisers, we are full of joy and excitement instead of suffering from headaches. Someday we should have sixteen thousand people in one of our races!

RB 642. *A knife fight in south Brooklyn*

This week I ran along the New York Marathon route twice, going by car to different sections of the course. The first time, we went from the start to the thirteen-mile point so that I could run all the hills. Between the eighth and ninth mile is the worst hill. It is 1,200 metres long.

When I was in South Brooklyn, between the third and fourth mile, I saw a Puerto Rican gang that had been challenged by a black gang. The blacks were coming from behind me, and the Puerto Ricans were coming towards them. There were about four or five on each side, and I was running in between them!

The blacks had on the proper uniform — all black. I was wearing a dark navy blue sauna suit that also looked black.

One of the Puerto Ricans showed the blacks such a big knife! I just smiled to myself and kept running, because I knew that the knife was not meant for me. The boys on the road crew also saw the knife. Dhanu got the shock of his life. What an experience!

RB 643. *All hills*

When we returned to the New York Marathon route on the second day, I started at the 17-mile point and ran to the 26th mile, again running only the hills.

Central Park was the worst. As soon as I entered the park, there were only hills going on, going on. During the marathon, once you come to Central Park you think you can heave a sigh of relief because you are almost finished. But O God, there it is all hills!

RB 644. *Why are you running now?*

While I was running on the marathon course, one black girl said to me, "You fool, next week is the marathon! Why are you running now?"

RB 645. *The sinking bridge*

At the start of the New York Marathon I thought that the Verrazano Bridge, instead of just shaking, was sinking. Many others also had the same experience.

RB 646. *Looking for the first mile*

At the first mile I didn't see the mile-marker or the clock. Finally I said, "I must have already passed it. I couldn't have taken nine minutes for the first mile."

RB 647. *Marathon handouts*

This year the water stations in the New York Marathon were peculiar. They didn't put them at every mile.

During the marathon people are always very nice. The spectators always give out oranges, ice and donuts. At one point this time it seemed that people were giving out tissues. At first I couldn't understand why everybody was grabbing the tissues. Then I saw what they were. They were sticks of gum.

RB 648. *Voirab's mother*

At one point I saw Voirab's mother holding two cups for the runners to take as they ran by. Other people near her were also holding out cups, but because I recognised her, I stretched my hand out to take water from her. Unfortunately, she did not recognise me, and she gave the cup to somebody else! She was so excited about the marathon that she didn't see who I was.

RB 649. *A discouraging story*

I started out on the men's side. Then, when the men's and women's sides came next to one another, I went to the women's side. I thought that on the women's side people would be more civilised, but I was wrong. After a mile and a half, they started throwing away the plastic garbage bags and all sorts of clothing they had worn to keep warm. Twice I almost slipped on the bags.

Afterwards I found out that when I went to the women's side, Chetana switched to the men's side, hoping to see me. She never saw me, but all the time she was seeing the boys from my road crew who were supposed to bring me water and run with me. She was seeing them, but from my side I couldn't find them at all. Two or three times I just stood still, only trying to see where the boys might be.

So many times I saw our disciples watching the marathon. But this side and that side I was looking for the road crew — without success — and they were also looking for me. For so many miles, ten or twelve boys were looking for me. I was running on the left side so I would not be blocked by people, but still they didn't see me.

When you want something and do not get it, it is very discouraging. Mile after mile went by but I did not see my road crew anywhere.

I didn't stop at all before 15 miles. Then I started walking and became cold. Thighs, legs, here, there everything became cold. And the road crew was nowhere to be found. It was very discouraging.

Finally, I saw Ranjana with some drinks for me, and soon after, at 17 miles, I saw the boys in my road crew.

RB 650. *The thirsty runner*

My road crew is always responsible for supplying me with drinks. This time when I was thirsty, sometimes I couldn't drink because I was in the middle of the road and could not get near the water station. If the road crew had been there, they would have given me ERG and water. Three times at the water stations I said "ERG" but they gave me water.

RB 651. *The helpful children*

While I was running, several times some black children patted me on the shoulder or tried to shake my hand. One said, "Buddy, go on."

They were very nice. They were giving the runners water and juice. Unfortunately, their fingers were inside the water. Twice after taking water from them and thanking them, I started running without drinking because the water was so filthy. Each mile I drank water from the water stations, but not the water that children were giving out.

RB 652. *Recognition*

I was so surprised that at least twenty people recognised me during the marathon. Even from the second mile people recognised me. My number was not listed in the marathon book because I got it late, and I was wearing something over my Sri Chinmoy Marathon Team singlet. Even so, at one point two or three black girls recognised me and called out, "Guru!" They were not my disciples.

RB 653. *Seeing the disciple runners*

Many times while I was running I thought that no disciples were near me. Then I would turn around to find some of the disciples only 50 or 60 metres behind me.

At one point I saw Shephali right ahead of me, almost touching my elbow, but she never saw me.

At another point I saw Pranika going ahead of me after she had been behind me for a while.

RB 654. *Pragati's parents*

At 14 miles I saw Pragati's parents, and smiled at them. They
have to tell the truth: at that time I was well ahead of Pragati.
Then afterwards, when I started walking, Pragati went ahead
of me and disappeared. Nirjhari was also behind me in the
beginning, but later she went ahead of me.

RB 655. *Toshiko D'Elia's marathon finish*

After finishing the New York Marathon, Toshiko D'Elia was so
disappointed with her time. She asked Tina to tell me. Toshiko
was so grateful to Tina for helping her after she finished. She
was in terrible agony. Everyone was giving her this and that to
drink. Tina massaged her and helped her like anything.

She is now quite old. She started running at the age of 40.
Her daughter inspired her. Before that she could not run even
one block. That means she was not a faster runner than I was
when I started. Now, in a few years she has become such a great
runner. She is a world record holder for women over 40. So still
I can have hope. The best thing for me is not to give up.

RB 656. *The marathon spirit*

Name and fame in marathon running was first won for America
by Frank Shorter. Frank Shorter really shook America out of its
lethargy or complacent feeling. It was he who made the start.

Now, people are running faster and faster. It will take at most
five years, perhaps even less, for someone to run a marathon
under two hours. How I wish that one of my disciples would
do it! It is wishful thinking, but sometimes dreams come true.
My disciples have an advantage because they have spirituality
behind their running. If I were twenty years old, I would try it.

RB 657. *Why do you get so exhausted?*

The day before the marathon I was running on 150th Street. At about the 800-metre mark, a dog came near me. The owner lifted his head and saw me. Then he became so excited. He shouted, "Sri Chinmoy!"

Three days ago I was doing intervals — walking 100 metres and then running 300 metres. The same man saw me on 150th Street while I was walking. He asked me, "Why do you get exhausted so soon?"

He thought I was only walking.

RB 608. *(p. 297)* 9 September 1982
RB 609. *(p. 297)* 13 September 1982
RB 610. *(p. 297)* 12 September 1982
RB 611. *(p. 298)* 14 September 1982
RB 612. *(p. 298)* 14 September 1982
RB 613. *(p. 298)* 14 September 1982
RB 614. *(p. 299)* 16 September 1982
RB 615. *(p. 299)* 16 September 1982
RB 616. *(p. 299)* 16 September 1982
RB 617. *(p. 300)* 19 September 1982
RB 618. *(p. 300)* 19 September 1982
RB 619. *(p. 300)* 26 September 1982
RB 620. *(p. 301)* 26 September 1982
RB 621. *(p. 302)* 26 September 1982
RB 622. *(p. 302)* 3 October 1982
RB 623. *(p. 303)* 3 October 1982
RB 624. *(p. 303)* 3 October 1982
RB 625. *(p. 303)* 3 October 1982
RB 626. *(p. 304)* 3 October 1982
RB 627. *(p. 304)* 3 October 1982
RB 628. *(p. 304)* 3 October 1982
RB 629. *(p. 304)* 9 October 1982
RB 630. *(p. 305)* 9 October 1982
RB 631. *(p. 305)* 10 October 1982
RB 632. *(p. 305)* 14 October 1982
RB 633. *(p. 306)* 14 October 1982
RB 634. *(p. 306)* 14 October 1982
RB 635. *(p. 306)* 14 October 1982
RB 636. *(p. 307)* 14 October 1982
RB 637. *(p. 308)* 17 October 1982

RB 638. *(p.308)* 17 October 1982
RB 639. *(p.308)* 21 October 1982
RB 640. *(p.308)* 21 October 1982
RB 641. *(p.309)* 21 October 1982
RB 642. *(p.309)* 23 October 1982
RB 643. *(p.310)* 23 October 1982
RB 644. *(p.310)* 23 October 1982
RB 645. *(p.310)* 25 October 1982
RB 646. *(p.310)* 25 October 1982
RB 647. *(p.311)* 25 October 1982
RB 648. *(p.311)* 25 October 1982
RB 649. *(p.311)* 25 October 1982
RB 650. *(p.312)* 25 October 1982
RB 651. *(p.313)* 25 October 1982
RB 652. *(p.313)* 25 October 1982
RB 653. *(p.313)* 25 October 1982
RB 654. *(p.314)* 25 October 1982
RB 655. *(p.314)* 25 October 1982
RB 656. *(p.314)* 25 October 1982
RB 657. *(p.315)* 31 October 1982

RUN AND BECOME, BECOME AND RUN

PART 13

This morning during our 24-hour race at Francis Lewis High School, people were bothering me while I was walking along the track. One man stood in my way and said, "Are you running 24 hours?"

I said, "Yes."

He said, "Crazy! They are crazy people!"

Then ten minutes later he came back to me and asked, "This is a meditation group?"

I said, "Yes."

Then he asked, "Are you connected with the meditation group?"

I said, "Yes."

I thought the conversation was over, but a few minutes later he came back to me again and asked, "Are you the teacher?"

When I said, "Yes," he started trembling.

Then he said, "I am going to a class taught by one of your students. His spiritual name I don't remember, but his American name is Jeremy. He is very tall. I like his teaching very much. But right now I am in trouble. Can you help me?"

I said, "What kind of trouble?"

He said, "Just before I joined his class, I ordered Edgar Cayce's tapes. Now they have come, but I have not listened to any of them yet. I wonder if I should listen to the tapes or continue with the classes."

I told him, "Continue with the classes and at the same time listen to the tapes. Then make your choice. If my teachings give you more joy, then continue with the classes. But if Edgar Cayce's tapes give you more joy, then follow his path."

The man said, "Such nice advice! Thank you."

RB 659. *Matter over mind*

During the 24-hour race, one runner was telling another runner, "We have to prove that mind can win over matter. But unfortunately, today matter has won."

RB 660. *Running in front of Susan's house*

Three or four important runners have said that in order to increase your stride you have to practise running down a very gradual hill for about 400 metres. We have found a gradual 300-metre hill on Union Turnpike and Baoul has marked the hill with 55-inch stride marks.

I was practising 100-metre intervals there, since Baoul had not yet put the marks for the second and third 100 metres. Baoul said, "Larry and his mother live somewhere near here." Two minutes later a bus stopped and who came out of the bus? Larry's mother, Susan! They live on the same side of the street that Baoul had put the stride marks on. She was so happy that I was practising in front of her house, and she stood outside watching me. At one point she was waiting for me to run by, expecting that I would continue. But I was leaving in the car, and we passed by her.

RB 661. *The VIP*

While I was running in Flushing Meadow Park, one of the boys on the road crew was driving behind me. Three girls who were visiting from other Centres were in the back seat — Sharon, Hladini and Kritagyata — and Vidhu was asleep in the very back

A middle-aged man came out of his car and said to me, "What do you think you are — a very important person?"

I said, "No, I don't think so."

Then I ran 200 metres. When I came back he again came up to me and asked, "Why do you need so many bodyguards, especially girls?" He didn't see Vidhu because Vidhu was still sleeping. He saw only the three girls. The man was smiling and joking with me.

RB 662. *Keep it up!*

The day before yesterday, when I was coming back after having run seven miles, Pranika was running nearby. After running seven miles, I was walking the last 20 or 30 metres. An old man who looked about 70 saw me running, and then he saw me stop. He said to me, "Keep it up, keep it up!"

RB 663. *Two prize winners*

Today I ran a three-mile race in Staten Island. They have these races every Saturday.

Alo was so excited; she was first in her age group — over 50. I was also first in the over-50 category. A little boy and three men finished long after I did. Tomorrow the results of the race will come out in the local newspaper.

RB 664. *The honour system*

In the three-mile race, a teenage girl with a bandage around her knee was ahead of me. Then she gave up.

The race counted on the honour system. Otherwise, in five or six places you could have taken a short cut.

The first mile, according to Pahar, I did in under eight minutes. But then the second mile was slower because at least twenty times I had to run through puddles.

RB 665. *The steep hill*

After the race I was walking up a hill that was at least 300 metres long. It was very, very steep. That will be one of the courses where I will practise running uphill for 300 metres. Even if you walk up, it is good exercise.

RB 666. *The Zurich Marathon*

I started running our recent marathon in Zurich before the other runners. Then I stopped during the race for fifteen minutes so that I could watch everyone run and see the styles of the disciples. Haridas had such a funny style! Even though I stopped, I finished before the first man.

It was difficult to run in the early morning hours. It was totally dark while I was passing through the woods. Three times I fell and both my knees went down to the ground. After the third time I said, "I am not going to fall again," and I was especially cautious.

Projjwal and Benny were going before me. Each one had a flashlight. Occasionally Kailash was able to come with the car and shine the headlights on the course.

Several times I was dying for something to drink, but Kailash could not come because the car could not drive on the course. Two or three times Shikha came running 600 metres into the woods to help me.

RB 667. *Running too fast*

Last night I was running slowly near my 700-metre mark. There were five or six boys around 17 or 18 years old watching me. They shouted, "Shrai, Shrai, you are running too fast!"

On the other side of the street I saw Saurjya. Saurjya was running much faster than I was, but those teenage boys didn't say anything to him.

RB 668. *The friendly dog*

This morning I ran three and a half miles and then I walked one mile. I started out down 150th Street and turned onto the Grand Central Parkway service road towards Parsons Boulevard. Right from there, a dog started running with me. He would run alongside me for a while, and then he would be inspired to go ahead 200 metres. Then again he would come back and run 30 or 40 metres with me.

The dog had a collar and he was very nice. He would come near me to smell my trousers, but he wouldn't bark. I didn't see any ferocious qualities in him, but a dog is a dog. God only knew what would happen next. When I was running down Parsons Boulevard to Union Turnpike, I saw a car going slowly and making a turn. At about my 1100-metre mark I stopped and stood looking at the car. The driver seemed to be very nice, so I said to him, "This dog is bothering me. Can you help me?"

He said, "Oh yes, I have been seeing that he has been following you. But what can I do?"

I said, "Can you please give me a ride for two blocks so that the dog won't see me?"

He said, "Oh no, I will be stopping in half a block!"

Then the dog went 40 or 50 metres ahead, hoping I would follow. I ran back very fast in the other direction and turned again onto the Grand Central service road. For about 300 or 400 metres I ran on the service road. Then I made a left turn and ran to Union Turnpike again. The dog was not to be seen. I had fooled the dog.

At about my two-mile mark on Union Turnpike, I was on the sidewalk when a car started honking. I said to myself, "What is this? I am doing nothing wrong. Perhaps someone wants to ask me for directions."

When I turned around, what did I see? The same car and the same man to whom I had spoken earlier. He said to me, "Mister, I feel very sorry that I didn't give you a ride when you asked me. Please come with me."

I said, "I thank you for your offer, but no thank you."

He was a nice-looking man. His conscience was hurting him, so he wanted to compensate. After that I walked half a mile and then turned around and started running back.

So these kinds of experiences I get no matter what hour of the day I go running. Always there will be some obstruction. Most of the time my road crew follows me in the car; but when I go alone, I always have wonderful experiences!

RB 669. *Running or meditation?*

When I was coming back, I saw Karabi the Great running. What did I do? I immediately looked at my wristwatch to see what time it was. I wanted to see if Karabi could have run that far if she had started after her six o'clock morning meditation. I wanted to catch her to see if she had missed meditation to go running.

RB 670. *A cold race*

During the three-mile race in Canada this morning, the Canadians were very brave to come and run in such cold weather. I was all bundled up, with long trousers and four layers on top. It was so cold!

RB 671. *Pavaka's Quarter Mile*

This time when I ran the Jersey Shore Marathon, every quarter mile Pavaka would come running to indicate the mark. After about five and a quarter miles, God knows if the place he indicated was actually the right distance. But at the third quarter of that mile he was at least 40 metres behind the 1200-metre mark. Then, when I was about to complete the mile, he came and stood right on the line.

RB 672. *The wrong turn*

This morning in Tokyo I ran for an hour and a half. On the way out I made four turns. I tried to remember two or three landmarks at each turn — the light, the telephone pole and so forth. Then, out of three things if I forgot one, no harm. In that way I wouldn't get lost.

Coming back, at one point I made a wrong turn. Instead of getting lost, I discovered that that way brought me back to the hotel sooner. If I had followed my planned route, I would have made the turn two or three minutes later.

Even at five o'clock in the morning there were so many people running! People in Japan love to run.

RB 673. *The steps up the mountain*

This morning in Okinawa I went out running while it was still dark. At one point I saw a series of steps going up a mountain, and I decided to climb them. After I had walked up hundreds of steps, I found a shrine at the top of the mountain. It was not a good place to go in the dark. Even the trees seemed to talk to you, telling you not to visit their mountain. But it was a very nice shrine.

RB 674. *The morning run*

Today I saw at least ten disciples running early in the morning. First I barked at Shephali and Pranika. I was asking them why they were out at that hour, but they didn't understand what I was asking them.

I also saw more than five Japanese disciples running together.

RB 675. *Seeing the disciples*

In my morning run today I averaged under a nine-minute pace. Of course, when I walked the pace was slower, but I ran more than I walked. I would run 200 or 300 metres and then walk 40 or 50 metres.

I saw at least 20 disciples while I was running. I saw some girls — Nayana, Sunanda, Begabati and Khudita — running past the four-and-a-half-mile mark, and I did not see them come back. They must have run at least ten miles, and they were going quite fast — definitely under an eight-minute pace. Runners like Sunanda and Snigdha never run at an eight-minute pace — always under! An eight-minute pace is only for us mortals.

I saw Savita and Chetana and said, "All right, you can run 40 or so metres behind me."

RB 676. *A boon from the soul of Japan*

Most people I saw running in Japan were very short, and their strides were also very short. They were very slow.

After I came back, the soul of Japan came to me and said she was so grateful that I had come to Japan. She said for that she would grant me a boon: "In this incarnation you will be able to run a marathon in under three hours."

I laughed.

RB 677. *The homeopathic remedy*

Last night during my 20-mile training run, I tried some homeopathic medicine. As soon as I take that medicine, my mind gets clear. Then, in my nose, eyes, ears and down to my neck, I feel a flowing sensation. But below the neck — to my legs, chest, heart, stomach, thighs, knees — the medicine does not reach. Each time I take it, almost instantly I feel that my head has become light. But unfortunately my head is not carrying my whole body. My chest, legs, heart — absolutely nothing below my neck works better when I take that medicine. For me, nothing works.

Perhaps if I had taken this homeopathic remedy at around ten miles, it would have helped me. When I took it at 16 miles, it was too late. It is a cream. At that point a cream will not take away my fatigue quickly.

RB 678. *A brave man*

It was so cold this morning while I was running that I saw almost nobody outside. Only two men greeted me. One said, "Good morning." The other said, "Hi!"

I was dying from the cold. Databir told me to take thick gloves, but I took thin ones. Then I had to put my hands in front of my chest to keep my fingers warm. I haven't run for a few days because I have been afraid of the cold. That means that today I was a brave man.

RB 679. *Late registration*

Long live Databir! Registration for the Orange Bowl Marathon was closed on the fifth of January, but Databir talked with the officials over the phone. They said that I could have a number but that they would not give me a T-shirt. In the end they gave me a T-shirt also.

RB 680. *Gloria*

Before I left for the marathon, I was waiting with the bags at LaGuardia Airport while Alo was getting the boarding passes. A lady with a dog like Sona came and stood near me. She said to me, "Do you want to have one?"

I said, "No, I have two. Just half an hour ago I was with them. I was thinking of them."

She said, "You are looking so affectionately at my Gloria."

The dog's name was Gloria — like Malati's name, Gloria.

RB 681. *Meeting with Bill Rodgers*

The registration place was the Holiday Inn in Miami. Savyasachi told me that Bill Rodgers was in the hall, so I got out of the car, thinking, "Let me say hello to him." He was just going out to run and was holding some running shoes.

I said, "Hello. Tomorrow you will be running?" He said, "Yes." I said, "I wish you the best of luck. Someday I wish you to go under two hours. Tomorrow I want you to be first and to go back to your highest glory."

He looked at me and said, "How I wish I could! "

I said, "Tomorrow you will try to do it. Do you recognise me?"

He said, "Yes." He was looking into my eyes very intensely and soulfully. He said, "Sri Chinmoy."

Again I smiled at him and he smiled at me. He thanked me and I thanked him.

RB 682. *An unexpected meeting*

After speaking with Bill Rodgers, I took two steps and who was waiting for me? Fred Lebow. I hadn't seen him, but he had seen me speaking to Bill Rodgers. He immediately grabbed my hand and introduced me to the race director. While he was introducing me, he was looking at me so lovingly and intensely. He told the race director, "This is Sri Chinmoy. He conducts races, especially marathons, and all his races are excellent. Whenever we need help, Sri Chinmoy's team always helps us."

The race director said, "Yes, I have heard about him."

Then Fred Lebow told me, "You must come to our club on the fifth of March. We are having a special banquet for excellent runners."

I said to Fred Lebow, "You have to finish tomorrow's marathon in under 3:30."

He said, "My best time is 3:40."

I said, "Isn't your best 3:30?"

He said, "No. Where did you get 3:30? My best is 3:40."

While he was talking to me, he was looking at me with such affection and loving concern. That kind of talk we were having!

RB 683. *A second encounter*

After speaking to Fred, I went into the rest room and then I went into the stationery store in the hotel to buy The New York Times. Who came up to me? Fred Lebow again!

He said, "I was looking for you. Here, I am giving you this T-shirt." On the T-shirt was written, "Training for the New York Marathon 1983."

He said, "I want you to have it."

I thanked him. Then I asked, "This time, are you going to Russia to run a marathon?"

He said, "No, not to Russia, but I am going to China next month." In another two weeks he was going to Shanghai to run. He also told me that two weeks earlier he ran a marathon in New Orleans.

I asked him, "Will you run one of our races? Have you ever run in Germany?"

He said, "No."

I said, "We have a few marathons in Germany. I would be so happy and honoured if you could run in one. I also will go once this year."

He said, "If you are going to run, then you let me know and I will come to join you."

He gave me the New York Road Runners Club schedule for the whole year. Then both of us said that we would see each other the next day at the race.

RB 684. *An expensive city*

When I went to pay for The New York Times, the funniest thing happened. Somebody had put a New Yorker magazine on top of my New York Times. So for the New York Times the cashier asked me for two dollars. I said, "Oh, in Miami it is so expensive!"

As I was leaving the cashier asked me, "Why are you not taking the New Yorker?"

I said, "I didn't buy it."

Then I saw Fred Lebow coming right behind me with a chocolate bar. He was trying to get his money out of his running shorts. I said, "I am paying for him." It was $1.58 or something. Everything is so expensive in those Holiday Inns. It is better not to buy anything there.

Fred Lebow grabbed my arm and thanked me. Then he said, "Oh, I forgot to tell you. You have to come tonight. I have got a videotape of the New York Marathon that I am showing here."

I said, "Three days ago I saw it in my house. First there were short, short races. Later you were waving your arms in circles. You were so happy and delighted when Salazar and the other big runners were finishing."

He asked me, "Where did you get it?" I said, "One of my students got it." He said, "Very few are released, and I have come here to show it." Then we departed.

RB 685. *The start*

The next morning before the race they were making announcements. Mr. Marathon was Bill Rodgers. Then they were saying that some great runners had come from Scotland and Ireland. They also said they were happy to have Fred Lebow running. I was happy that Fred Lebow's name was mentioned. While this was going on, five or six helpers were making such noise!

Three thousand people were running. This is the sixth year they have had this marathon. Five minutes before the race began, the wheelchair racers started. One fellow didn't have legs even. He was lying on his stomach, moving the wheels with his hands.

RB 686. *Running with Fred Lebow*

After two miles I felt as if I had run a whole marathon. The humidity was so bad, and also it was drizzling. I didn't mind the rain, but the humidity was so bad that after two miles I wanted to give up. With greatest difficulty I continued.

After four miles I started running and walking. After nine and a half miles, I was absolutely walking for four or five hundred metres at a time. Then whom did I see? Fred Lebow! He came from behind me. When I saw him, I said, "Oh, you were behind me?"

He started running with me. He asked me how many marathons I had run. I said, "This is my twentieth."

He said, "I am fifty years old and this is my fiftieth marathon."

I said, "I am congratulating you! For each year of your life you have run one marathon."

Then he said, "Look behind me. The man there has run a hundred and one marathons."

I was running with Fred Lebow for some time. I often complain about my stride. His stride is also short, but very quick. He was complaining about the humidity. Finally, he went ahead of me.

RB 687. *The crazy lady*

There were four or five middle-aged men and women running together. One of the middle-aged ladies, a crazy lady, came from behind me and pushed my elbow. She said, "Sweetheart, don't walk. You can make it. Run!" Then she and her friends went away.

I continued walking and jogging. When I ran, I ran fast, so at some point I must have passed that lady, although at the time I didn't know it. After eleven and a half miles, again she saw me walking. She came and stood in front of me. She was very mad at me and said, "Don't do that! I told you to run!" Her friends were all laughing at her while she was barking at me.

After thirteen and a half miles, I saw the same lady coming in my direction from the other side of the road. She had already made the turn at fourteen or fifteen miles, and she was coming back in the other direction. When she saw me she said, "Honey, I am so glad you are running. Keep running!" Again her friends were laughing, but I could see that she herself was also tired. Although she was telling me to run, she was absolutely dead. When I looked at her face, she looked like she would collapse. God knows how many miles she kept running.

RB 688. *Fred Lebow's encouragement*

After I saw the crazy lady for the last time, I went about four hundred metres farther, and whom did I see? Fred Lebow. He was practically a mile and a half ahead of me. He said, "Oh, Sri!" His face was so tired. I was not tired because I was walking.

After sixteen miles Saraswati saw him walking, but when I saw him, he was still running.

The humidity was unbearable, but Fred Lebow was encouraging me.

RB 689. *The perfect gentleman*

When I was at nine and a half miles, it started raining so heavily! Everybody was miserable. After I had made the turn and was coming back — at around sixteen miles — I saw a middle-aged man coming from the other direction. He had only run thirteen and a half miles and had not yet made the turn.

He was a perfect gentleman, cleanly shaven and nice looking. He said to me, "You are a gentleman and I am a gentleman. So you don't mind." Then he turned around and joined me. He had only run thirteen and a half miles, but now he was running with me at sixteen miles. I said, "Wonderful!"

At first he was running with me, but after fifty metres he started walking.

RB 690. *The five grandmothers*

One fellow who was running near me had five grandmothers. At one point he went off the course and kissed an old lady who was giving out water and oranges. He said to her, "I am okay, Grandmother." The "grandmother" was so happy. Like that, five times during the race he went out and kissed a grandmother. Then the grandmother would be so happy.

RB 691. *Learning from the elite*

One runner who was doing his first marathon had been told never to stop while drinking water. This is what he learned from the elite runners. When he took a cup of ERG, half went into his eyes and half into his mouth and ears. Then he was apologising to the people who were around him. It came out in an article afterwards.

RB 692. *My friend Mark*

Every mile Savyasachi would come to give me something to drink. He would come either at the end of the mile or somewhere in the middle of it — wherever he could bring the car.

Many people were running on the sidewalk, so that the trees would protect them from the heavy rain. But I didn't like the leaves on the sidewalk and also I was afraid I would step in a puddle. At least on the street I could see where I was running.

At seventeen miles I found a friend. A young man, about thirty years old, was driving by in a car. He said to me, "I want to drive with you."

I said, "Fine!"

Whenever I would walk, he would stop the car and wait for me. He was following me and encouraging me, saying, "Yes, you can make it."

After driving with me for one mile, the man said to me, "My name is Mark. What is your name?"

I said, "Chinmoy."

Mark said, "Come into the car. I will take you secretly a few miles ahead and nobody will know."

I said, "I can't do that."

He said, "You are a nice gentleman. Good luck."

RB 693. *Old ladies*

When old ladies go ahead of you, you say, "O Lord, You have destroyed my pride. What else will You do?"

Then later, when a sixty-year-old lady starts passing you, you say, "O Lord, You have left some competitive spirit in me still."

I was trying to keep up with a sixty-year-old lady who was passing me, but her strides were so short that I couldn't run with her. Finally, after five hundred metres, I stopped, and she went away with her shorter than the shortest strides.

RB 694. *People at the end*

From eleven to thirteen miles, I practically walked the whole way because I saw that walking was far better than running. At twenty miles I said, "I am not going on. I am not running one more mile!"

Then Saraswati came, and for the last six miles she walked in front of me. While I was walking, I saw that people who were running were going slower than I was. I was walking, but I was passing people who were running! Some of them looked like real athletes — very strong. Some were getting cramps, and some were lying under the trees, giving up.

After nine miles, at least four or five hundred people went ahead of me. But after twenty-two or twenty-three miles, I was doing the passing. I passed at least twenty people that way. I knew that I was not going to get a cramp if I ran, but my speed was so bad that it was faster to walk.

RB 695. *Reaching the stadium*

The last three hundred metres of the marathon were in the stadium. You did not even have to run around the whole track — just three hundred metres. I said, "For God's sake, let me run."

But when I tried to take one step running, there was no power inside my lungs. I had no strength. Walking was far better.

RB 696. *"Super" finisher*

When I finished the marathon, the person who took off my number said to me, "Super!" He was saying that because we were so brave to finish.

Afterwards, we drove three miles back along the course to see the people who were still running. We saw at least twenty people still running! I had walked quite a lot, so what kind of speed could they have had?

At the end some people collapsed from the heat. Bill Rodgers saw one person at the finish and said, "Major dehydration!"

RB 697. *Marathon difficulties*

There was such humidity, plus pouring rain, during the marathon. Bill Rodgers had wanted to give up twice. He said that he never suffered so much because of the humidity. If anybody had come near him around twenty-three miles, he would have given up. It was all in the newspaper. He ran a 2:15 marathon.

Alo ran seven and a half miles. She was so happy that there were people behind her. Then, after seven and a half miles, she stopped. God knows how many other people also stopped and didn't finish the marathon.

There were big puddles, and in some places there were cars on the course. The mile markers were only very small numbers on the ground. So many times I did not see them. I had to ask Savyasachi how many miles I had covered. Sometimes there would be a small marker on a pole. They gave water at intervals of about three miles. It was mostly water, with some Gatorade.

My time was 5:33:33. It is not that my capacity is decreasing. I am doing cycling on my machine and practising running like anything. Just recently in Japan, and also in Switzerland and New Jersey, I finished around 4:30. Even in Puerto Rico my time was under five hours. So it is not that my capacity is decreasing. It was just circumstances.

RB 698. *Suffering*

In some ways the Orange Bowl Marathon was worse than the Greek marathon. In Greece I didn't suffer until after seven or eight miles. Here I began suffering after two miles. Then for six or seven miles it was drizzling, and for six or seven miles it was raining heavily. The newspaper said it was raining cats and dogs. Sometimes you could not even see anything in front of you because of the rain. The first two miles I wore a hat. Then it was so hot that I took it off and gave it to Savyasachi. "I will manage without it," I said. Then when it started raining so heavily, I didn't have the heart to put it back on.

Once while I was walking, an old man who was helping at one of the water stations put a sponge on my head and then brought it down along my spinal column. Such relief! He didn't say a word. He just moved the sponge from my head down my spine. He knew how much we were suffering. Everybody looked so pitiful.

RB 699. *The future of the marathon*

Often people say they will never run a marathon again. During or after the race they say that this is their last marathon. Then after four days they start thinking about their next marathon.

In ten or twenty years, people will regard the marathon the way we regard a ten-mile race today. People will consider forty miles or seventy miles or a hundred miles as long distance. Long distances will be as popular as the marathon is today. People will pay more attention to fifty-milers and hundred-milers.

Now people are doing so well in the marathon. In four or five years the best runners will run the marathon in under two hours. In twenty or thirty years people will run at a five-minute pace for fifty or a hundred miles. The children of people who are running the marathon now will run at the present marathon pace for thirty or forty miles, and then even farther. They will have such stamina. Sports are like that. Roger Bannister's four-minute-mile record lasted for years. Then the hundred-metre record stayed for years. Jesse Owens' long-jump record stayed for twenty years before it was broken by Bob Beamon. But ultimately all records are broken.

RB 700. *Two jokers*

The morning after the marathon, I ran seven miles. That shows what kind of marathon I ran! I hardly had to walk forty metres. There was no humidity, and I didn't even have to drink. During the marathon sometimes I drank every eight hundred metres!

After five and a half miles I started walking. At that time a man ran by me and said to me, "No walking, no walking!"

Then I started running again, and after half a mile, I saw the same gentleman, walking. I said to him, "It is not good to walk."

He said to me, "But while I was running, I was running faster than you are running!"

So we were two jokers.

RB 701. *Visit from a soul*

While I was in Florida for the marathon, I went into a bookstore with Savyasachi. When I opened up a sports book, what did I see? The face of the little girl who lives next door to me in New York. Her soul appeared right in front of the page, looking at me. I said, "What is she doing here?"

Then when I came back to New York, as we were driving up to my house, she came out of her house and stood looking at me, not saying anything.

In Florida her soul came for my blessings, although outwardly I never talk to her.

RB 702. *Let it be known!*

Today, Databir ran with me for three miles. He had no trouble keeping up with me while we were running. But the fourth mile we race-walked, and let it be known that then he had trouble.

RB 703. *The police search*

This morning I was running on Hillside Avenue at about ten o'clock. Just before I reached Parsons Boulevard, I saw several policemen with guns and walkie-talkies. Somebody had told them that a man on the street had a gun. For one man who was reported seen near that place, how many policemen were there!

As soon as I ran by, a black man who was smoking said to me, "Shrai, Shrai, you are here? You invited me to come to a concert of yours, but I could not come. Can I have an interview with you?" He even wanted to shake hands with me. Four or five Puerto Rican children nearby started saying, "Sri, Sri." Then one of the policemen looked at me and gave me a big smile.

RB 704. *Singing my songs*

During my solo marathon in Flushing Meadow Park, each hundred metres I would hear a different one of my songs.

At one point Robin was singing, *I am a member of the New York Road Runners Club.* Fred Lebow's name was there in the song.

Sometimes the Canadians were singing my songs in French. At one point they were singing *O Good Canada's Oneness-Heart*. Then my America songs I heard. One group was singing songs from *Transcendence-Perfection*. One group only sang *Phule phule*. It went on and on. Their repertoire was very limited.

Some groups had songbooks and were singing the old songs that we never sing nowadays. O God, some songs I knew were mine, but they were so unfamiliar to me. Some of them were songs I had composed eight or ten years ago for the first group of non-singers, *Eternity's Patience-Pride*. I wrote those songs for the absolute beginners. The people singing them as I ran had not even been my disciples at that time. They were singing songs like *Milbena bhai milbena*. When I heard that song, I couldn't believe that someone was singing it after so many years.

RB 705. *The running Master*

People who don't run marathons feel sad that they don't run them, and people who run marathons feel sad that they do run them. So many problems human beings have! Why do they have to create additional problems by entering into the world of marathoning? By running a marathon has anybody realised God? I don't think any spiritual Master other than me has ever run a marathon. Perhaps they were wise people. Perhaps it is because I am not wise that I run marathons.

RB 706. *Mutual appreciation*

Carla is going to run tomorrow's Inspiration Marathon. Several years ago she finished last in the New York Marathon, but now she has improved her time by over two hours. With utmost sincerity we appreciate her present speed. She should also try to appreciate the patience we had in the past while we waited for her to finish.

RB 707. *Praying for speed*

Many, many years ago, before my disciples were even born, I gave up praying and started meditating. Once you enter meditation, you don't get joy from praying any more. But now I shall have to start praying again. I have to pray to God for speed and stamina and also not to get cramps in tomorrow's marathon.

RB 708. *A tremendous success*

I was very happy with this year's Inspiration Marathon. I am very grateful to Bipin and Pulin, to all those who helped them and also to those who ran. To me it was a tremendous success, plus improvement. Improvement is what we need. I am very proud of my disciples' excellent performance!

RB 709. *Do you want to get run over?*

One morning when I was running in Fort Lauderdale, Savyasachi was following me. Since he was following right behind me in the car, I was running practically in the middle of the street. I wanted to run seven miles.

After four and a half miles, a young man saw me. He looked as if he hadn't gone to sleep the night before, and he had a bottle in his hand. He said, "Hey! Do you want to get run over? Why are you running in the middle of the street?" He didn't know it was Savyasachi's car following me.

RB 710. *Olympic runner*

While I was running my solo marathon in Long Island this morning, so many times I had to run over bridges. Each bridge meant a very bad hill.

At one point Niriha and Chetana told a man that they were videotaping a famous marathoner. The man asked if I was in the Olympics. Indeed, I can go to the Olympics. I can be a spectator.

RB 711. *The disciples' aspiration*

During my marathon in Long Island the Canadian boys were inspired to sing *O Good Canada's Oneness-Heart* so many times! Chandika's group was the best. Then came the Canadian boys and then Viresh's group and Hladini's group.

I may be the world's most absolutely useless runner, but God is so kind to me. He has given me the world's most encouraging disciples. They have such enthusiasm, inspiration and aspiration! It was all their aspiration that was carrying me from the first to the last mile.

My road crew plus the singers and others who helped me in various capacities in today's marathon did me a very signal service. They were not my helpers; they were my saviours. I don't have enough gratitude to offer them, but my Beloved Supreme will definitely, definitely give them something very special in the inner world.

How hard it is to remain outside for five and a half hours cheerfully, soulfully, unreservedly and even unconditionally — helping me in my own way!

As I said before, my Beloved Supreme, my Inner Pilot, will definitely give them something very special in the inner world. My marathon assistants kept me alive.

RB 658. *(p. 321)* 31 October 1982
RB 659. *(p. 322)* 31 October 1982
RB 660. *(p. 322)* 4 November 1982
RB 661. *(p. 322)* 4 November 1982
RB 662. *(p. 323)* 4 November 1982
RB 663. *(p. 323)* 13 November 1982
RB 664. *(p. 323)* 13 November 1982
RB 665. *(p. 324)* 13 November 1982
RB 666. *(p. 324)* 13 November 1982
RB 667. *(p. 325)* 23 November 1982
RB 668. *(p. 325)* 2 December 1982
RB 669. *(p. 326)* 2 December 1982
RB 670. *(p. 327)* 12 December 1982
RB 671. *(p. 327)* 14 December 1982
RB 672. *(p. 327)* 21 December 1982
RB 673. *(p. 328)* 3 January 1983
RB 674. *(p. 328)* 4 January 1983
RB 675. *(p. 328)* 7 January 1983
RB 676. *(p. 329)* 8 January 1983
RB 677. *(p. 329)* 9 January 1983
RB 678. *(p. 329)* 18 January 1983
RB 679. *(p. 330)* 24 January 1983
RB 680. *(p. 330)* 24 January 1983
RB 681. *(p. 330)* 24 January 1983
RB 682. *(p. 331)* 24 January 1983
RB 683. *(p. 332)* 24 January 1983
RB 684. *(p. 333)* 24 January 1983
RB 685. *(p. 333)* 24 January 1983
RB 686. *(p. 334)* 24 January 1983
RB 687. *(p. 335)* 24 January 1983

RB 688. *(p.335)* 24 January 1983
RB 689. *(p.336)* 24 January 1983
RB 690. *(p.336)* 24 January 1983
RB 691. *(p.336)* 24 January 1983
RB 692. *(p.337)* 24 January 1983
RB 693. *(p.337)* 24 January 1983
RB 694. *(p.338)* 24 January 1983
RB 695. *(p.338)* 24 January 1983
RB 696. *(p.339)* 24 January 1983
RB 697. *(p.339)* 24 January 1983
RB 698. *(p.340)* 24 January 1983
RB 699. *(p.340)* 24 January 1983
RB 700. *(p.341)* 24 January 1983
RB 701. *(p.341)* 24 January 1983
RB 702. *(p.342)* 27 January 1983
RB 703. *(p.342)* 31 January 1983
RB 704. *(p.342)* 31 January 1983
RB 705. *(p.343)* 31 January 1983
RB 706. *(p.343)* 5 February 1983
RB 707. *(p.344)* 5 February 1983
RB 708. *(p.344)* 6 February 1983
RB 709. *(p.344)* 12 February 1983
RB 709. *(p.345)* 20 February 1983
RB 710. *(p.345)* 20 February 1983

RUN AND BECOME, BECOME AND RUN

PART 14

I know my disciples will forgive me, but God won't forgive me for exploiting their devoted oneness by asking them to come at such an ungodly hour — midnight — to help me in my training run in Flushing Meadow Park last January.

The day before, of all days, I decided I would run seven miles during the day, although I knew that I would try to run a training marathon at night. Who asked me to run five or six miles? I did one mile of hill work up 150th Street in the morning. Then I ran two miles. Later I did one mile of speed work and one mile at an eight-minute pace. Then how I suffered during my long training run!

Was it my mental hallucination that it was so cold? Usually I go out at five in the morning, but it is not as cold as it was that night. At times I felt as if a bullet were passing through my chest. Then I stepped in a puddle and my left foot started burning. Inwardly I was screaming because my sock and shoe were burning with the absolutely icy cold! I always wear long underwear under my trousers, but that night I wore only a nylon running suit. Right from the beginning, the muscles in my legs were so cold. I wasn't wearing enough on my hands either, although I had on two pairs of gloves.

I said, "If I finish 20 miles, then I will be satisfied." I had already given up the idea of doing a whole marathon.

I am so grateful to each of the disciples who was there. All those who ran with me and those who sang throughout the night, standing at different places, were so compassionate. Hundreds of songs they sang. Each one deserves my very special gratitude. When they make such sacrifices for me, I hope they feel my heart's undying gratitude. If I have gratitude in any form, is it not for these disciples? Luckily I have them as my disciples. Had I been their disciple, I would have stayed in bed. I am speaking very sincerely. I would have said, "I am sick. I have got this to do, I have got that to do." Next time, if I do a midnight training run again, perhaps all of my disciples will say they have fallen sick. That is why they could not come.

RB 713. *Attack by dogs*

Early in the morning, around 5:30, I went out to run four miles. As I was running back, I was in my highest meditation. Right near my house, two huge, ferocious dogs — no exaggeration — came chasing after me from the other side of the street. They were barking and jumping up at me. One was right in front of me and one was on the side. One jumped right up to my chest and one was at my elbow. They were almost touching my chest and elbow — it was a matter not of a foot but of inches. I couldn't jog, I couldn't walk. I had to use my occult power — I still have some left — so they wouldn't bite me.

For four miles I had been meditating, so was it my karma? You might say that perhaps the previous day I had done a bad meditation, but I knew for the past half hour what I had done. The mind was not thinking at all; it had not yet started with Centre problems. I was doing only prayer and meditation, but the hostile forces are all around. Luckily, my prayer-power saves me always. I was praying to the Supreme, "Save me, save me!" and the Supreme did save me.

Then I went onto my porch and was sitting on the couch watching the dogs. For three or four minutes I was on my porch looking at them and they were looking at me. One was brown and one was black and white. The brown one stood right in front of my house.

I called Ashrita, and he came with Thomas, Bipin and Pulin. I told them, "Please try to solve this dog problem!" Ashrita put a hole in his pants and blood on his arm and pretended he had been bitten. Then they went to complain to the lady who allows the dogs to stay behind her house. They also went to the police.

Four months ago I had the same experience. It is not like silly barking. These dogs are really attacking! This has been happening again and again with the same two dogs. They always come chasing after me from behind this lady's house. The lady says they are not hers, but she and her husband won't let anyone take the dogs away.

A few months ago I was going down the street and five or six dogs came. What are you going to do? I wanted to enter into the house of the old lady who is my friend. I stood in front of her house, hiding behind a tree. I said, "O God, this is the time for me to knock on her door — at 4:30 in the morning!" I was about to knock on her door, but then the dogs went away.

This time I didn't get a chance even to stop. If you see them five or ten metres ahead, you can pretend you are walking and maybe they won't attack. But this time I didn't have a chance to stop, because the dogs came from behind. The best thing is to have something in your hand. One time I looked for something and found a ball, so I pretended it was a rock.

RB 714. *Welcoming committee*

Around five o'clock when I go out to run immediately one of my dogs, Kanu, starts crying. Then, when I come sneaking back like a thief, Kanu is up waiting for me on the porch. Even if I turn off the light, the dogs know it is me.

RB 715. *Puddles*

This morning I went out running in shorts. It was so bad outside — raining cats and dogs! On the sidewalk there were so
many puddles! But when I descended to the street I came across
even more puddles. Then I would go back up onto the sidewalk
again. Everywhere there were puddles. The rain was falling like
arrows, but I still ran two miles.

RB 716. *Looking at my picture*

During our 12-hour walk, some of the walkers were looking
at my picture. I thought they were reading. At 3:30 in the
morning, when I saw Agraha go by holding something in his
hand, I thought he was learning songs. I knew he was not a
singer, so I wondered why he was learning songs. No, he was
looking at my picture for inspiration.

For some people to do something on the physical plane is
such a difficult task! I am the pioneer. I walked 19 miles today.
I am extremely proud of myself. The first time I stopped after
eight laps. The next time I did five laps, and then I did six. So
it came to 19. If I could have continued from the beginning to
the end, I could have done 30 miles.

RB 717. *You have to drink!*

In the Boston Marathon I ran for a while and then walked slower
than the slowest. An old man grabbed me by the shoulder and
said, "Your heart is working very hard. You have to drink!"
I said, "No, thank you."
But he said, "You have to!" and he forced me to drink.
Because I was tired, he sympathised with me.

RB 718. *Can I shake hands with you?*

While I was practising before the start of the Long Island Marathon, someone came up to me and asked, "Are you Master Sri Chinmoy?"

I said, "Yes."

He said, "Can I shake hands with you?"

So I shook hands with him. He was saying to his wife, "He is such a kind man."

At the start of the marathon, one lady ran with me for three or four miles. She was wearing all yellow. Then she asked Lucy if I was Sri Chinmoy.

RB 719. *Nature is so cruel!*

Nature is so cruel to us! To run 26 miles is not enough. It also has to be so windy and cold! Is it a joke? We say nature is kind. We are all the time trying to be as natural as possible and become one with nature's beauty. But nature has been so hostile to us — both in the Jersey Shore and the Long Island Marathons.

RB 720. *Under three hours*

At least three times Janani has been kind enough to remind me of the promise that the soul of Japan made to me — that I would do the marathon in under three hours. I said to her, "All right, I will ask your husband to do it on my behalf, since he and I are one."

RB 721. *Oneness with the soul*

Last night I ran four miles and walked two miles. Then we drove six miles in the car.

Databir's calculations were going wrong because his mind was not functioning. Indian kindergarten students could have done better arithmetic. Mentally I knew he was wrong. I was writing the figures on a paper plate and calculating mentally. His calculations were three or four seconds off.

Just as I finished writing my calculations, I saw Anugata's soul inside the car. I smiled at the soul and blessed it. Then, not a minute later, Databir told me that he had written down a message from Anugata on the other side of the plate.

Anugata had called the previous night from California to say he had found a place on Long Island that has a belt to support my back. The place has 24-hour service, so Databir and Pulin had phoned up the place. It was 2:30 in the morning. Today they will go to get the belt.

Last night Anugata's soul had also come to me for special blessings and love. Perhaps the soul had come to me right after he had finished talking with them. And this morning, when they were about to tell me that he had called, his soul came a second time. So this is our oneness with the soul.

RB 722. *The screaming man*

I was walking and running around 6:15 this morning. Some people who had crossed to the other side of the street came back when they saw me to say, "Good morning!"

Then I saw a black man on a bicycle. He was so excited to see me that he started screaming, "Sri Chinmoy, Sri Chinmoy!"

How do these people know me? I was wearing a hat that practically covered my head, and it was early in the morning.

Databir was following me in his car, and he was wondering why the man was screaming.

RB 723. *The dispute*

Yesterday, when we were running four miles at a little over a 7:30 pace, Databir had no trouble running with me. But when we started race-walking, he fell behind me. Ashrita said he was 400 metres behind, but Databir said it was only 200 metres!

RB 724. *Some unique running styles*

This year, after the Long Island Marathon, I couldn't believe the way Pulak surrendered to one of the helpers at the finish line. It was absolutely unconditional surrender! After finishing he was so helpless.

Pulak's running style is unique! Then comes Saurjya's style — he wants to touch the ceiling with his head while running.

The other day I saw Sudhir running early in the morning. His hands were stretched straight out.

Once, while race-walking, Baoul looked as if he was doing archery with his arms.

RB 725. *The clock*

One night I was in my room reading my walking book. At about 1:45 a.m. I called the San Francisco Centre. Susan and 10 or 12 people were there. Then I saw the time — 2:05. So I rested. Then I heard the clock say, "It is three a.m." so powerfully. Every hour this clock announces the time. I said, "I am not going running yet. I want to hear it say another hour."

Again at 4:00 it was so faithful. It said, "It is four a.m." But I was just sitting there, praying and praying for God-realisation. Then it became 5:00. I started getting ready, doing a few stretching exercises. At exactly 5:30 I phoned up Databir. In ten minutes he found me with his car. He always catches up with me on Union Turnpike.

RB 726. *Watching our races*

Running is a serious part of our manifestation. I wish to say that the races we hold or participate in have a very special place in our manifestation. And this manifestation is nothing short of our aspiration. So even those who do not or cannot run in the races should have a considerable interest in our efforts, which are our self-giving to the Supreme. This is especially true of the races in which the disciples and I run; they are absolutely necessary in our life of dedication.

RB 727. *So happy to get prizes*

In our ten-mile race today two ladies over fifty were so happy and excited to get prizes! They never expected in this lifetime to win anything. They never imagined that they would come in first and second in their age category and they were so thrilled. They were in tears because they had won. One of the ladies was very spiritual.

RB 728. *Bits and pieces*

In our ten-mile race today Kalatit surrendered to Pahar. But last Sunday, in the Long Island Marathon, it was a different story.

After running five miles, Prakash was telling us that he was not the body, he was not the body.

RB 729. *My running was all walking*

I had wanted to run ten miles before our ten-mile race began. But my problem was knee pain. After 20 metres I started walking. So my running was all walking.

RB 730. *Running mantra*

Every day, as soon as I start running, I have the same mantra: "Today let me go slowly."

But "today" becomes "every day," and then relaxation starts. Never does the mantra come: "Today let me go fast!"

RB 731. *A sense of satisfaction*

With tennis, I get such joy while playing, but then afterwards, nothing. But with running or walking, no matter how badly I do, afterwards I get such satisfaction. I am relaxed and I get such a sense of accomplishment.

RB 732. *Losing weight*

Whenever I want to lose weight, I start walking. Walking is my salvation. When I run, I don't lose as much weight. In seven or eight days I have lost thirteen and a half pounds from walking. My body doesn't register it, but my scale does.

RB 733. *False alarm*

I was walking in front of my house. Two dogs were barking like anything. One of them — a big dog — came running towards me. They came up ten or fifteen metres and then went away.

RB 734. *Mistaken identity*

This morning when I was in front of my house walking, a funny thing happened with the neighbour who is on our right side. He is a young man whom I do not know very well. It is not like the neighbour across the street, whom I know so well.

I thought my right-side neighbour was in his car, so I said, "Good morning, good morning!" Then he said to me, "Good morning!"

Five minutes later the actual neighbour came out of his house and said "Good morning!" to me. Then he entered into the same car. So I said, "Good morning." The first one was my neighbour's brother perhaps, but I thought it was him.

His older daughter always looks at me with such respect. When little children are cycling on the street, bothering me like anything, she is always very nice to me.

RB 735. *Everything is contradictory!*

Everything is contradictory! In the morning I decide to be a sprinter. Then in the afternoon I decide to be a marathon walker — even though I know that sprinters are never supposed to walk because they will develop certain muscles that are not good for sprinting.

RB 736. *I know your name!*

On our street we have a Filipino family. There are two brothers. As I was walking yesterday, one of them said to me, "I know your name! Your name is Sri Chinmoy."
Then his brother said, "Shut up, shut up!"
The first one was so happy to tell me my name.

RB 737. *Recognition*

While I was watching the 50-mile race in Central Park, so many people who were running and riding bicycles recognised me. But when I looked at them, I couldn't recognise them at all. Some people from our 24-hour race were so nice to me. Nathan Whiting did so well.

RB 738. *The Chinese doctor*

When I ran the Sri Chinmoy Marathon in San Francisco, for the first 13 miles hundreds of people were behind me. Even a Chinese doctor who had given a clinic before the marathon was behind me. He had given a talk on how to run a marathon, but this was his first marathon.
Then I got cramps. I was screaming, and Nirvik and Pradhan were both massaging me in the street.

RB 739. *I need admirers!*

This morning, near my 100-metre mark, I saw a man with a dog on a leash. He was an old man, fat and tall; he was totally out of shape. He was admiring my running. I said to myself, "I need admirers!"

RB 740. *Delayed start*

The 10-kilometre race in Prospect Park was supposed to start at 10:00, but it started at 11:10. When the police came, I thought they were going to disperse us and throw us out. But then they made an announcement that when the police car came a second time, the race would start.

RB 741. *Rivals*

When we started the race, I was absolutely the last person. A young girl went ahead of me and told me that she was not going to be last. What an insult! But after two or three hundred metres, she surrendered.

Then, after 600 metres, whom did I see? Vince! He was my first rival. I was watching him and watching him, following him very faithfully. After 1200 metres I saluted him and passed him.

Then I saw Sarama just before we came to a hill. The hill was my worst enemy. I said, "Perhaps those two will go ahead of me." But fortunately they did not go ahead of me.

RB 742. *Beat that sissy!*

During the race at least 12 people recognised me. They called out, "Sri, Sri!" They said I could make it.

There was a girl from our Montreal Centre who kept going ahead of me. Sometimes I would come very close to her. Then she would get tremendous inspiration and run ahead and disappear.

When I had completed five miles, a very nice black man who was watching came up to me to give me special advice. He told me, "Inhale, exhale three times. If you do that, then you will be able to beat that sissy!" He was encouraging me, telling me to defeat her.

RB 743. *Life is most precious*

I never take water from those helping in a race, but life is most precious. Today there were two women giving out water. I was only looking to see where their fingers were — whether they were inside the water or outside on the cup. They were inside the water.

I said to myself, "Which is more precious, my life or a finger?" I decided my life was more precious, so I took the water. Afterwards, Ranjana gave me a Tab. I did not think I would feel thirsty in only 6.2 miles.

When I see children giving out water, I never look at their fingers. Children are God. But with grown-ups, I look at their fingers first before taking the water.

Runners like us, who are dying all the time, need water. But when you are at the back of the pack, you find that there is often no water left.

RB 744. *Appreciating our races*

In the race, a 16-year-old boy named Stanley could easily have gone ahead of me. But when I started walking, he also started walking. Then he started appreciating our races like anything. He said our races were much better. He said, "Here there are no split times, no mile markers. There is absolutely nothing!" He also said he liked our T-shirts, especially our half-marathon T-shirt.

RB 745. *The quarter-mile that never ended*

Towards the end of the race people were telling us, "After the turn it is only a quarter of a mile." But that quarter of a mile never ended.

After I finished the race, I took a few steps and somebody said to me, "Are you the last guy?"

I said, "Oh no, no! There are people behind me."

RB 746. *Our friend the announcer*

After the race while we were having prasad, our friend the announcer, Kurt Steiner, came up and I offered him some ice cream. He enjoyed it. He was saying that definitely our boys have the national team record for the 50-mile race.

RB 747. *My excuses*

Today I ran the three-mile fun run for Queens Day in Flushing Meadow Park.

After running one mile at a seven-minute pace, I drank water. I was walking very nicely for 100 metres. After two miles again I started.

At two and a half miles I said, "Go, go!" to Lucy. At first she didn't see me, because I was so far ahead. Then she went ahead of me.

My timing was better than my best three miles, but when our boys measured the course, it was 100 metres short.

In the morning I had played 30 or 40 games of tennis. Then I took so much exercise. And I hadn't eaten for the previous two days. These are all my excuses why Lucy finished 100 metres ahead of me.

RB 748. *Meeting Fred Lebow*

At the start of the Westchester Half-Marathon, I was standing in the eight-minute-pace section. Whom did I see? Fred Lebow! As soon as I saw him, I greeted him and said, "Good morning."

He said, "I will see you next week at the hundred-miler."

I said, "Definitely I will be there."

Every year our team counts laps at the hundred-mile race.

RB 749. *Seeing the front runner*

During the Westchester Half-Marathon I saw the man who stood first. I was heading one way and he was coming the other way. He was taking such long strides, as if he were running on flat ground rather than on such big hills.

RB 750. *Watching the disciples*

In today's half-marathon, Chandika defeated Lucy, Chetana and Nilima on my behalf. Deliberately I was staying seven metres behind Chandika, saying to myself, "I will defeat all of them." After two miles I surrendered, but Chandika went ahead and defeated them.

At one point, Sarama was going ahead of me with such devotion and surrender. Great, Sarama!

When I saw Thomas, he gave me such a wonderful smile. Then I found out that it was because he had gone ahead of Pahar. To get a smile from Thomas is no joke! Mahiyan and Thomas were running together. Then, at the last moment, Thomas had to defeat Mahiyan.

As you know, I didn't have the courage or strength or stamina to finish. From the first mile I wanted to surrender.

At the finish line I was sitting in the car. Sundar came up and told me of his deplorable performance with such sincerity and soulfulness. There was no false modesty — only sincerity and soulfulness. I was so proud of him. How I wish all the disciples, when they don't do well, would maintain this kind of cheerful and soulful consciousness!

RB 751. *Disobeying the sign*

While I was running on my course near Jones Beach, I saw a fat woman and a fat man riding bicycles. When they came to the bridge, the wife started walking but the man kept riding, even though there was a sign saying to get off your bike and walk it over the bridge.

RB 752. *You were going so fast!*

This morning I phoned up Baoul and told him to meet me along the course going towards Flushing Meadow Park. Usually he comes when I am at the 500 or 600-metre mark. But this time, O God, even after I completed one mile, there was still no sign of him. I said to myself, "That means he is asleep!"

Then I said, "Since he is not here, let me watch the time myself. Let me run a second mile. Then perhaps he will come."

In my second mile, when I came to 1100 metres, I got inspiration to walk a little. So I walked for ten or fifteen metres. When I finished, I couldn't believe my time 6:51. Baoul saw me after 1100 metres and told me afterwards, "You were going so fast!"

Then I ran another 300 metres, only blessing Trishul. He is responsible for that course. There were so many branches there and Trishul had done nothing about them. Then, after two or three miles, there were the old marks.

RB 753. *Everything can be a blessing*

Today I went to Yonkers to run my hill course. Vincent and Databir were with me. After some time, Databir entered into his trance. Vincent was not feeling well. It was so hot. What an experience! Instead of running, I walked four miles.

Always you have to take advantage of the situation. If I want to run on 150th Street, I can do it again and again and again. But during the trip to Yonkers, I will write poems and do many things, whereas I may not get inspiration at that hour to write poems in my house. So I force myself to go to Yonkers to run the four-mile hill course there.

It usually takes 45 minutes to drive there. Today it took one hour and fifteen minutes. While in the car, I could have slept, played my flute or read the newspaper. But I took the opportunity to dictate poems. Everything can be a blessing! You can have a comfortable life and stay home and accomplish nothing. But each time I go to Yonkers I can dictate 40 or 50 poems.

RB 754. *100-mile-race experiences*

I was watching the 100-mile race at Shea Stadium when Cahit saw me. He walked to the sprinkler and washed his hands. Then he came over and shook hands with me and said, "Sri Chinmoy, it is so nice to see you here." He was one of the runners, but he came to a complete stop and washed his hands so he could shake hands with me.

James and Arpan were running together. Both of them were in a very good consciousness, and they smiled at me very soulfully. Then Trishul passed by me, not even one foot away, almost dashing into me, but he did not even see me. Databir was forty metres away from me. He saw Databir and said, "Hi." Then he saw me and stopped, smiled and folded his hands

When Nathan saw me, he said, "Sri, I have something to tell you. I am studying your books."

RB 755. *The 100-mile race*

At the 100-mile race Arpan was so excited because he got number 27, which is the day of my birthday.

Nathan doesn't like to talk to people when he is very exhausted. At 74 miles he said, "These people, what are they telling me? They should come and start a marathon in my state." He had 26 miles left. But when he came near me, he smiled at me and his mood changed.

The great Stu Mittleman was hit by a bicycle at midnight. He was jolted. Of all people, he was the one who had to be attacked!

Seven women joined the race. Four finished. Many men also gave up. The runners had to have completed a 50-mile race before this.

They gave us a very big prize, a plate, because Arpan, James and Trishul won the 50-mile National Team Championship.

At six in the morning George Vallasi ran over to greet me. I was shivering. It was so cold, and Baoul didn't have any jacket in his car. It was foggy and drizzling.

George told us that many excellent runners say that they used to dream night after night about baseball. But we have created so much interest in running that people are losing interest in baseball. Running is giving them so much joy that they are no longer interested in baseball.

RB 756. *Poetic aside*

Nathan Whiting said he has read thousands of poetry books, but he has never read anybody who writes in the English language in such a natural way as I do.

I had told him that I liked his poetry book, so he told me that. I said, "Nathan!"

He said, "Yes, I mean it!"

RB 757. *Watching the six-day race*

During the six-day race, a runner from Colorado came up to me and said, "Sri, I always feel for you. Whenever other people misunderstand you, I say, 'His philosophy is totally different.' I read your books.

"My wife is so nice. She says, 'As long as you don't get injured, you can run.' After eight days I am running another six-day race."

Then, after some time, he said to me, "Sri, you have inspired me so much that I have already run three miles."

Cahit Yeter came up to me and said, "I took a long rest, and as soon as I opened my eyes, I saw you." I hadn't seen him.

As soon as Stu Mittleman saw me, he started clapping. Don Choi gave me a little smile.

Kim Cavanough calls me "Guru." She said, "Guru, this is one of your races. Your people have made it into your race. I am getting the same feeling here as at your races."

Nathan Whiting came by and I said, "I have read the article about you."

Nathan said, "I have not read it."

I said, "It is excellent."

Nathan was begging me to give a spiritual name to James. Nathan is always so nice to me. I asked him how he survives. He said, "Oh, a difficult task! I work a little and then I run."

George Vallasi was also in a clever way trying to get me to give James a spiritual name. He was saying that James was not talking to the cameramen and that he himself wanted to speak to the camera people on James' behalf. So he asked me what he should say — what James' good qualities are.

RB 758. *A visit from Indira*

When I was coming back from running today, I saw Robin. He was going straight and I made a turn.

O God, Robin's third eye is not open, so he could not see Brihaspati's wife, Indira, standing right in the middle of the street. Her soul had come to me for blessings.

RB 759. *Looking at my watch*

As I was coming back from running, I saw Ranjana driving to practise sports. As she passed I looked at my watch. I said to myself, "Perhaps she is thinking that she is late, and that is why I am looking at my watch." But actually, I was looking to see how long I had been out.

RB 760. *Dying to lose weight*

I feel such joy and such sorrow when I see the disciples running early in the morning on 150th Street, trying to lose weight.

The other day, first I saw Anupadi. I said, "Good!" Then I saw Anna. As soon as she saw me, she increased her speed. I said, "O God, she can run so fast!"

All are dying to lose weight!

RB 761. *The deaf became dumb*

At our West Coast triathlon, I was supposed to draw a number in a kind of lottery. It was read out over the loudspeaker — number 644.

The woman with that number could not hear; she was almost deaf. A man did something with his fingers, and then she understood. Then she came up and became speechless because she had won. So the deaf became dumb.

Then she said that she had been dying to go to Hawaii, and now she had got the round-trip ticket free. Over 700 people joined and she won the ticket!

RB 712. *(p. 351)* 1 April 1983
RB 713. *(p. 352)* 2 April 1983
RB 714. *(p. 353)* 2 April 1983
RB 715. *(p. 354)* 3 April 1983
RB 716. *(p. 354)* 13 April 1983
RB 717. *(p. 354)* 20 April 1983
RB 718. *(p. 355)* 1 May 1983
RB 719. *(p. 355)* 1 May 1983
RB 720. *(p. 355)* 3 May 1983
RB 721. *(p. 356)* 3 May 1983
RB 722. *(p. 356)* 7 May 1983
RB 723. *(p. 357)* 7 May 1983
RB 724. *(p. 357)* 7 May 1983
RB 725. *(p. 357)* 7 May 1983
RB 726. *(p. 358)* 8 May 1983
RB 727. *(p. 358)* 8 May 1983
RB 728. *(p. 358)* 8 May 1983
RB 729. *(p. 359)* 8 May 1983
RB 730. *(p. 359)* 12 May 1983
RB 731. *(p. 359)* 12 May 1983
RB 732. *(p. 359)* 12 May 1983
RB 733. *(p. 360)* 12 May 1983
RB 734. *(p. 360)* 12 May 1983
RB 735. *(p. 360)* 12 May 1983
RB 736. *(p. 361)* 14 May 1983
RB 737. *(p. 361)* 22 May 1983
RB 738. *(p. 361)* 29 May 1983
RB 739. *(p. 361)* 1 June 1983
RB 740. *(p. 362)* 4 June 1983
RB 741. *(p. 362)* 4 June 1983

RB 742. *(p.362)* 4 June 1983
RB 743. *(p.363)* 4 June 1983
RB 744. *(p.363)* 4 June 1983
RB 745. *(p.364)* 4 June 1983
RB 746. *(p.364)* 4 June 1983
RB 747. *(p.364)* 6 June 1983
RB 748. *(p.365)* 12 June 1983
RB 749. *(p.365)* 12 June 1983
RB 750. *(p.365)* 12 June 1983
RB 751. *(p.366)* 13 June 1983
RB 752. *(p.366)* 17 June 1983
RB 753. *(p.367)* 17 June 1983
RB 754. *(p.367)* 17 June 1983
RB 755. *(p.368)* 18 June 1983
RB 756. *(p.369)* 22 June 1983
RB 757. *(p.369)* 6 July 1983
RB 758. *(p.370)* 8 July 1983
RB 759. *(p.370)* 8 July 1983
RB 760. *(p.370)* 14 July 1983
RB 761. *(p.371)* 2 August 1983

RUN AND BECOME, BECOME AND RUN

PART 15

While I was running this morning at 5:23, on the bottom of my mouth I was wearing my mouth retainer, which I use while exercising. Unfortunately, the retainer for the top of my mouth had been eaten by my dogs.

As usual, I was doing my hill work and speed work on 150th Street. First I was running up and down the hill. I would go down 20, 30, 40, 50 and 70 metres. Then, on the flat part, I would run from my starting point to my 500-metre mark. I always run on the side of the street with the cars. Otherwise, the lights blind me. They are so bright, so bright!

A Puerto Rican man was watching me from the top of the hill, where he was waiting for the bus. He was smoking like anything.

This time I ran to my 500-metre mark and kept walking to the 600-metre mark. I saw nobody on the street. But when I reached my 600-metre mark, suddenly I heard a lady 150 metres behind me screaming to me, "Hey Mister, save me, save me!"

So I started running as fast as possible towards the lady to save her. The robber who was bothering her got frightened and ran away.

The lady said, "Thank you, Mister, you saved me. You saved me. This black man tried to take my bags. He had a gun. (Actually it was a toy gun.) I had so much money on me because on Fridays I go to the bank. You saved me! I am so grateful to you. Please take this $20 bill."

I said, "No, please." I wouldn't take her money.

Then I said; "Have you heard of Sri Chinmoy?"

She said, "No, I don't believe I have."

I asked, "Have you heard of Guru?"

She said, "Oh yes, of course I've heard of Guru. He is a nice guy, a very nice guy!"

So I smiled at her. But right then the bus came. At that moment she was more interested in catching the bus, so she never knew that it was that "nice guy" who had saved her. Then I ran back to my starting point, next to the bus, and the bus went slowly by me.

The bus drivers are all my friends; they all know me because I run so much on 150th Street. They like me so much!

So this is the kind of thing that happens when I go out to run. Then I went home and did my 100 push-ups for the day.

RB 763. *The garbage bag*

During the New York Marathon, Suradhuni took off the garbage bag she had around her and threw it on the street. I blessed her, because I was right behind her.

RB 764. *What determination can do*

Nemi's boss, Sandy, completed the whole New York Marathon! Look what determination can do when God's Grace descends! There is a Sanskrit saying that when God's Grace descends, it can give eloquence to the dumb and enable the lame to scale mountains. Here God's Grace descended, and through his determination he completed the marathon even though he recently had suffered a stroke.

One person will run the marathon in two hours and another will have to exercise patience and run it in 10 or 12 hours. The race goes to the swiftest; that is one theory. But in the inner world, the race goes to the one who has utmost patience. Because of our infinite patience, our hope of realising God will one day be manifested into reality.

RB 765. *Running blind*

So many times I have seen Madhuri running in the street and invited her to come into the car with us, but she doesn't see me.

Today I was in the car near my 1200-metre mark, almost at Main Street. The car was going slowly, but Madhuri was running without her glasses, so she was doubly blind. She didn't see me.

RB 766. *Saved by the notebook*

Today I came out of the house carrying a notebook and a tape recorder, because I had decided I would do hill work in Westchester and dictate some poems in the car on the way there. As soon as I came out of the house, I dropped the notebook — not the tape recorder, luckily. So I bent down with difficulty, because of my back pain, to pick it up.

My notebook had fallen on my left foot. When I looked down I saw that my right foot was dark but my left foot was so white. I said, "How can it be?" On my right foot I had no sock. So I had to go inside and make the right foot white. I always get blisters if I don't use socks. So the notebook saved me. Otherwise, perhaps when I started running I would have been in another world and I would have gotten blisters.

RB 767. *A cheerful and soulful consciousness*

During the 70-mile race, I was admiring Trishul's consciousness. Four or five times I saw him. Each time he saw me, he smiled and folded his hands. He was in a very, very cheerful, soulful consciousness. I was very, very pleased and proud of him.

RB 768. *The glass wall*

Once when I was in Madras, I was running quite fast and I didn't see that there was a glass wall in front of me. I thought that side of the building was open. I ran right into the glass. The shock that I got! Fortunately, I was not hurt.

RB 769. *Malicious pleasure*

This morning while I was walking, some car drivers were getting malicious pleasure by bothering me. First they would go to this side and then to that side — only to draw my attention. Nine or ten boys were with me. Would the drivers have been able to escape if they had done anything? They were just showing off.

RB 770. *The Maracaibo race*

During the three-mile race in Maracaibo this morning, I was admiring the way T was running. He was just going on — like an eternal runner. He was running and running — quite cheerfully.

Long live Senani! He never runs three miles, but today he defeated quite a few.

RB 771. *Breathing loudly*

Today I saw Premik and I couldn't believe how loudly he was breathing. From a hundred metres away I could hear, "Hee! Hee!" I thought something serious was taking place while he was approaching me.

When he came near me, he stopped making those noises, but then after ten metres he started again. Such a loud noise! Other runners also make noise when they run, but Premik was really something!

Once I was running a marathon and I was breathing very loudly. A man running by me said, "Did you check with your doctor?"

RB 772. *Two useless runners*

I will never forget my 5-kilometre race today in Caracas. I am such a useless runner! Towards the end Nayana was behind me. I knew she had been struggling, but I thought she had finished and that now she just wanted to run with me. I said, "No, I do not want to run with anybody."

But she said she had pulled a muscle and she was still running the race. She was smiling and running. I thought she was coming to sympathise with me.

Last week I walked a mile and a half during a race. Today I had to walk four or five times, but the rest of the time I ran.

RB 773. *I could not laugh*

Yesterday Prasannata was running in the race. Other times I would have laughed and laughed at her, but now my standard has gone so high, I could not laugh. How slowly she was running! But I did not laugh at her.

RB 774. *Chasing Kanchan*

During the marathon today in Puerto La Cruz, a dog chased Kanchan. Of all people, she was being chased! The dog was not even a metre behind her, barking and barking, and Kanchan was also barking at the dog. Then we went behind Kanchan and screamed, and the dog ran away.

RB 775. *Thinking of the dogs*

When you are running, sometimes it is like a morning walk. You only look to this side and that side and think of the dogs. If you run on the sidewalk, they will come and bite you. They are undernourished. As soon as they start barking, they never stop.

RB 776. *The old man with a beard*

During the marathon an old man with a beard saw me three times. Each time he recognised me, he raised his hands and clapped and screamed.

RB 777. *Two jokers*

One fellow was running the marathon in sandals. Vidura gave him his running shoes and they fit him.

In the last two miles Virendra ran so fast that he passed four or five runners.

He came in second.

The two brothers, Aviram and Pravaha, are such jokers. At thirteen miles I saw them stop and go into the hotel. The tall one said, "Guru, after thirteen miles we realised we were not wearing your T-shirt, so we went into the hotel."

Then the little one said, "Guru, we got a little tired, so we stopped!"

RB 778. *No short cut!*

During the marathon Kailash was running behind one particular runner. Then, in the last 100 metres, Kailash went ahead of him. The man could not believe it. He said Kailash took a short cut. In this world people say anything they like.

RB 779. *Innocence was flowing*

When I was giving prizes after the marathon in Puerto La Cruz, how much innocence was flowing! It was a little group, and the people were so simple.

RB 780. *False information*

I was running by my 600-metre mark, and Baoul and Kailash were 200 metres behind me in a car. Then I saw Neeta in a car, so I smiled and waved.

When I mentioned it to Nishtha, she told me that Neeta doesn't drive; she doesn't even have a car. Then I began doubting myself. Am I so blind? Later I found out that Neeta does have a car, and it was Neeta I saw.

RB 781. *Lose ten pounds!*

Yesterday I ran John's one-mile course in Flushing Meadow Park. Kailash took my timing. I have made tremendous progress — from 13:40 to 11:40! If I can make progress, all of you can make progress.

If you lose seven to ten pounds, you will not die. But the result is something else. If you lose ten pounds, even three pounds, you simply fly when you run. You don't need to be a bird to fly.

So, overweight people, lose ten pounds!

RB 782. *Two unforgettable moments*

In the Inspiration Marathon last year, Chris' brother, Carlos, was behind me. I will never forget how all of a sudden I heard him scream, "Guru!"

At that time he stood fourth.

I will also never forget what happened four or five years ago on the course in Breezy Point. There he stood first in our four-mile race. Like a horse he was galloping! He is so short, but his stride was so long. Such a big stride! He was returning, and I had not yet gone half the way.

RB 783. *Invisible runners*

At the last marathon in Puerto Rico, all those who won were shorter than the shortest and thinner than the thinnest. After the race, when I stood in front of the winners, I could not believe how thin human beings could be. They were all practically invisible!

RB 784. *Even Pulak makes progress*

Everybody makes progress, even Pulak. Last week in the 6.2-mile race I was observing him. I was so proud of the way he has made such tremendous progress in his style.

RB 785. *Central Park experiences*

During the 20-mile race in Central Park today, one old man was
looking at me and telling another old man, "He is the director
of the Sri Chinmoy Marathon Team!" Then two ladies — not
disciples — started calling me, "Guru, Guru!"

The first two miles Prabhir was ahead of Sarama, although
she was running and he was walking. She had her jacket around
her waist. People were dying and she was carrying extra weight!
Then she went ahead of Prabhir.

RB 786. *Imagination-power succeeds*

During the five-mile race, I was running behind Durga. She
saw me and went to the other side, but I was so tired that I
stayed behind her. Then we came to a hill. I said, "Where is
she? Where is she?"

I used to do hill work every day, and while I was running I
was thinking of my hill work. I was running and she was running
too, but because I was thinking of my hill work I went ahead
of her. Only by thinking of it was I able to go ahead of her, or
perhaps she deliberately showed me compassion.

RB 787. *Only one mile!*

One man in the five-mile race, wearing green, was walking. He
told me, "Don't go ahead of me; stay with me!"

A black girl who was 50 metres ahead of me stopped. Her
boyfriend and her brother were so sympathetic.

An old lady said, "Sri, are you not walking? Are you not
walking?" She saw how tired I was — that I was dying — so she
was begging me to walk. She was very kind to me.

When I start running, my mantra is, "Only one mile, only one mile!"

RB 788. *Mistaken identity*

One man was walking, and I thought it was Prabhir. I was coming from 40 or 50 metres behind him. I said, "Prabhir, I am so proud of you," but he did not turn around. Then, when I was only one step away, I said, "Prabhir!" Finally he turned around, and I saw that it was someone else, so I smiled at him.

RB 789. *Burning, burning*

In this five-mile race I ran the whole distance. It was difficult. After 4 miles I was calling Databir, but he did not come. So I waited.

When he came, he took my yellow jacket. Once you start running, after 10 or 15 minutes, you want to take off everything. My upper body was burning, burning. Some people wore shorts, but I didn't.

When Databir took my jacket, I was greatly relieved. At least 10 or 15 seconds definitely I lost, but my last mile was my best mile.

RB 790. *No sense of distance*

Pulak has no sense of distance. When I was nearing the finish of the five-mile race, he told me, "After the bend, it is just half a mile." After the bend, it was not even 400 metres!

RB 791. *The missing poodle*

Whenever I run alone, people talk to me. After God knows how many months, I went out to practise. Bipin and Pulin were following me in the car. After 1300 metres, a little boy came right in front of me in an intersection and said, "Please stop, stop, stop!" So immediately I stopped. Cars were coming on this side and that side, but they had a red light, so I could stop.

He said, "Have you seen my little white poodle? Have you seen my little white poodle?" It was so pathetic.

I said, "I have not seen it."

He said, "You have not seen it?"

Then he started looking for it again.

RB 792. *A perfect joke*

We had a marathon in Germany that was a perfect joke from the beginning to the end. It touched the height of absurdity. Our organisation reached the highest height. Fortunately, this was only a family gathering. The most important thing for the German disciples was their concert, so they paid all attention to that.

One reporter said I ran 26 miles. It was six, but he added 20 miles.

RB 793. *What are you doing?*

Today at 4:30 a.m., after many, many months, I went out to walk. I was enjoying myself like anything. After one mile I came back.

At my 800-metre mark a short but very fat lady was waiting for the bus. As soon as she saw me, she said, "Mr. Chinmoy, what are you doing at this hour?" Then she said, "Have a very nice day."

I said to her, "The same to you." She smiled.

"What are you doing?" she was asking me. She could see that I was walking! I had never, never seen her before.

RB 794. *Thrilled to see me*

Then I went down the 150th Street hill. I saw a van that said something like, "C. S. Company." A young man with curly hair said, "Hello, Sri Chinmoy! Hello, Sri Chinmoy!"

Then I started to walk another mile. When I had walked about 1500 metres, I saw a cyclist coming. I went another 100 metres to complete my mile. Then I saw him stop. I said to myself, "Something is wrong with his bicycle."

He started saying, "Sri, Sri, Sri Chinmoy!" He was so happy to see me.

I smiled. Then, very slowly, he rode with me to Main Street, beaming with joy. He made a right turn and I made a turn towards my mile mark.

Both these young men were so thrilled to see me.

RB 795. *A young admirer*

As I was walking in front of my house at 1:30, a young man came out of a car and said, "Run and become, become and run." He was not joking. He was showing tremendous admiration for me and sympathy with my pain. He was asking, "How did you get hurt?"

He said, "I tell my friends about you, and they don't believe that you live in that house. I tell them that the picture on the Santana and John McLaughlin album was taken right in front of your house. They don't believe me."

Then I came back and told Databir, who was in front of my house, to go and talk to him. The young man had said that he was a pianist, so Databir told him about Haridas.

Databir also told him about the Cologne concert. Then he asked Databir, "How can a famous person like Sri Chinmoy walk all by himself in a poor community?" He lives in Manhattan. He had a good conversation with Databir. Databir came to my house to get a book for him.

All of a sudden he got a call on his beeper, so he left to call his company. He said, "Tell him I will definitely come back."

RB 796. *I will be right back*

At the 70-mile race, George Vallasi shook hands with me. He is so nice to us.

Then he said to me, "I will be right back," and he started running with his friend, whom he was helping. I thought that he meant he would run 100 or 200 metres, but he went on and on.

During the race I saw Nathan. I said, "Run! Run!" He didn't hear me. He just kept running.

RB 797. *A marathon wait*

When I was coming back from Boston, a man on the plane said he had waited for the plane for three hours.

The stewardess said to him, "It seems you have just run a marathon."

He said, "Yes, I did. It took me three hours to run the marathon and three hours to wait for the plane."

RB 798. *Inspiration leads to manifestation*

Avery informs me every day about the six-day race in England.

One runner, an Englishman, was leading right from the beginning. At one point he said, "Now I am going to speak to Sri." Then he left the track and for five minutes he looked at my picture. He is not a disciple.

The person who is third also looks at my Transcendental Picture every time he comes near it.

One man tells Avery every day to say hello to me, and another runner was appreciating our races. Beverly Nolan and Bob Cannata were wearing our T-shirts right from the beginning.

Avery is helping all of the runners — not only Trishul. Our London disciples come every day also, to inspire the runners. If there is inspiration, there will be aspiration; and if there is aspiration, there is bound to be manifestation.

RB 799. *No experiences*

Every day while running I see disciples, but today I did not see even one disciple. I went out at 5:15 in the morning. I didn't see anybody and I didn't have a single experience. Only once I saw a car, when I had completed my first mile.

RB 800. *Trying to catch Pramoda*

In the 1200-metre walk at our World Family Day, I tried so desperately to catch Pramoda. One, two, twenty people I passed, but I couldn't catch her.

RB 801. *Sitting beside the world*

When I was watching the Olympic marathon trials on video, I was looking for Gary Fanelli, but I could not see him anywhere. They were showing only the lead runners — the first five or six. He ran 2:18 and his position was 23rd out of 160. The next time he comes to New York I will definitely honour him.

He is such a great runner! A few months ago he had an operation. He is not fully recovered. Only two months ago at our race in Connecticut he asked me to pray for him. He is very receptive; that is why my prayers work for him. He told me that he prays and meditates on my picture every day.

Once when he was sitting beside me at Madison Square Garden, he said, "Guru, to sit beside you is to sit beside the whole world."

His brother and also a friend of theirs join our races in San Francisco.

RB 802. *Harassment*

This morning I went out to walk fast. First I saw Nilima, then I saw Bhikshuni and then I saw Agamani — three!

After four and a half miles, three other girls — not disciples — were a little ahead of me on the sidewalk and would not allow me to cross the street. With greatest difficulty I crossed. Then I thanked them.

They started running behind me, saying things which I couldn't understand. For 100 or 150 metres they were harassing me. I turned around and looked at them, and then they all turned around and started running away. Then I went ahead.

In spite of seeing the boys following me in the car, they were harassing me.

RB 803. *Another street encounter*

In the afternoon also there was a car following me. Around my 700-metre mark a middle-aged man saw me. He said, "Sir, I do not know your name, but you are a very nice person. I have seen your picture in the train."

So I looked at him and thanked him.

Then I made a turn at 800 metres. Lucy was running by. She thought it was the same story as in the morning — that the man was harassing me — so she came quite fast to my rescue. But the man was so nice — so happy to see me in the street.

Altogether, today I walked 13 miles.

RB 804. *A long running career*

Tomorrow is my sixth running anniversary. When I think of my marathon-life, it seems to me that I have been running for the last ten or eleven years — especially when I think of the cramps that I used to get during the marathon!

RB 805. *A surprise meeting*

Today I was running all by myself. I wanted to run seven miles, so I was taking the loop near Mohan and Anjali's house. At six miles, all of a sudden I saw Vidhu and Bipin in a car. Bipin said that they were going out to buy some juice.

RB 806. *A sensation!*

While I was running today, at one point I saw Chanakhya. He was going so fast! I said, "He is an excellent runner."

In the street if you run under a six-minute pace, it creates a sensation. But coming back, he was going so slowly!

RB 807. *Recognised*

Seven or eight boys, schoolchildren, recognised me while I was running. I was making my turn off the Grand Central service road onto 188th Street when they saw me. They said, "Guru, Guru, Guru!" They were not joking with me. They were showing respect.

RB 808. *You are doing well!*

While I was running the 3.1-mile race at Flushing Meadow Park this evening, one of the officials greeted me. He said, "Guru, Guru, you are doing well!" Not bad — considering I have had six months' vacation!

Then after the race, a boy came up and talked to me. He had recognised me.

RB 809. *A very hard time*

What was wrong with Anupadi? She didn't run the two-mile race tonight at Flushing Meadow Park. I would have given her a very hard time in the race!

Then I saw her running on 150th Street. She was running by as Snigdha was coming out of her house.

Sandhani ran the race — very good!

RB 810. *Better late than never*

I went to a 3.1-mile race tonight on Long Island. We were 20 minutes late, and the first-class runners were all finished. Then Trishul got a map of the course and Pahar followed it exactly — with no mistakes.

The course was excellent — 100 per cent flat. On either side of the road there were trees and so forth. It was very beautiful — a good panoramic view.

When we finished, they had already started distributing the prizes. There were about 300 people there — very good!

RB 762. *(p.377)* 14 October 1983
RB 763. *(p.378)* 24 October 1983
RB 764. *(p.378)* 27 October 1983
RB 765. *(p.379)* 29 October 1983
RB 766. *(p.379)* 29 October 1983
RB 767. *(p.379)* 6 November 1983
RB 768. *(p.380)* 19 November 1983
RB 769. *(p.380)* 24 November 1983
RB 770. *(p.380)* 18 December 1983
RB 771. *(p.380)* 18 December 1983
RB 772. *(p.381)* 27 December 1983
RB 773. *(p.381)* 28 December 1983
RB 774. *(p.381)* 8 January 1984
RB 775. *(p.382)* 8 January 1984
RB 776. *(p.382)* 8 January 1984
RB 777. *(p.382)* 8 January 1984
RB 778. *(p.383)* 8 January 1984
RB 779. *(p.383)* 8 January 1984
RB 780. *(p.383)* 21 January 1984
RB 781. *(p.383)* 21 January 1984
RB 782. *(p.384)* 2 February 1984
RB 783. *(p.384)* 2 February 1984
RB 784. *(p.384)* 2 February 1984
RB 785. *(p.385)* 26 February 1984
RB 786. *(p.385)* 3 March 1984
RB 787. *(p.385)* 3 March 1984
RB 788. *(p.386)* 3 March 1984
RB 789. *(p.386)* 3 March 1984
RB 790. *(p.386)* 3 March 1984
RB 791. *(p.387)* 15 March 1984

RB 792. *(p.387)* 29 March 1984
RB 793. *(p.387)* 2 April 1984
RB 794. *(p.388)* 2 April 1984
RB 795. *(p.388)* 3 May 1984
RB 796. *(p.389)* 5 May 1984
RB 797. *(p.389)* 12 May 1984
RB 798. *(p.390)* 25 May 1984
RB 799. *(p.390)* 27 May 1984
RB 800. *(p.390)* 27 May 1984
RB 801. *(p.391)* 27 May 1984
RB 802. *(p.391)* 31 May 1984
RB 803. *(p.392)* 31 May 1984
RB 804. *(p.392)* 31 May 1984
RB 805. *(p.392)* 18 June 1984
RB 806. *(p.393)* 18 June 1984
RB 807. *(p.393)* 18 June 1984
RB 808. *(p.393)* 22 June 1984
RB 809. *(p.393)* 26 June 1984
RB 810. *(p.394)* 1 July 1984

RUN AND BECOME, BECOME AND RUN

PART 16

RB 811. *The six-day race*

At the six-day race, so many runners knew me. I smiled at them and they smiled at me. But my Cahit! He came off the track — he had to shake hands with me, talk to me and give me gifts. He couldn't believe that I gave him such a big gift. All the runners smiled at me, but he came off the track to see me.

Fred Lebow was all appreciation for our Marathon Team workers. He spoke to me most gratefully about our contribution.

The leader, a Greek named Yiannis Kouros, is something! Once he ran 200 miles at a seven-minute pace.

RB 812. *Bringing sunshine*

Yesterday it was raining during the six-day race, so I left the track and went inside the car. Cahit came running to shake hands with me. He said that I bring sunshine to him. Then he said he was sorry he was unshaven. Where can I find another Cahit?

Sue Medaglia was so happy to see me at the race. She said, "Because of you, because of your group, I am alive, I am running."

Today I saw divine Kim, with folded hands. She was smiling and smiling. Such a soulful consciousness she maintained throughout!

RB 813. *The best*

The other day I went to run a 3.1-mile race in Flushing Meadow Park. When I finished, a runner came up to me. He had finished long before me. He said that our races are by far the best. He has run in California and various places, and everywhere our races are the best.

RB 814. *The over-fifty champion*

The man who won the special prize in the over-fifty category in our Runners are Smilers race today is an excellent runner. He will always win, unless somebody else comes. He should bring all his friends by saying that he has got nice gifts. He should show them his trophy. Then his friends will come and challenge him. There is no other way.

RB 815. *Have a cup of coffee!*

The first day I was in Los Angeles for the Olympics, I went out running early in the morning. I asked a man where the stadium was. He said, "Forget the stadium. Go have a cup of coffee!"

On another day, I was walking on the sidewalk when I saw three men — simply undivine — coming towards me. I jumped into the street to avoid them. Very loudly one said, "Jesus!"

In silence I said to him, "Thank you for invoking a very good friend of mine!"

RB 816. *The mini-swim*

Today in the mini-triathlon only Databir, Pahar, Pulak and Dhanu couldn't swim. In the big triathlon, they would be forbidden — we cannot afford to lose four or five lives.

On the boys' side Kripan was the best! Luckily Kripan was not driving; he was swimming. First he would go to one side, towards Anugata. Then he would go to the other side. His wife was screaming. How much time he was wasting going to this side and that side! He totally forgot about geometry.

RB 817. *Giving out oranges*

When I was giving out oranges to the runners finishing our half-marathon in Flushing Meadow Park yesterday, some of them were mad. One fellow heard he was tenth or twelfth and his friend was eighth. I think his friend was also his rival. He was very disappointed and he said, "Damn it!"

Some runners didn't take oranges. One or two perhaps didn't like oranges, but others were mad at themselves. One or two, when they calmed down, came and took.

RB 818. *Blessings from the elderly*

During the race two or three runners were so nice to me. Some elderly runners were saying, "Guru, Guru!"

One of them was so happy. Another patted my shoulder with such affection. He was blessing me. He was running near me and then he went ahead.

RB 819. *Ali, Ali, Ali!*

Yesterday I was walking near the tennis courts behind P.S. 86 and Hillcrest High School. Six or seven young black boys saw me and started saying, "Ali, Ali, Ali! Champion 1999!" Then one of the boys told the others, "Shut up!" They were calling me Muhammad Ali!

Databir, Pulin and Bipin were following me in the car only 10 metres behind, but the boys didn't notice them.

RB 820. *What speed I have!*

I was running at 6:30 in the morning on the Grand Central service road. When I stopped for a red light, I saw that Nemi was 50 metres behind me — at least. Then, in a minute she smiled and passed me very nicely. Then Sulochana came up and just went ahead of me. What wonderful speed I have!

RB 821. *My only rival*

In today's two-mile Runners are Smilers race, Saroja was my only rival. The first mile I was ahead of her, but the second mile I was 10 or 15 metres behind her.

RB 822. *Smiling like anything*

This morning I ran four miles. The first mile I ran in 12:13. I said, "Great! Very near 13, my lucky number."

The second mile I ran in 10:21. I couldn't believe it! Instead of descending, I went faster. This was all because I got inspiration from Chidananda. After the first mile I saw Chidananda drive by in his car, and he was smiling like anything.

I said to myself, "Definitely he didn't meditate at six o'clock. Otherwise, he wouldn't be out at this hour." Sunirmalya was in the car with Chidananda. They were going to play tennis. Later Sunirmalya told me they had left the house at 6:16, right after meditation.

My third mile was 9:37. Then my fourth mile was 8:57.

RB 823. *The challenge*

In today's two-mile race, I saw Kritagyata and Pratyaya so far ahead of me during the first mile.

Then I challenged Lucy and Nilima. I was a few metres behind them, but I felt that I would be able to catch them at the one-mile point. Then, after I passed them, I started walking.

RB 824. *You must run!*

The other day while I was walking, a gentleman with a cane grabbed my left arm and said, "You are not doing the right thing. You must run, always run!"

I said, "Do you run?"

He said, "I can barely drag my leg, so I cannot run."

A nice gentleman! But he didn't realise that I also have serious leg problems!

RB 825. *Cahit's race*

In the five-mile race that Cahit Yeter organised today in the Bronx, Carlos was encouraging me and I was begging him to go a little faster so he would get a prize. In the race, the disciples were encouraging me all the time, singing, *O grant me the fastest speed*. But the people watching the race were laughing at my speed.

After killing myself for some time, I saw no life inside my body. Then I saw Anne Alaimo 400 metres ahead of me. First I passed Chameli, then Anne, Godavari and Chandra. Then I passed Chetana long after them. But Sarama was beyond my reach.

During the race, at least fifteen people recognised me.

RB 826. *Patience replaces capacity*

When I see my disciples running now, many times they are 600 metres or one mile ahead of me. But I used to be right behind them or even ahead of them.

They have to admire how much patience I have. When you lose capacity, you have to give credit to your patience.

RB 827. *Maybe he doesn't understand English*

Yesterday I was running in Flushing Meadow Park near our 1,000-mile race. Two men were also running. One of them saw the poster about the race and said to me, "Why are you not also competing?"

I just smiled at him.

Then the other man said, "Maybe he doesn't understand English."

RB 828. *Coming from behind*

The day before yesterday I was running behind John in the 1,000-mile race. I said, "I will never be able to pass him."

But then I went ahead of him. I also went ahead of Trishul two times. I said to myself, "Can you believe it? Never did I think I would be able to pass these two excellent runners! I will give both of them very nice gifts."

Of course, Trishul had been running for four days. He is planning to complete the 1,000-mile race. And John had also run more than 200 miles by that time.

RB 829. *He walks faster than I run*

Still I have not been able to pass Kirit while running in the 1,000-mile race. Sometimes he walks, and then I say, "This is the time when I will pass him." But he walks faster than I run.

RB 830. *A birthday run*

The other day was Yury's birthday. He had completed 23 years, so he walked and ran 23 miles at the 1,000-mile race. Now I think he has become an invalid.

His mother came yesterday to Annam Brahma. She got an orange as prasad and asked her son if she had to preserve the seeds because the orange was sacred.

RB 831. *A rare smile*

So many times I have seen Bob Wise walking in the 1,000-mile race. Previously he never smiled at me. But today, on the fifth day of the race, he smiled at me and started clapping.

RB 832. *Running and running*

Today in the 1,000-mile race, so many times I got joy from passing Trishul. I was forgetting that he had already done 300 miles.

RB 833. *Good morning!*

Today at five o'clock in the afternoon, Bob Wise, the walker in our 1,000-mile race, looked at me and said, "Good morning!"

I told him also, "Good morning."

RB 834. *I am nearing 75*

This morning at a quarter to seven, I was walking on 150th Street. I saw an elderly man get up on a bike with difficulty. As soon as he saw me, he got off the bike. He had only covered 20 metres.

He said to me, "You are running and I am cycling. I am 75. How old are you?"

I said, "I am nearing 75."

He was so happy to hear that.

RB 835. *Walking ferociously*

I had an experience near Queens Boulevard at four o'clock this morning. Just near the top of the hill a respectable-looking lady was waiting for the bus. She saw me coming towards her, from about 20 metres away. I was walking so ferociously that she got frightened and ran away. I felt sorry, so I called out to her, "Don't be afraid of me!" Then she came back to the bus stop.

RB 836. *The Queens fitness Guru*

The end of the 1,000-mile race was on the 6:30 news last night on television. When they mentioned my name they had trouble with "Sri"; they said, "Sir." They called me "Sir Chinmoy, the Queens Fitness Guru."

RB 837. *Struggling towards 1,000 miles*

Originally I wanted to run seven miles every day during the 1,000-mile race. I felt that if I tried to do 13 miles, I would not be able to continue. But at the end of the race I had completed 208 miles — an average of 13 miles a day for the 16 days of the race.

Three people completed the full distance: 1,000 miles! Here is the proof that there are a few things the mind cannot understand — when the soul operates through the heart or through the vital. To run 1,000 miles is beyond the comprehension of the mind; the mind cannot imagine it!

Perhaps now people will be inspired to sponsor 1,000-mile races.

By the first week of August I do hope to complete my 1,000 miles. I am going on, going on. God knows if I can do it!

RB 838. *Nayak's soul preceded him*

The day before yesterday I was at the 800 metre point on the 1,000-mile course, near the circle, walking. It was in the morning. All of a sudden Nayak's soul appeared for blessings. I thought, "Nayak didn't inform me he was coming to New York. Usually he informs me." But it was not actually Nayak, but only his soul, which appeared so vividly.

Then a few hours later I saw Nayak himself standing at the same spot, near the circle. He had come to New York quite suddenly on business.

RB 839. *My imagination gets frightened*

I have run a little over 200 miles during the 1,000-mile race, but already I am blessing my forefathers that I have promised to run 1,000 miles. Even my imagination gets frightened!

But I am sincerely proud of those who have completed the race. Look at Trishul! The race ended just yesterday, and already he is here at the meditation, enjoying his spiritual life.

RB 840. *A slow run*

The other day Pulak and Saral ran with me. I asked them if they ever run as slowly as they were running with me. Both of them remained silent. That means they never run that slowly. One day they will run long distance — 70 miles — and I will see how slowly they run.

RB 841. *I am blind*

Yesterday morning at about 5:30 I was running on 150th Street near Sandhani and Snigdha's house. Suddenly Navina's soul came to me for blessings. I said, "Fine. Why did you not come to New York after the April celebrations?" I decided to ask Kailash why Navina had not come.

In the afternoon I was walking to circus practice. On Snigdha and Sandhani's steps I saw three persons standing: Snigdha, Durga and a third person. So I smiled at them. Snigdha was pointing out the third girl to me, but I couldn't recognise her. I am blind! Then I saw it was Navina. Navina was with them, but her hairstyle had transformed her face.

RB 842. *I surrendered*

The other day during our two-mile race, Barada waved at Radha as she went ahead of her. I said to myself, "Yes, I am seeing you, Barada."

Seven years ago during a 10-mile race, Barada and I had our first rivalry. Then I surrendered.

RB 843. *No competitiveness*

Early in the morning I walk at a 20-minute pace — very solid. One morning, when I had covered a mile, all of a sudden I saw a lady pass by me. She had a bag on her shoulder. My ego came forward. How could she go faster than me, carrying a bag on her shoulder? O God, I tried to defeat her.

That was the morning I had taken an oath that I wouldn't go very fast. After five minutes, I saw another lady. This one was running for the bus, and she also was passing me. I said, "This is too much!"

Then I walked very fast. I was on the street and she was on the sidewalk. I managed to pass her, but it made me very tired. Was it worth it? In three or four seconds, again she was going ahead of me. I asked myself, "Why did I compete with her?" Then I decided not to compete with her anymore.

RB 844. *Tricking the mind*

When I run mile after mile, I meditate. When I don't feel like meditating, I sing in silence. I have lists of songs that I play on the double bass, cello, violin, Moroccan instrument, Chinese instrument and harp. There are about 40 songs altogether. While running I sing each song inwardly, only once. In this way, when I go out of the house I kill three or four birds at once.

This morning at 7:00 I went four miles. I sang very soulfully, in a prayerful way.

When I walk, my mind says, "Once upon a time, you used to walk at an 11 or 13-minute pace. Now you are walking at a 17 or 18-minute pace." So the mind brings discouragement. But then I play a trick on the mind. I say, "Yes, it is a 20-minute pace, but I am gaining in another way. I am meditating longer."

At home I have millions of problems to deal with. In these 20 minutes when I am walking, I am all by myself; so I am very happy. If I take three minutes more, who cares? Nature is helping me. With nature's beauty I am meditating. The mind brings discouragement, but then I tell my mind that for 20 minutes without interruption I am able to meditate. So the mind remains silent. We have to be super-smart when the mind wants to discourage us.

RB 845. *I want your outer blessings*

The other day I was walking to the tennis court. On the way an elderly Indian man came out of his house and said, "May I speak to you?"

I said, "Why?"

He said, "You are a great man. My daughter is getting married this Friday. I wish to invite you and your disciples. I wish to honour you."

I said, "Your daughter is getting married. This is her day. Why do you have to honour me?"

He said, "If you come to our house, you will bless our house and bless us."

I said, "You have my inner blessings."

He said, "I want your outer blessings."

"Please forgive me," I said, "I will not be able to come."

Then we shook hands and I went on.

RB 846. *The hat*

Today, first I walked two miles. Then I covered another eleven miles by running for 1400 metres and walking for the last 200 metres of each mile. I call this combination "running." Then I walked another half mile — for a total of thirteen and a half miles.

After the 1100-metre mark, near my seven-mile point, my hat was bothering me, so I took it off. Then I saw a beautiful lawn with a fence. I put the hat on one of the bars of the fence very nicely and left it in charge of God. I said, "God will take care of it. If it is His Will, He will keep it here."

Then I started jogging. After 40 metres I saw a gentleman smiling at me. God knows why he was smiling at me, but I also smiled at him. We were two gentlemen.

I went to the nine-mile mark and then started returning home. When I came to the seven-mile mark, I remembered that I had left my hat on the fence. I was about to look for it when I saw the same gentleman who had smiled at me holding the hat. He gave it to me and said, "I feel you are a nice man."

I said, "I know you are an excellent man!" Then he started laughing, and we shook hands.

This all happened right in front of his house. When I had left the hat there, at that time he had been 40 metres away. But when I came back, he was standing right in front of his house holding the hat. Can you imagine!

RB 847. *The water pistol*

After I ran about four miles today, two little boys on bicycles came up behind me. One of them said to me, "I can easily beat you."

I said, "Fine!"

Then they passed me, and one of them turned around and shot me with a water pistol. Then they both rode away very fast. I thanked them.

RB 848. *Enjoying the argument*

Last week two children came up to me while I was walking and wanted to walk with me. One asked why I was wearing the belt that I always use to support my back. I smiled at him.

The other one said, "Can't you see that he is fat?" So they had an argument. They walked with me for about 400 metres arguing back and forth. I was enjoying the argument.

RB 849. *Driving backward*

The other day a car was about to drive away from a gas station. It was waiting for the other cars to pass by so it could enter into the street. The driver was looking to this side and that side. I was running on the sidewalk.

The car was not disturbing anybody, and I ran behind it. But just when I was behind it, the driver suddenly got the inspiration to go backward instead of forward. I shouted very loudly, at the top of my voice. What can you do with people like that? Luckily I escaped.

RB 850. *Running in Quebec*

When we were in Canada this weekend for the two seven-hour meditations, I went out running early in the morning in Quebec City. First I saw Pratyaya running. Then I saw Hashi right near me. The next moment, when I looked around, Hashi was already 100 metres ahead of me!

RB 851. *I know why you are strong*

One day I was walking in front of my house and also exercising at the same time. The old German lady who lives on our block — the one who has the dog — came up to me and said, "Now I know why you are very strong and why you are very skinny."

Then she came near me and pushed my left shoulder. Whenever she sees me, she always pushes my shoulder in an affectionate way.

RB 852. *We love you!*

While I was out walking, two people came up to me and said, "We love you!"

I gave them a smile.

Can you imagine people who are not my disciples saying that to me!

RB 853. *I am the wrong person!*

While I was taking pictures at the L'eggs Mini-Marathon, a man came up to me and wanted me to help him put film in his camera. He was giving me his camera and the roll of film.

O God! I know next to nothing about cameras! Even my own camera, I ask one of my students to load for me. So I said to the man, "I am the wrong person!"

He said, "Thank you!"

RB 854. *Wearing the American flag*

Whenever I see a T-shirt with something written on the back, I think it is a shirt from one of our races.

Last week while I was running, I saw a lady ahead of me with quite a few lines written on the back of her shirt. I thought it was Tanima. I ran so fast to catch up with her, but then I saw it was some other lady. And when I came close, I saw it was an American flag on the back of her shirt!

RB 855. *Not in the mood to talk*

I was outside walking up and down my street. Radha, the little girl who lives two doors down from me, came up to me and said, "Guru, will you be walking for a long time?"

I said, "Yes."

She said, "I will ride my bicycle with you."

She rode alongside me for about a mile. She was talking and talking, and I was meditating. Finally she said, "Guru, you are not in the mood to talk!"

I smiled at her.

Then Radha's sister introduced me to their father. We both smiled at each other. We didn't know how to talk.

RB 856. *Mother Earth should bless me now!*

When I used to practise running in the ashram when I was young, I used to feel sorry for Mother Earth because my legs were so strong and powerful. I felt I was hurting the ground when I ran. When I did the hop, skip and jump, my hop was so powerful that again I felt I was hurting Mother Earth. But now when I run, I find the ground so hard that it hurts me. Mother Earth should bless me now!

I even feel the difference between the sidewalk and the street. The sidewalk is so much harder than the street. Even when I run on the track at St. John's University, the track hurts my legs.

In the ashram I used to go out running barefoot at four o'clock in the morning, and I wouldn't even notice that the ground was hard. Then when I went out at six o'clock, after it had become light, I would see pieces of glass in the places where I had been running. So the Supreme had saved me!

RB 857. *The candy store*

I walked many miles today. At one point, after covering about 11 miles in my slowest possible walk, I entered a candy store. I bought all kinds of things, including candy that looked like little baseballs.

I spent lots of money — about $15. Then, after I had paid for everything, I wanted to buy four more of the little baseballs. The lady said, "They are 25 cents each."

I gave her a dollar. She took the dollar and then said, "But there is tax." Can you imagine? After I spent so much money, she had to ask me for tax on one dollar!

I never keep any change in my pocket, but I reached into my pocket and found a five-dollar bill. In the meantime, the lady put the first dollar I had given her into the register. When she gave me change for the five dollars, she gave me three dollars and some coins.

I said, "I gave you a dollar before."

She said, "Oh no, you didn't give it to me."

She had been holding it while I was getting out my five-dollar bill. In this world there are good people and bad people. She was very, very bad!

RB 858. *Perhaps she thought I was tired*

After buying the candy I started walking again. Near my four-mile mark I saw Atala the great in her car. She was smiling and smiling and inviting me to enter into her car.

I said, "No, no!"

Perhaps she thought I was tired.

RB 859. *Prasad*

After I saw Atala, I kept on walking. At my mile-and-a-half mark I saw Ranjana, Amita and Savita at the St. John's University track. I still had some candies with me, so I gave them the candies. Unfortunately, I had eaten a lot of the candies while I was walking.

RB 860. *The nice man*

When I came to Parsons Boulevard, at my 1,000-metre mark, I was really tired! All of a sudden I heard a very frightening noise in the street. I was on the sidewalk, so I didn't have to worry, but I looked back.

There I saw that a red car had stopped very abruptly. A middle-aged man opened the door and started calling to me,

"Sri Chinmoy, you are so tired! Please come into my car. I will give you a lift. I will be so honoured."

How abruptly he stopped the car! He was ready to have an accident just so he could offer me a ride. I don't think I have ever seen him anywhere before.

So God wanted me to have this experience. After seeing that bad lady in the candy store, I met this nice man.

RB 811. *(p.399)* 2 July 1984
RB 812. *(p.399)* 8 July 1984
RB 813. *(p.399)* 27 July 1984
RB 814. *(p.400)* 31 July 1984
RB 815. *(p.400)* 8 August 1984
RB 816. *(p.400)* 3 September 1984
RB 817. *(p.401)* 19 November 1984
RB 818. *(p.401)* 19 November 1984
RB 819. *(p.401)* 1 February 1985
RB 820. *(p.402)* 7 March 1985
RB 821. *(p.402)* 20 April 1985
RB 822. *(p.402)* 22 April 1985
RB 823. *(p.403)* 27 April 1985
RB 824. *(p.403)* 27 April 1985
RB 825. *(p.403)* 28 April 1985
RB 826. *(p.404)* 28 April 1985
RB 827. *(p.404)* 4 May 1985
RB 828. *(p.404)* 4 May 1985
RB 829. *(p.405)* 4 May 1985
RB 830. *(p.405)* 4 May 1985
RB 831. *(p.405)* 5 May 1985
RB 832. *(p.405)* 5 May 1985
RB 833. *(p.406)* 10 May 1985
RB 834. *(p.406)* 14 May 1985
RB 835. *(p.406)* 15 May 1985
RB 836. *(p.406)* 17 May 1985
RB 837. *(p.407)* 17 May 1985
RB 838. *(p.407)* 18 May 1985
RB 839. *(p.408)* 18 May 1985
RB 840. *(p.408)* 18 May 1985

RUN AND BECOME, BECOME AND RUN

PART 17

RB 861. *You are running too slowly!*

One day when I was in Pondicherry recently, I was running near the Bay of Bengal. A little Tamil boy said to me, "Sir, you will not be allowed to run here tomorrow."

I asked, "Why?"

He said, "Because you are running too slowly!"

I said to him, "All right. I will not come this way tomorrow. Tomorrow I will go to some other place."

Then he said, "No, come here! No matter how slowly you run, come here. I like you."

All this was in Tamil.

RB 862. *Looking for Auroville*

Another day, I started my run at four o'clock in the morning. But even at that hour you can't run more than 400 metres before you start perspiring! And the Pondicherry streets are so uneven and full of holes! Still, I ran fifteen miles — seven and a half out and back.

They had told me that Auroville is about six miles from the Ashram. So I set my timer-beeper at ten minutes. After it rang six times I thought that I should definitely have reached Auroville. From the light in the sky I saw that an hour had gone by, so I knew for certain that I had heard the beeper six times.

Then I started asking people driving bullock carts where Auroville was.

One person said, "Oh, you have already passed it!"

I asked myself, "How can it be? Did I run so fast?"

Another person said, "It is one mile ahead." So I kept running until I reached it.

When I was coming back, three or four dogs attacked me at the same time — out of the blue. I stood there and shouted at them. While I was shouting, the owners of the dogs also started shouting. Then they started laughing at me, and I started shouting at them in Tamil.

RB 863. *The devotee*

One day I was walking along the Bay of Bengal. A young man was running by. When he saw me, all of a sudden he stopped and folded his hands.

I couldn't understand why he would show such devotion to a stranger, since he was a European. Then he started running again.

The following day I was walking in the Ashram taking pictures when I saw this same young man running along the other side of the street. As soon as he saw me, he stood still and folded his hands. Then he came and stood in front of me with folded hands. He said, "I was your disciple once upon a time."

I said, "You were my disciple?"

He said, "I come from Heidelberg. I was your disciple. I even came to New York once to see you."

I said to myself, "O God, he came to New York and still I can't recognise him!"

He told me his name. I asked, "What do you do?"

He said, "I am a taxi driver. Now I have become Sri Aurobindo's disciple. But please tell me what I should do about my spiritual life."

I said, "If you are Sri Aurobindo's disciple, I am not the right person to tell you what to do."

He kept asking me, so finally I said, "Now that you are inspired by the Ashram, you can go back to Heidelberg and do something for the Ashram there."

He said, "But I don't know any seekers there."

I said, "Just try. From one it becomes many." Then I asked, "Do you know Renate?"

He said, "Yes, I know her. She has gotten her Indian name, Minati." I didn't think he would know her Indian name, but somehow he knew it.

Then he said, "I am very grateful to you because I got the inspiration to run from you. You encouraged me to run. In New York I started running."

RB 864. *Lost in London*

One morning in London I started running at 3:30 in the morning. I had no idea what streets I was going on, so I started remembering landmarks: "Here is a light, there is a mailbox, here is a store called Aladdin's Lamp." Like that I got six or seven landmarks to remember.

After running about three and a half miles, I turned around to go back. But I had forgotten two of the landmarks. I had no idea where I was, and I didn't have any money with me. Anyway, where could I get a taxi at that hour? If I could have found a taxi, I could have gone back to the hotel and gotten some money from there. Then I got angry with myself. Why did I have to meditate while running instead of paying more attention to the landmarks?

At that very moment, when I was totally annoyed, one of my inner beings started making fun of me because I thought I was lost. Usually they are terribly afraid of cutting jokes with me. But this inner being said, "Although you have made a mistake, you are off by only half a block."

I believed my inner being. I went just half a block in the direction it showed me, and I saw "Aladdin's Lamp." Then I had only two more landmarks to find. I had been out only an hour or so, but one of the landmarks had disappeared. Perhaps it had blown away; it was such a silly landmark! My inner being told me, "Definitely that is the place. Make a left turn there." Again I believed my inner being, and soon I came to the last landmark, which was a mailbox.

If I could have gone into the park, there would have been no problem. I would have remembered the big building — Kensington Palace. But the park didn't open until 5:30 or 6:00, and the streets were not at all familiar to me. As I passed a bicycle shop, the burglar alarm was ringing and ringing. Even after I had gone at least two blocks more, I was hearing the alarm so loudly! It was about 4:30, and at that hour there were absolutely no policemen out — not even one! Whom to tell? I didn't see any person and perhaps only one car.

RB 865. *The San Juan Marathon*

At our marathon in Puerto Rico the runners had to run three times around the stadium at the start of the course. Our singers had taped running songs that were played over the loudspeaker, and they inspired the runners considerably.

Because of the heat, many people suffered after completing the race. For many it was a very painful experience.

The man who won had a time of around 2:30, and his wife stood first among the women. So husband and wife stood first together, with one hour difference.

The former champion finished in 2:51. I had a long talk with him, and many pictures were taken. He said this was his worst time in ten years. He blamed the heat. Also, the day before he had eaten Kentucky Fried Chicken, and he said that ruined everything. So remember, don't eat chicken before a marathon!

RB 866. *The kiss*

During the awards ceremony after the Puerto Rico marathon, I was so embarrassed! I was giving a prize to a black lady who had placed in the marathon, and she leaned forward to kiss me. I immediately put my hand in front of my forehead. She said, "Pardon, pardon!"

RB 867. *The Puerto Rican Indian*

When I went to the World Masters Games held in Puerto Rico in September, on the registration form I wrote down my nationality as Indian. But the officials cancelled it and instead put Puerto Rican. That is how I became Puerto Rican and held the Puerto Rican flag during the march past.

Every day I got such tremendous joy and inspiration from the Masters Games. I enjoyed them like anything! They really created a Kingdom of Heaven on earth. The inspiration from the Games will last for some time. Now I want to break my own records. My goal is transcendence.

RB 868. *An unfair race*

In one race I saw a 92-year-old man running; he came in third. Quite good! But he came to me after the race and said, "Is it fair? I have to run with 85-year-olds!" Poor man. How could they have another category for runners over 90? So he was only third. He was a nice man. He had been a revolutionary in his youth, and had been in jail for 16 years. They wrote a nice article about him in the San Juan paper.

RB 869. *The brave hurdler*

There were 19 people registered in the over-40 category for hurdles. Out of these, only six actually came and participated. The rest were all injured. On the very first day of events people were practising hurdles. I saw at least two fall down. They seriously injured their knees and they were lying down. Most of them had very bad style. I don't know how they can run like that. For old people like us, the organisers should lower the height of the hurdles.

One of the hurdlers was really brave. From the very first hurdle he was last. When I did hurdles in India I used to think my stride was horrible, but his was definitely worse. Dhananjaya took a very nice picture of him after the third hurdle.

At the fourth hurdle, he fell down and rolled three times. Then he got up and again started running! I could not believe it. He was so brave! I thought he would remain on the ground and they would bring a stretcher.

RB 870. *Autograph hunters*

In the 35–40 category, there was a woman who looked very small, but she was so fast! She stood second or third. After the race she came and stood in front of me. Her boyfriend came, too. They are from Chile. They wanted my autograph on a very small brochure. Dhananjaya was asking them their names. They gave him their names and I signed their brochures.

Then two people came who lived near Cologne. They also took my autograph. I told them I was going to Cologne next March to give a concert. Where is Cologne and where is Puerto Rico?

RB 871. *Begging for a photograph*

One Indian got four gold medals, one silver medal and one bronze medal. He was begging Dhananjaya to take a nice picture of him with all his medals. Then his manager became so jealous that he would not talk to him.

RB 872. *Coming in last*

Poor me! I always come in last, last, last. But how can everybody get a place? Just because some slow people like me also run, some faster runners stand first, second and third. If we did not join, there could be no competition.

Still, I am quite happy. The prayers of the San Francisco disciples worked: I have broken my 100, 200 and 400-metre records. Of course, these are my best times since I came to the West — not my Indian records!

RB 873. *Young but useless*

In the ladies' group some of the participants are a little over-weight and have grey hair. Others look quite thin and smart; in comparison, they look quite young. But when the race starts, sometimes those grey-haired ladies go so fast, and the younger-looking ones, who are thin and light, are useless.

RB 874. *Sometimes it is better to watch*

Twenty minutes before the semi-finals of the 400-metre race, my Filipino friend told me that the officials had allowed more people to join, and that I was definitely qualified to participate. When they announced that everybody was allowed, he said that he was prepared to compete. But since I had not qualified in the heats, I had not come prepared to run. Even if I had been prepared, I would not have been able to compete with those really good runners. Sometimes it is better to watch than to run.

RB 875. *Strong bodies and strong minds*

Some 60-year-olds are more energetic than 35 or 45-year-olds. I saw a very fat 75 or 80-year-old man practising the high jump alone. Each time he was about to jump, I got a heart attack. Twice he fell on the mats. Once his right leg crossed the bar but his left leg was under the bar. I thought that a serious accident would take place. But no, each time after he fell, he stood up and gave me a smile. Such adamantine will he had! The height he was jumping was quite negligible, but he was so happy that he could jump at his age.

For 75 and 80-year-olds to do the pole vault, hurdles and hammer throw is really something! They were not carried away by the weight of the hammer. They were strong, strong people, with strong bodies and strong minds. Everything about them was strong!

RB 876. *Saying nice things*

There were quite a few former Olympians at the Masters Games. Another 10 or 15 per cent were not Olympians but were previously national champions. So the standard was quite high.

One former Olympic hurdler from California said nice things to me at least seven or eight times. He is a poet and he told me that he had read some of my poetry books. Sometimes he would see me three times in the interval of four hours, and each time he would stop and say something nice and smile. What nice people!

RB 877. *Strong ankles*

Mr. Mikio Oda, the Japanese man who visited our Centre in San Juan, failed miserably in the 1920 Olympics. Then, in the following Olympics, he was first. His event was the hop, skip and jump. He was quite short, but he gave all the credit to his ankles. He had strengthened his ankles like anything. He was the Japanese national champion, but he was very, very humble and modest. He told us that he never gives talks about his event or about his Olympic experiences, but he was kind enough to speak at our Centre. He said this was because my simplicity had touched his heart.

RB 878. *Cycling with bullet speed*

The other day I was running on Union Turnpike at my three-and-a-half-mile point when I saw Dhananjaya on his bicycle. How fast he was riding! He was so happy to see me that he called out to me, "Hello, Guru!" But before I could open my mouth, he was gone. With bullet speed he was riding although there were so many cars!

RB 879. *Smart horses*

Last Friday, when I was running on Union Turnpike, I saw a police car pulling a trailer with horses inside. I was amused because for the first time I was seeing a police car pulling horses. The horses were not facing me; they were facing the police car. They were very smart horses.

RB 880. *Shame!*

This evening at a quarter to seven, as I was going to the tennis court, I saw an elderly lady walking a big dog behind Jamaica High School. The dog was on a leash so I was not at all afraid of it.

The lady said to me, "Hi! Good evening."

I said, "Good evening."

She said, "Do you recognise me?"

I couldn't recognise her.

Then she said, "You can't recognise me? I know your name — Sri Chinmoy." She said my name correctly.

I smiled at her and said, "Now tell me what your name is."

She said, "Shame!"

What was I going to tell her? She knew my name, but I didn't know her name. I have never seen her, but she knew me.

RB 881. *Good morning, Sri Chinmoy*

On the way to Flushing Meadow Park today, I was walking towards Main Street. After my 1200-metre mark, a bearded young man in a van saw me as I was waiting for the red light. He had the green light in his favour but he waited, allowing me to cross.

I was looking at him and he was looking at me. Then he said, "Good morning, Sri Chinmoy. It is so nice to see you again."

God knows when I had seen him before!

RB 882. *Ruining somebody's joy*

After being greeted by the man in the van, I made a left turn. At the Kew Motor Inn, two water pipes had broken, and there was a flood, so I had to take a detour. At the one-mile mark also the water was knee-deep. I had to turn one block before that.

But that was not enough adventure for one morning. Before I reached two miles, a Puerto Rican man in a car stopped and said, "Hi! How can I get to the Triboro."

I smiled and said, "I don't know how to get there."

He said, "The hell with you!" and drove away very fast.

Just a mile before that, somebody saw me and was so happy! His morning started with such joy because he saw me. Then a mile later I ruined somebody else's joy.

RB 883. *The first and last time*

Today, the day of the U. N. Peace Run, I walked over 22 miles. From my house I walked to Flushing Meadow Park on a particular course which is five miles. Then I walked two miles on our Flushing Meadow Runners are Smilers course. After that I took a little rest.

Then, for the first and last time, I walked along Queens Boulevard into Manhattan to the U.N. It is very bad to walk that way into Manhattan. There were so many undivine things, but the noise of the cars was the worst. It killed me. Why did I have to listen to so much noise? I took an oath that it would be the last time.

RB 884. *A wrong turn*

There were three cars following me while I was walking on Queens Boulevard. Pranika was following me to give me drinks. In another car, Databir was driving Jason, my masseur. Niriha and Chetana were in the third car, videotaping. In spite of the fact that three cars were following me, at one point I got lost.

Chetana told me I had to cross the 59th Street Bridge and then turn right. But on Queens Boulevard there is a small bridge before the 59th Street Bridge. So after I crossed this bridge I thought I had crossed the 59th Street Bridge. I didn't see any of the three cars following me, so instead of continuing straight, I turned right. Nobody saw that I was going the wrong way. Because of that wrong turn, I started going back towards Jackson Heights. I was totally lost, and there was nobody to give me directions.

RB 885. *Only fools run*

Finally I saw an old man walking. I asked him if this was the right way to get to Manhattan. I had gone astray, but he brought me back to the right path. We became friends.

Then he became very undivine and started criticising everything. He felt the world was very bad, everything was very bad. He was not interested in anything. He was very happy to see that I was walking, because he hated running.

The man said to me, "Only insane people walk in the street. Always walk inside the park where there are very few people."

At one point he said to me, "Are you injured?"

I said, "Yes."

He asked, "How?"

I said, "From running."

He said, "So now you are wise. You are walking."

He did not want me to run anymore. He said, "Only fools run. You and I are wise."

I smiled at him, and just then we saw a young man with a headband, running very fast. When he ran by me, he said, "Hi, Sri! You are here!"

The man said to me, "Your name is Sri?"

I said, "Yes, my name is Sri."

He said, "Who is he?"

I said, "I don't know."

Look at this! Only a minute earlier, the old man had said that only fools run. Then a runner came to greet me.

RB 886. *Two greetings*

The other day I was running near the outdoor flea market on the corner of Parsons Boulevard and Union Turnpike. Some young boys were playing near the street. One of them stopped playing and came running towards me. He folded his hands and called out, "Sri Chinmoy!"

Only two hours before that, in the Queens shopping mall, someone else had stood in front of me and folded his hands when I was there shopping.

RB 887. *How is your tennis going?*

The following day I was walking to the tennis court. As soon as I made the first turn away from my block, a bald man came up and started begging me to let him drive me to the tennis court.

Then, two houses before Niriha's house, a man called me by name and asked, "How is your tennis going?"

RB 888. *An inner story*

A few days ago in Connecticut a boy was running, when someone came up to him and smashed his head with a hammer and stole his wristwatch. The boy was admitted to the hospital in a coma. The doctors gave up hope even before the operation.

But after a day or two he came out of his coma, and the first thing he did was to write down "Sri Chinmoy" and then "Love and Serve."

His mother went to Love and Serve restaurant today and told the disciples how grateful she is to me. She felt that I had done something for her son inwardly. Her son had been to Love and Serve a few times, but he had never seen me.

RB 889. *Interview in an intersection*

Three days ago I was walking, and Ranjana and Durga were following me in the car. I was near my two-and-a-half-mile mark on Main Street — in the middle of a big intersection — when a young man stopped his car abruptly and got out. He said, "O Guru, I am one of your new disciples!"

Master and disciple were in the middle of a big intersection — with cars this side and that side.

I asked, "What is your name?"

He said, "Michael. I am in the Blue Centre." He was so happy to see me; he was jumping with joy.

He said, "Yesterday I was at the tennis court."

The night before, new disciples had been invited to the tennis court.

RB 890. *Unknown disciples*

Five or six years ago I was running in London in front of
Kensington Gardens. A car came so close to me that I got
frightened and jumped onto the sidewalk. A man came out of
the car and said, "We are your disciples."

Then the whole family came out. It was Kaivalya, Bhavani
and their two boys. I did not recognise them, even though they
had already come to New York. Now I know the family so well.

RB 891. *Morning walk*

Today there was a racewalk in Central Park. I started walking
long before the race began. A tall young man, 25 or 26 years old,
saw me twice. The second time he saw me, he came up to me
and asked, "How is it that you are walking faster than I am?"

I said to him, "How is it that you are walking slower than I
am?"

Then he patted me on the shoulder. He looked as if he were
taking a morning walk.

RB 892. *The racewalk*

Luckily some disciples joined the racewalk today. Otherwise,
there would have been only five or six walkers. We contributed
nine walkers. The organisers said, "We are so happy. Today we
have the largest number of participants in this race."

Our people were singing songs very loudly right in front of
the counters. Five or six girls were singing *Aspiration-Sky* and
other songs to inspire the walkers. I thought they would be
scolded by the organisers, but nobody said anything.

RB 893. *Don't bother him!*

When I had walked only two or three hundred metres, one of the scorers said I was not straightening my legs properly. There were two judges — the supreme judge, who would throw people out of the race, and another man. A girl who was the assistant to one of the judges was telling him about me, saying, "He is not walking properly."

The big shot said, "Don't bother him!" He knew I was last. If you are last, why do you have to get a warning?

Later, the judge introduced himself to me. His name was Howard Jacobson. He was the one who organised the race.

RB 894. *Warnings*

Howard was going to this side and that side to check if people were walking properly. He was very serious. While he was moving around, so many articles of clothing he took off: his trousers, jacket, red tie and hat!

Howard would show the walkers a particular card when they were not walking properly. If he showed them a card with a "V" on it, it meant they were out of the race.

Poor Subarata got one or two warnings. She was ahead of me, but she was nowhere near the other walkers. They were up to eight miles and perhaps she was struggling at one or two miles. Still, she got a warning. Then her husband also got a warning.

RB 895. *Soft legs*

At one point Howard told me, "All your people have soft legs."

What he meant was that they were not racewalking properly. They were not straightening their legs.

He said you have to strike always with the heel first. Our people were touching with the toes or the middle of the foot.

RB 896. *Advice from the racewalking expert*

Howard is the great authority in New York on racewalking. He has written a book about it. When I had walked 800 metres, Howard came over to me and said, "You are in pain, I can see. Do you want to walk?"

I said, "Still I will try to walk a little."

After I walked two and a half miles, he came up to me again and grabbed me in a very kind, affectionate way. He said, "Can you do me a big favour? I want to speak to you."

Then he took me off of the course and told me, "When you are in pain, never walk. It is hurting me to watch you."

I said, "I was in pain. That's why I gave up running."

He said, "Now you should give up walking."

I said, "I have read your book. I have learned so much from it."

He said, "Thank you. Do you have a chiropractor?"

I answered, "I have four or five, but they cannot cure me."

"I had the same experience," he said. "But at last I went to a chiropractor who is so good that she cured me. If you go to her, she will cure you. Where is your pain?"

I explained where my pain was and he said, "I had exactly the same thing. Do you know the source? This doctor found the source: right under the shoulder, near the right side of the spine."

Then he sat on the ground and straightened my leg, and then pulled it. I was in such pain! He said, "I had the same pain. You should go to my chiropractor."

After that he said, "I won't allow you to walk anymore. First you have to be cured."

I asked him about breathing. In his book he had mentioned inhaling for two counts and exhaling for two counts. He demonstrated this, going two or three metres from this side to that side. He was breathing in and out: "Hoo! Hoo!"

He asked me, "Can you hear me?"

Then he ran away to give advice to some of the other walkers.

Later I sent Bipin to talk to him and get his chiropractor's name. Her name is Dr. Kirk. I have asked Laurajean to learn from her, and then teach her husband, Avery. Then Avery will treat me.

RB 897. *Starting at the back*

I started the 5-kilometre race in Flushing Meadow Park yesterday evening way at the back. I am always afraid that the other runners will stamp on me when they start. I was just five metres behind Lucy. Only one person was behind me — a lame, fat man. I felt sorry for him.

Then, one by one, I started passing people. My first victim was Mitali. Mitali is a rogue! As soon as she saw me passing, she stopped and started tying her shoelaces.

After one mile and 400 metres I saw a man with an artificial leg ahead of me. Can you imagine! What was I doing so far back?

Then I saw that Varayuvati and Prasannata were ahead of me. I felt that they were going so slowly, but I was going even slower! Eventually I passed them. I also passed quite a few others.

RB 898. *Stuck behind two ladies*

I was running behind two ladies — an old lady and her friend. For a while I got stuck there. First I was behind them. Then I went ahead of them 15 or 20 metres. When the old lady saw I was going ahead of them, she couldn't bear it. She started running side by side with me. Then I started taking long strides. My knee was hurting me, and I said to myself, "Is it worth it?" Then I said, "Yes, it is worth it!"

Finally the old lady gave me a smile and fell back. Near the end I looked behind to see where she was, but I couldn't see her at all.

RB 899. *Go ahead of him!*

As I was finishing the 5-kilometre race, I saw many people near the finish line. In the last 100 metres, an old man was telling an old lady, "Sri Chinmoy is finishing. He is going ahead of you. Go ahead of him!" But I was sprinting and she could not go ahead of me.

After we finished she asked me what our timing was. But how could I tell her her timing when I was ahead of her? I heard 31:07 for myself, but she was 10 or 15 metres behind me.

RB 900. *My secret promise revealed*

After the race a man came up to me and asked, "Sri Chinmoy, how is your leg injury?" He was not a disciple, so how did he know about my leg?

I said, "I am getting better."

Then he said, "I understand that by your birthday you want to complete a thousand miles. How many miles have you completed?"

I said, "Not even 600."

He said, "You must finish it before your birthday!"

He was not a disciple, but he knew all about my secret promise!

RB 901. *Good ones and bad ones*

Last Tuesday I was walking very slowly near Annam Brahma at around a quarter to six, just before I went to run at Runners are Smilers. I saw Databir's car guarding the tennis court. Databir sometimes sleeps in his car, but this time he was not to be found there. His car was empty.

Six or seven boys were behind me. Some were mocking me, and some were showing respect and were happy to see me. Four or five followed me right up to Niriha's house, calling me "Shry." Then children from another block also started shouting "Shry!" They didn't even see me, but when they heard the others call "Shry," they also started saying "Shry! Shry!" It was like one jackal barking and all the other jackals starting to bark in response.

Then, when I came near Niriha's house, three little boys on bicycles rode by. One came up and smiled at me and then went away. He was nice. Another came up to me, laughing and coughing, and then went away. This one was very bad. The third boy followed me right up to my 100-metre mark on 150th Street, near Ranjana's old apartment. He was a young boy, 10 or 12 years old. He came up to me and said, "Shry, Shry, I have a question. Will you please answer it?"

He looked like a nice boy, so I said, "What is your question?"

He said, "Is it really true that you saw God at the age of 12?"

I said, "Yes." Then I asked him, "How old are you?" But he didn't hear my question.

He said, "I am going to tell my friends that you have spoken to me." He was so happy that I had spoken to him. Then he rode away hurriedly. So he was among the good ones.

When I go out alone, all kinds of incidents take place. But when my disciples follow me in a car, people usually do not come near me.

RB 902. *A promise to Radha*

Today I was walking near my house when Radha, the little girl who lives on my block, saw me. Even if she sees me ten times during the day, every time she has to say something to me. This time she said, "Guru, Guru, please wait! You have to give me the book with the story you have written about me!"

I said, "Tomorrow I will give it to you."

She said, "What time tomorrow?"

I said, "Tomorrow, anytime."

She said, "No, please give me a time."

Then I said, "Then come tomorrow at four o'clock."

I totally forgot that tomorrow we will be having our own annual Masters Games, and I will be away all day.

RB 903. *Seeing "Shry"*

While I was walking near Agni Press, two little sisters were eating at the dining table as I was passing by their house. As soon as they saw me, the little one said, "Shry Chinmoy! Mommy, Shry Chinmoy!" They were so excited to see me.

RB 904. *A very cute smile*

The other day at around 4:00 I was coming back from Queens Boulevard. At my one-mile-and-400-metre mark a young man stopped his car and said, "Can you tell me how to get to Roslyn Park?"

Where is Roslyn Park? I smiled at him and said, "I do not know."

He said, "You have a very cute smile."

So he forgave me. Sometimes when you can't give people directions, their mantra is, "Go to hell!"

About three weeks ago I was near Flushing Meadow Park. Always I have problems there. A Puerto Rican man asked me how to get to the Triboro Bridge. When I told him I did not know, he said, "Go to hell!" He also got my smile, but he didn't appreciate it.

RB 905. *Powerful laughter*

I was running near Agni Press when I saw Anupadi. Perhaps she brought me bad luck, because right after I saw her, my hat blew off! Anupadi started laughing, and then some little boys also started laughing. Since everybody was laughing, I also started laughing, very powerfully. When the little boys saw that my laughter was more powerful than theirs, they stopped.

RB 906. *You look so smart!*

Yesterday I was walking to Circus practice. As I was passing my mile-and-a-half point, near the St. John's University tennis courts, all of a sudden I heard my name: "Sri Chinmoy!" A man who was playing on the courts was greeting me through the fence. He had come to pick up his ball and saw me walking by. He said to me, "You look so smart!" I was walking very smartly. I do not know who he was. I couldn't see his face.

RB 861. *(p.423)* 28 March 1982
RB 862. *(p.423)* 28 March 1982
RB 863. *(p.424)* 28 March 1982
RB 864. *(p.425)* 28 March 1982
RB 865. *(p.426)* 5 December 1982
RB 866. *(p.427)* 11 December 1982
RB 867. *(p.427)* 2 October 1983
RB 868. *(p.427)* 2 October 1983
RB 869. *(p.428)* 2 October 1983
RB 870. *(p.428)* 2 October 1983
RB 871. *(p.429)* 2 October 1983
RB 872. *(p.429)* 2 October 1983
RB 873. *(p.429)* 2 October 1983
RB 874. *(p.429)* 2 October 1983
RB 875. *(p.430)* 2 October 1983
RB 876. *(p.430)* 2 October 1983
RB 877. *(p.431)* 2 October 1983
RB 878. *(p.431)* 16 June 1985
RB 879. *(p.431)* 16 June 1985
RB 880. *(p.432)* 17 June 1985
RB 881. *(p.432)* 23 June 1985
RB 882. *(p.433)* 23 June 1985
RB 883. *(p.433)* 23 June 1985
RB 884. *(p.434)* 23 June 1985
RB 885. *(p.434)* 23 June 1985
RB 886. *(p.435)* 23 June 1985
RB 887. *(p.435)* 23 June 1985
RB 888. *(p.436)* 27 June 1985
RB 889. *(p.436)* 27 June 1985
RB 890. *(p.437)* 27 June 1985

RB 891. *(p. 437)* 30 June 1985
RB 892. *(p. 437)* 30 June 1985
RB 893. *(p. 438)* 30 June 1985
RB 894. *(p. 438)* 30 June 1985
RB 895. *(p. 439)* 30 June 1985
RB 896. *(p. 439)* 30 June 1985
RB 897. *(p. 440)* 13 July 1985
RB 898. *(p. 441)* 13 July 1985
RB 899. *(p. 441)* 13 July 1985
RB 900. *(p. 441)* 13 July 1985
RB 901. *(p. 442)* 26 July 1985
RB 902. *(p. 443)* 26 July 1985
RB 903. *(p. 443)* 26 July 1985
RB 904. *(p. 444)* 26 July 1985
RB 905. *(p. 444)* 28 July 1985
RB 906. *(p. 444)* 3 August 1985

RUN AND BECOME, BECOME AND RUN

PART 18

RB 907. *This guy is everything!*

Yesterday, when I was running a race in Australia, two runners went ahead of me. As they were passing me, one of them told the other, "This guy is everything! Turn around!" Both of them turned and looked at me.

Then, right after the race, somebody else came up to me and started asking me about food. He said, "Why do you not allow people to eat meat and fish?" I simply smiled at him.

This second experience happened immediately after the race, when I was so tired and exhausted. That is why I was not in the mood to answer the question.

RB 908. *I bow to thee!*

When I was out walking, just across from Agni Press, about five young boys around twelve or thirteen years old came right up in front of me and stood there with folded hands.

One of them said to me, "O great man, I bow to thee!"

I said to the boy, "I bless you."

The boy was so startled: "What! You bless me!"

I said, "If you are bowing to me, then why should I not bless you!"

Then the boys ran away.

RB 909. *Watching the New York Marathon*

During the New York Marathon, I was crossing the street around the six-mile mark. All of a sudden somebody grabbed me and embraced me.

It was an older gentleman from Hawaii who had run one of our races. He said, "My wife and I are your great admirers.

We ran your 24-hour race, and tomorrow we shall come to your concert at Lincoln Center."

He was wearing all kinds of plants and leaves around himself and a Hawaiian skirt. It was his costume for the New York Marathon.

RB 910. *The university student*

When I was coming back from a walk around three-thirty in the afternoon, I saw a girl with a heavy bag of books on her shoulders. This was near St. John's University.

When she saw me, she jumped with joy. "Sri! Sri!" she screamed.

RB 911. *A Tokyo running adventure*

I came down to the lobby of the Sun Route Hotel in Tokyo around five o'clock in the morning in order to go running. I wanted to run for forty-five minutes or so. I was determined that I would not make any wrong turns or get lost, because I wanted to come back in an hour.

But God wanted me to run longer! I was running and running and, as usual, I totally forgot my landmarks. So I got lost very nicely.

Finally, at six-thirty, I said, "Now I have to make inquiries." So I started asking people where the Sun Route Hotel was. When I said, "Sun Route," they did not understand my English. I had to say, "Sun Routo." But even then nobody could help me.

I said, "Fine, nobody knows where it is!" So I continued my journey.

Then I saw a taxi driver and I asked him for directions. He spoke English well. He said to me, "It is quite far. You get in."

I said, "But I have no money."

He said, "Oh no, you do not have to pay."

I told him, "But I want to run."

"It is quite far," he said again.

I said, "I will enjoy running."

He was so nice. He took a sheet of paper and wrote down the directions. "You go to the station and make a right turn."

So I continued running and came to the station, which was quite far. But instead of making a right turn, I made a left turn and got lost once more. Then I saw a policeman, who showed me which was the right direction.

Finally, I got tired and started walking. God knows where I was. Then I saw Projjwal and Pravaha running along the street. I said, "That means the hotel is very near."

They told me, "Make a left turn and then a right." Then they continued running.

For me, right and left are all the same! So again I got lost. Finally, I took a taxi back to the hotel because I was tired of running. The taxi ride lasted seven minutes. Altogether, for two hours I was out running and walking.

RB 912. *Lost souls in Tokyo*

Today I saw Ila and Nirvik running and running and running. When I went this side, I saw them running. Then, when I went that side, again I saw them running. Later, Nirvik told me that they had tried to take a short cut, but it had not worked.

Like me, they were lost souls in Tokyo!

RB 913. *The short cut*

During our race in Fukuyama, I was running along the one-mile course. I saw Padmasini running about forty metres ahead of me. She was alone.

There was a big stone marking the turn-around point, but she did not go up to the stone. Before reaching it, she just turned around and went back. I thought, "How clever Padmasini is! There is such a big mark at the turn-around point, but she pretends not to see it."

I thought that since nobody was there, she was taking a short cut. But I did not have the heart to say anything. Afterwards, I found out that she had already finished the race and was just doing some more walking and running.

RB 914. *Senani running in Japan*

Four or five times in Japan I saw Senani running. When I see somebody who is older than I am jogging and running, it gives me such joy and inspiration. I can only walk and limp; but he is so tall and his strides are so long. I was admiring him from the bottom of my heart.

When elderly people run or do physical exercise, it inspires the younger generation. In the Sri Aurobindo Ashram, Nolini started running again after turning 65. Some of you people are 28 or 29, but you are acting as if you were ancient.

Those who do physical activity give me immense joy, and those who do not take exercise have to develop a new heart to feel my sadness.

RB 915. *The 300-metre mark*

Always people stop me at the 300-metre mark of our race course in Flushing Meadow Park. Yesterday, before the Runners are Smilers race, somebody stopped me at that mark and said, "Can you tell me how to get to the train station?"

Then today it happened again. I was warming up before the start of our five-mile race. At about my second mile, which was at the 300-metre mark on the course, a runner came up to say hello. "Do you have the time?" he asked.

I said, "I have no watch, so I am not sure. It is around seven-thirty. The race has not started, so you will not miss it."

He said, "But I want to practise."

Then he went to one of the disciples to ask the time. That disciple told him, "It is exactly seven-thirty." Then the runner was reassured and he went to practise. Every time I go to the 300-metre mark, somebody comes and asks me for something. That is the place!

RB 916. *The soul's reality*

When I was meditating early this morning, at exactly a quarter to three Trishakash's soul came to me for very special blessings. So I blessed and blessed his soul, pouring utmost divine light into it. I was very pleased with how much his soul received. When his blessing was over, I blessed other souls.

At 3:15 Alo happened to call. After my conversation with Alo, I took some stretching exercises. Then I went downstairs to attempt to lift 200 pounds. Unfortunately, I only pushed the weight up about four inches; so I still have eight more inches to go! Then I lifted some other weights and did various exercises. How many exercises I took upstairs and downstairs!

Shortly before 5:30, I went out for a run. As soon as I came out of my house, I said to myself, "How I wish Trishakash would come down this weekend so I can tell him the juicy story about this morning's blessing."

As usual, I began running on the edge of the street because the asphalt is softer than the cement sidewalk. When I reached my 300-metre mark on 150th Street, all of a sudden I saw a car come to a stop very close to me.

A very tall, strong man came out of the car. O God, it was Trishakash! What was he doing there in Queens at that hour of the morning!

Another disciple, a young boy, was in the car. He was astonished to see me at that hour. They had both just arrived from Canada.

Trishakash screamed, "O Guru!"

He was standing on one side of the car, and I was standing on the other. I was shouting at him — as if he were deaf — telling him the story about his soul.

When I was looking at him, I was seeing not his body but his soul; his soul was on his face. His face, his eyes, his ear — everything — was all soul!

So you see, there is something called the soul. You have to believe it! The body is unreal, but the soul is so real. The real thing you do not see or value. But when the real thing is pleased with you, then it is something! And when the real thing is displeased with you, at that time everything in the inner world is dislocated.

So today Trishakash's soul was very pleased with him.

He told me, "O Guru, today is my birthday." A few days ago I had known his birthday was coming soon, but this morning, when his soul had come to me, it was not in my mind.

RB 917. *Enjoying the race*

After I finished this morning's five-mile race, I was standing relaxed, drinking some water.

A man came up to me and said, "Here is someone who is really enjoying watching the race!"

A disciple immediately came up and said, "Oh no, he has just finished running."

RB 918. *Morning blessings*

This morning I went out to run at around six o'clock. At that time my disciples were all meditating at home, but I was meditating on the street while running. As usual, my route was along Queens Boulevard. I stopped only once, at the Main Street intersection, and rested a little because my body demanded it. So I surrendered to my body and then started running again.

On the way back, I was in a very high consciousness — in another world. All of a sudden, I saw the soul of one of our newer disciples from the New York Centre. Her soul asked me for special blessings so she could fulfil the inner promises she had made this year. I was very pleased. Immediately I blessed the soul with utmost concern and poured solid determination into the soul.

Then, shortly afterwards, I saw someone on the street who looked like my rabbi, Sanatan. I was on the street and he was on the sidewalk. There was a van and a car in between us, but his vibration I still got.

Around my 400-metre mark on 150th Street, I was dying with exhaustion. Then I saw someone running towards me, but I could not recognise her. When she passed me, immediately I felt the vibration of her soul. Although my eyes could not recognise her, I got a vibration from her soul. It was the same New York disciple whom I had blessed earlier.

So I stopped and screamed at her. She also stopped. I told her, "I just blessed your soul. Go straight and make a left turn to my 900-metre mark. Then stand there and meditate."

Hundreds of things like this happen every day. I do not tell you people how many times your souls come to me for special blessings, affection and love. But your souls come to me only if you are in a good consciousness. If you are in a bad consciousness, your souls know how to sleep!

If you are sincere, if you are determined, then your souls will definitely come to me again and again for extra blessings, affection, concern and determination to fulfil your promises.

RB 919. *British enthusiasm*

At the inauguration of the Sri Chinmoy Peace Mile in London, the weather was mild and excellent. It was very unusual for England. Believe it or not, the sun actually came out! Everybody was so happy that we were blessed by the presence of the sun.

All around the one-mile loop there were beautiful blue flags, quite small, and large pictures of important runners. They started with Robert de Castella's picture, then some English runners, and ended with Sebastian Coe's picture — as if he were finishing first.

There were also twelve stone plaques on the course with the inscription "Sri Chinmoy Peace Mile". There was also a big plaque that told our ideals and philosophy in a nutshell.

Thirty metres away from the starting line there were four golden statues of Lord Buddha in a peace pagoda. Right near the start was the River Thames, which runs along about 800 metres of the course. It was all very beautiful!

I always speak about enthusiasm. This time the British have shown enthusiasm from beginning to end. How cheerfully they worked together! In terms of happiness, enthusiasm, warmth and oneness, this race far surpassed all the races we have ever held, including those in New York. I always say, "Become, and then go beyond." So they have become one with all the good qualities that New York offers in its races, and they have gone far beyond.

The big shots who came were so nice! How kindly and respectfully they talked to me. I was so deeply moved.

RB 920. *On one condition*

The Mayor and the Commissioner of the Park were at the opening ceremony of the London Peace Mile. There were also a Nobel laureate and a Minister on the stage. For the opening they asked me to release peace doves. I said that I would like the Mayor to release them.

The Mayor said he would do so only on one condition: I had to be on the stage beside him. So we stood together, and he released the doves.

RB 921. *The great runners*

So many runners came to the inauguration of our Peace Mile in London. Many were former Olympians — some from 1948, some from 1956. There was also a British Olympian who had stood fourth in the 10,000-metre race in the Los Angeles Olympics in 1984. Now he is training for the next Olympics.

I had a very long talk with him. I said, "You will get another chance in Korea."

He replied, "This time, if I do not get a medal, I will give up." He had seen a video of me lifting 200 pounds and he was very impressed. He said he used to lift 40 pounds, but it was too much for him.

I said, "You do not need to do it."

There was also a runner from Iran who holds eight Asian records. He was very humble and very nice. He was appreciating me like anything, and I also was appreciating him. He feels I have special blessings from Allah. He also gives all credit to Allah for his running success.

Then, an ex-Olympian from the 1948 Olympics came over to introduce himself to me. He said, "I am a friend of Dhrubha Hein's father." This world of ours is so small! Here I was in London and I met a friend of Dhrubha's father.

RB 922. *Running with the children*

The BBC came and interviewed me for a long time at the inauguration ceremony. Then they wanted me to run with the children. So I ran with the children.

From the beginning to the end my place was fixed: last. When I started, I had barely covered 100 metres when the children were at 400 metres. They were so fast!

One lady was wheeling her child in a perambulator. She was ahead of me. Then something happened at around 300 metres, and she fell down. I felt miserable!

Afterwards, the father of the girl who had stood first in the competition begged me to be in a photograph with his daughter. She had defeated me badly, so he was very proud of her. The father was the photographer, and he took a very nice picture.

RB 923. *The Buddha pictures*

The Mayor came up to me because he wanted to have a picture taken with me in front of one particular statue of the Buddha, which he liked very much.

Unfortunately, I did not care for that statue. So after we had taken the picture that he wanted, I asked him to stand in front of another statue for another picture. According to me, this second statue was infinitely better.

At that time his photographer was missing. We had two photographers of our own, but he wanted to have his own photographer. So we had to wait.

The Mayor was shouting: "Where has he gone! Where has he gone!" Finally, his photographer came and took the picture.

RB 924. *The victory*

In the two-mile race in London I walked and ran. Even then I defeated Chameli. I said, "Oh, Chameli! Two months ago you gave me a heart attack during our Christmas vacation. At that time, I tried to defeat her, but she went ahead of me.

RB 925. *Good morning, Mr. Summer!*

This morning I went out shopping to buy doughnuts. I had come back from jogging, so I was still wearing shorts. When the lady selling doughnuts saw my shorts, she said, "Good morning, Mr. Summer!"

Then she asked, "Are you Pakistani?"

I said, "No, I am Indian."

She told me, "Pakistanis always wear shorts."

RB 926. *You have made my day!*

This morning I went running in shorts and a T-shirt. When the old German lady who lives on my street saw me, she said in broken English, "You don't feel cold?"

I said, "No!"

Then she said, "You want me to feel that I am an old lady!" She was wearing a brown coat.

I told her, "No, you are quite young."

She said, "You have made my day!"

She is the lady who has a dog. She always says something funny to me.

RB 927. *The idiot*

Yesterday when I was running, a little girl called me an idiot. She was in a car. She put her hand out of the window and said, "You are an idiot!"

I said, "Thank you, thank you!"

Her mother, who was driving, felt sorry, She said, "Sorry, sorry, Mr. Sri."

Perhaps the little girl saw me as an old man dying of exhaustion, so she was saying, "You are an idiot. Why do you have to run?"

RB 928. *The lousy runner*

Yesterday I ran our dear friend Cahit Yeter's races. The one-mile race I managed, but in the five-mile race that came next, I suffered so much.

Cahit had given me the number '1' for my running number. At about a mile and a half into the five-mile race, a little girl was running near me with her father. He said to the child, "Look, number 1 is running with you."

At the time I was struggling and struggling. The little girl said, "Number 1 is a lousy runner."

The father said, "Don't say that!"

Then she went ahead of me. We were competing with each other.

Finally, what happened! I went ahead of her towards the finish of the race.

Cahit gave me the number '1,' so number one got wonderful appreciation from that little girl.

RB 929. *The impossibility-challenger*

Joe Michaels is really an impossibility-challenger. He is now running our 1,000-mile race after having suffered from so many heart attacks.

Today he was telling me, "You are supplying us with everything. It is a perfect day; everything is perfect!"

I said, "We are all aiming at perfection. That is why this race is happening."

RB 930. *The happiest of runners*

Sometimes Joe Michaels folds his hands when he sees me. But Dan Coffey likes to shake hands with me. He is the happiest of runners, as cheerful as a butterfly.

Dan comes from England, but he acts like an Indian; his soul is all joy. He is like a heavenly angel. His smile, his movements, everything about him is angelic. Each time you see him, it is like seeing a continuously blossoming flower.

Dan is so nice. How many times he has come up to me to shake hands! Sometimes I am in a serious mood, but his smiling face immediately takes away my seriousness.

Alan Fairbrother is all British. He is measured and very strict and disciplined. But he smiled at me quite a few times; he also is very nice.

RB 931. *Nothing will happen*

The other day, when Stu Mittleman was hit by a baseball during our 1,000-mile race, he said to me, "Nothing serious will happen to me."

Stu was telling one of the disciples that he had been seeing my Transcendental Picture on his third eye for hours.

RB 932. *A quick response*

I was running near the 700-metre mark in our 1,000-mile race when, quite unexpectedly, a new soul came up to me. The soul was quite unfamiliar, but I did my part. I blessed the soul and then I made a nice promise to the soul about a matter on the outer plane.

Then, when I came to the 800 metre mark, one of the runners ran by me. After going three or four metres ahead, he turned around and gave me the broadest smile. His soul was on his face; so when he turned around, it was his soul that smiled. It was the same soul that I had seen and blessed at the 700-metre mark. His name is Siggy Bauer.

In just thirty or forty seconds from the time I blessed his soul, his soul was able to convince his mind, and that was his response.

The first time he took prasad, he told someone that he felt he was in Heaven.

RB 933. *Running in agony*

When Sulochana sees me, she smiles. Then I see that she is in absolute agony. So instead of smiling back, I try to make a sorrowful, sad face to sympathise with her.

She suffers so much, but even then she smiles at me. What am I going to do?

RB 934. *Making history*

When Fred Lebow visited our 1,000-mile race, he said we are so efficient. I laughed, because at every second we are having a heart attack!

He told me that we are making history. It is so true; the race is a real victory for America. Where else can they hold this kind of race! And this year it was won by an American.

RB 935. *Don Choi speaks*

Believe it or not, today Don Choi said "Good morning!" to me. I could not believe it.

I promptly said "Good morning" back to him.

Usually he does not say anything while he is running.

RB 936. *Only heart-power succeeds*

In this life there will be a few things that the 1,000-mile runners will never be able to forget. This 1,000-mile race is one of them.

The runners will feel sad today that the race is over and that they are not on the course running. The handlers will feel happy.

We do not have much money-power, but we have heart-power. Other organisations may have so much money and thousands of people. But money-power does not work and man-power does not work. It is with our heart-power that we put on the 1,000-mile race.

RB 937. *A Marathon Team member*

I was running near my one-mile mark by Main Street, wearing a Madal Bal T-shirt. God knows what it says on the back. A man with a little umbrella came up to me and said, "Are you a member of the Sri Chinmoy Marathon Team?"

I said, "Yes."

He said that he had read about the 1,000-mile race in the newspaper. Then he said, "Oh, how I would love to meet Sri Chinmoy!"

Then I said, "I am Sri Chinmoy."

He dropped his umbrella.

RB 938. *Faces worth seeing*

This morning we had our Father's Day Marathon. The faces of two runners were worth seeing. Satyajit's face was by far the best. Then came Saurjya's face. These two are such good friends. Satyajit had such concentration that he looked like he was going to attack somebody.

RB 939. *You should always go first!*

This morning I left my house at quarter to six in the morning to run to Flushing Meadow Park. At an intersection I was standing on the sidewalk waiting for a car to pass. But when the car came up to me, it just stopped.

A young man and a few girls were in the car. The young man said to me, "Good morning, Sri Chinmoy. You should always go first!"

Then he signalled for me to cross in front of him. I smiled at him and he smiled at me. Then I crossed the street.

RB 940. *The drink of water*

The other day I got thirsty while I was out running. So I stopped at a small restaurant and asked for a drink of water. But the man working there said, "No, you have to bring your own cup or a glass." He was so unkind!

So I went somewhere and bought a paper cup. Then the man at the first store gave me some water.

RB 941. *Wisdom dawns*

When I see Snehashila running at our races, sometimes the monkey in me wants to laugh at her style. At every moment she seems to be taking her last agonised breath.

Then wisdom dawns. She is running, whereas I am seated in my chair just watching. I have to succeed in admiring her!

RB 942. *Kindness or duty?*

This afternoon I went out walking. As I was coming back, I saw an older lady mowing her lawn. The lawn was on a small hill that came down to the sidewalk. She must have accidentally pulled out the electric plug to her lawnmower and let go, because suddenly it started rolling down the hill towards the street. The lady was standing there screaming, "Oh! Oh! Oh!"

Nowadays I am unable to run at all, but when I saw the lawnmower rolling towards the street, I came running over to grab it. I was afraid it might hit a car and cause an accident.

The lady was holding her hand on her heart. "Oh, thank you, thank you! You are such a nice man," she said.

But her friend, who was standing next to her on the lawn, said, "Why do you have to thank him? It was his duty!"

RB 943. *I did not have the heart*

Today the picture of me lifting twenty-six runners from our Marathon Team has appeared in New York Newsday. While we were watching the New York Marathon, Ranjana found the newspaper in a candy store.

The owner of the candy store asked me, "Are you from Trinidad or India?"

I said, "I am from India."

He told me that he was from Gujarat.

I said, "Gujarat has produced many eminent persons," and I named one very famous Gujarati.

He asked, "Is he still alive?"

I said, "Unfortunately, he is dead."

"Are you sure?" he asked.

"I am sure," I replied. "His wife is also dead."

He said that he had been in America for fifteen years, so he was not in touch with what was happening in Gujarat. I did not have the heart to tell him that I have been in America for twenty-two years.

RB 944. *Screaming "Sri Chinmoy"*

During the New York Marathon, Ranjana kept screaming "Sri Chinmoy" to get the disciples' attention as they ran by. When she would call the disciples by their own names — like Abarita and others — they did not respond. It seems they had forgotten their own names. But when Ranjana screamed "Sri Chinmoy," they looked over.

One disciple went at least fifty metres past me. Then, when he heard "Sri Chinmoy," he came back fifty metres just to look at me.

RB 945. *The curious photographer*

One photographer heard Ranjana screaming my name so many times that he climbed on top of the wall where she was standing to ask how to spell and pronounce it. Then he asked all about me.

RB 946. *Running in the seventh heaven of delight*

Two times I saw Mohan and Anjali running together. The first time, at three or four miles, they were laughing and laughing. I was screaming at them, but they were in the seventh heaven of delight, and they did not notice me.

After eight or nine miles, the course became very narrow and everybody had to go to one side of the street. At that time I saw them and they also saw me.

RB 947. *Give me five!*

While I was watching the New York City Marathon from the sidewalk, many times I raised my hand when I saw disciples running.

Four or five times other people hit my hand with their hand as they were running by. They hit me so hard!

One or two recognised me, and while touching me said, "Sri Chinmoy!" But some just gave me a slap.

RB 948. *A hug from Jack*

One runner, when he saw me, stopped and hugged me. He said, "You have helped me so much in my life!"

The man was wearing a T-shirt that said, "Jack."

His running partner could not believe what he was doing. He kept asking Jack, "Who is it? Who is it?"

RB 949. *Crossing between the runners*

I was crossing from one side of the street to the other because somebody told me that Lucy and Nilima were coming on the other side. As I was crossing, one of the runners said, "Look at that idiot!"

Afterwards, I became more alert. I would run a little ahead of the people coming and then cross.

RB 950. *Already dead*

At the eight-mile point, a thin, old man came up to me and grabbed my hand. He said, "Sri Chinmoy, Sri Chinmoy, God bless you! Please pray for me." At eight miles he was already feeling dead.

RB 951. *No sympathy*

After the marathon, one runner was making a phone call. I heard everything he said because I was standing behind him, waiting to use the phone. The runner had a bandage around his right quadricep. He was begging his brother to come and pick him up. God knows what the brother said.

Then the man called someone else, whom he called "Honey." But this person also did not want to come.

Then he called "Mum." But Mum also said no. She was the third person to refuse him. Then he said such a nasty word to his mother over the phone.

Afterwards, I saw him cross the street to get the bus. Poor fellow, once he had to cross the street to make the phone calls, and again he had to cross to go to the bus stop.

RB 952. *The phone calls*

I made calls to four different places: Annam Brahma, my house, Ashrita's house and one more place.

The man behind me was so annoyed. Perhaps he thought I was dialing the same number each time.

He said, "What is the matter with you? Why are you dialing again and again?"

First he had to wait for the injured man to call all his relatives. Then he had to wait for me.

RB 953. *Running insults*

While some of the slower runners were still running, the organisers started taking down the equipment.

Many years ago I had that experience when I was running the New York City Marathon. What an insult! The first insult was not enough — that Chameli went ahead of me! Then came the second insult: I saw the police taking down the wooden barricades while I was still running.

RB 954. *Running with Greta Waitz*

John has my heart's deepest appreciation for two reasons. First, he did extremely well; his timing was 2:32. Also, he was running side by side with Greta Waitz for such a long, long time. So many times his Sri Chinmoy Marathon Team T-shirt was clearly visible on television. I was so delighted and excited to see it on TV. It had a very special inner significance.

RB 907. *(p. 451)* 12 September 1984
RB 908. *(p. 451)* 15 August 1985
RB 909. *(p. 451)* 11 November 1985
RB 910. *(p. 452)* 25 November 1985
RB 911. *(p. 452)* 17 December 1985
RB 912. *(p. 453)* 20 December 1985
RB 913. *(p. 454)* 1 January 1986
RB 914. *(p. 454)* 13 January 1986
RB 915. *(p. 455)* 19 January 1986
RB 916. *(p. 455)* 31 January 1986
RB 917. *(p. 457)* 2 March 1986
RB 918. *(p. 457)* 3 March 1986
RB 919. *(p. 458)* 15 March 1986
RB 920. *(p. 459)* 15 March 1986
RB 921. *(p. 459)* 15 March 1986
RB 922. *(p. 460)* 15 March 1986
RB 923. *(p. 461)* 15 March 1986
RB 924. *(p. 461)* 16 March 1986
RB 925. *(p. 461)* 3 April 1986
RB 926. *(p. 462)* 3 April 1986
RB 927. *(p. 462)* 3 April 1986
RB 928. *(p. 462)* 21 April 1986
RB 929. *(p. 463)* 4 May 1986
RB 930. *(p. 463)* 4 May 1986
RB 931. *(p. 464)* 4 May 1986
RB 932. *(p. 464)* 4 May 1986
RB 933. *(p. 465)* 4 May 1986
RB 934. *(p. 465)* 8 May 1986
RB 935. *(p. 465)* 8 May 1986
RB 936. *(p. 465)* 11 May 1986

RB 937. *(p. 466)* 13 May 1986

RB 938. *(p. 466)* 15 June 1986

RB 939. *(p. 466)* 6 July 1986

RB 940. *(p. 467)* 30 July 1986

RB 941. *(p. 467)* 10 August 1986

RB 942. *(p. 467)* 23 October 1986

RB 943. *(p. 468)* 2 November 1986

RB 944. *(p. 468)* 2 November 1986

RB 945. *(p. 469)* 2 November 1986

RB 946. *(p. 469)* 2 November 1986

RB 947. *(p. 469)* 2 November 1986

RB 948. *(p. 470)* 2 November 1986

RB 949. *(p. 470)* 2 November 1986

RB 950. *(p. 470)* 2 November 1986

RB 951. *(p. 470)* 2 November 1986

RB 952. *(p. 471)* 2 November 1986

RB 953. *(p. 471)* 2 November 1986

RB 954. *(p. 472)* 3 November 1986

RUN AND BECOME, BECOME AND RUN

PART 19

RB 955. *Running with joy*

This morning I saw Mitali running. When she saw me, she started screaming with joy.

If all my disciples ran with so much joy, they would all be world champions.

RB 956. *Kokila's juicy story*

This morning I went out for a two-mile walk. At my 250-metre mark, all of a sudden Kokila's soul came to me. I said, "I liked your article about my weightlifting so much. I will print it in a pamphlet. Then I will either sell it for 25 cents or give it away free. If I sell it for 25 cents, I will give you all the money." Then I blessed her soul, and the soul went away.

As I came near Main Street on my way back, I saw someone 200 metres ahead of me. I could not see who it was, but I felt a vibration was coming from Kokila's soul. Then, after I turned onto 150th Street, I saw someone about 300 metres ahead of me, and again I felt Kokila's vibration.

When I reached my 250-metre mark, I saw that Kokila had just turned onto the street where she lives and she was waiting there for me. I said, "Kokila!" She turned away her face and started giggling. She would not look at me.

I said, "I liked your article so much. I will print it in a brochure form." Then I told her I had seen her soul at this very spot just a few minutes ago and had blessed it. Again she started giggling.

What can be a greater juicy story? I blessed her soul on my way out, and I saw her on the physical plane on my way back — at exactly the same spot!

RB 957. *This is the man!*

When I was walking near my house, two little kids saw me. One of them said, "This is the man!" He meant that I was the one who lived in this house.

The other one said, "No!" So they were having an argument.

Then I said, "Good morning, good morning," and smiled. I made them feel that I was the person who lived here.

RB 958. *Appearing again*

Recently when I was at my 1,200-metre mark, I saw Anna running. The following day, I was walking along the same route, looking at the ground. When I came to that spot, I said to myself, "Yesterday I saw Anna here."

Then I lifted up my eyes, and whom did I see? It was Anna again! She was about thirty metres ahead of me.

RB 959. *The early bird*

Another day I saw Namrata running. I said, "O God, Namrata is running so slowly." But after two minutes she was even farther away from me.

Then I saw somebody in front of Namrata. I said, "Somebody is running much faster than Namrata." The person looked like Lucy, but I said, "She usually does not run at this hour. How can it be Lucy?" She was far ahead of me, and she turned down a side street, so I did not see who it was.

Then, when I was coming back, I saw that it was Lucy. I smiled at her and talked to her for a minute. At that hour for Lucy to run!

RB 960. *Like Sona and Kanu*

Two days ago, when I was coming back from my run, I turned my head only to see Kokila sitting on a car, looking at her feet. She would not have seen me at all, but I took the trouble of saying, "Kokila!" Then she jumped up.

As soon as I call her, she turns her head away, like my dogs Sona and Kanu.

RB 961. *The circus clowns*

When I was at my 1200-metre mark, I saw two runners who looked like circus clowns: Pranika and Dipali. They were wearing tights and hats; they reminded me of circus monkeys.

My outfit was just the opposite: a heavy coat and other warm clothes. It was very cold outside.

RB 962. *Out of the blue*

Three days ago, before going out to walk, I saw a poem by Shephali the great about my piano performance. The poem was lying on my white table. I was pleased that she had been so inspired by my piano.

Then, at my 200-metre mark, whom did I see? Shephali! As soon as you think of someone, out of the blue that person appears.

RB 963. *The eavesdropper*

Two or three days ago I was coming back from my one-mile walk. Two old ladies were walking side by side ahead of me. They were going so slowly. Finally, one of them turned around and said, "Why do you have to listen to our conversation?"

They thought I was dying to hear their conversation! I wanted to go past them, but they were blocking my path.

A few moments later they stopped at an intersection to wait for the red light to change. I stopped at least thirty metres away from them because I did not want to be insulted again.

When I was in my own meditative consciousness, at that time I had to get their blessings!

RB 964. *The sick guy*

Today at my 700-metre mark on 150th Street, two Puerto Rican boys drove by in an old red car. Their hands and heads were sticking out of the car. They were not in a good consciousness.

I was limping, so they shouted, "Look at this sick guy!" They were enjoying themselves.

Later, after I had crossed Main Street, again I saw the same car with the same boys. And the same message I got: "Look at this sick guy!"

RB 965. *Desire fulfilled*

Today I was wearing the grey Bill Rodgers running suit that Nemi gave me a year ago. I said, "This is Nemi's uniform. Nemi should see me wearing it."

O God, I had not gone even 600 metres when I saw Nemi driving by in a car. I said, "Look at this! Here I am saying Nemi should see this, and she comes by in the car!"

So God fulfils that kind of desire!

RB 966. *The soul's connection*

Every month Anjali makes me a special cake or pie, which I give out as prasad. But this month I was out of town, so she did not give me any.

Early in the morning, just as I was going out to run, I was thinking, "Just because I was not here, she did not give me prasad."

Then, when I came back, she and Mohan were waiting there in the car. This is called the soul's connection.

RB 967. *Oneness-sacrifice*

I am so proud of Aaron and Anna. Twice I have seen them running together.

See Aaron's oneness-sacrifice! Look at his speed and her speed, but still he runs with his wife.

But their daughter was not with them. I asked, "What is she doing?"

They told me, "She is sleeping!"

RB 968. *The drunk couple*

I was running on Queens Boulevard at five in the morning. After a mile and a half, I saw a young Chinese couple who were very drunk. The poor husband was trying to hold up his wife, but she was fat and he was thin. With such difficulty he was holding her up!

At that hour, at five o'clock in the morning, old people sit at the bus stop reading the newspaper!

RB 969. *Averting a wild goose chase*

Last night I told Pratyaya I would go out running at six-thirty this morning. But then I got inspired to go out at five o'clock, and it was not yet six-thirty when I came back.

I said, "Oh my God, if I do not inform Pratyaya, then she will go out looking for me on the street because she likes to see me run. She will be going on a wild goose chase."

So I phoned her and told her I was already back. She was all ready to go out looking for me, but I stopped her in time.

RB 970. *The young man*

Yesterday as I was walking near my 1 1/2-mile mark, I saw a man who had just bought a New York Times from a street booth. He was about my age.

When he saw me, he said, "Hey, young man! Inside the park a car has been totally smashed. Can you go and see what is wrong?"

I smiled at him. Then he said, "Young man, you cannot go? Then take care, and have a nice day!"

RB 971. *The clean car*

Today, while I was out running I saw a very nice car parked near Flushing Meadow Park. I said to myself, "These people keep their car so clean! I shall have to bless the car."

I put my left hand on the car to bless it. But then, O God, all my fingers became dirty!

From a distance, the car looked so nice.

RB 972. *The handshake*

While I was out walking this morning, I came to an intersection. There was a car coming, so I was going to wait for it to go by. But the driver waved for me to pass first.

As I crossed in front of him, the driver called out, "I know you! You are Sri Chinmoy!"

I smiled and went by. Then he said, "Wait a moment! I want to shake hands with you," and he started coming out of the car.

I said, "Oh no, you do not have to come out of the car." Then I went over to him and put out my hand. He was so surprised that I went to him.

Poor me, I do not know how to shake hands, so I held my hand in a peculiar way. Anyway, he took my hand and shook it. He was of Spanish origin. I think he was a construction worker.

RB 973. *Believing in me*

A few days ago I was at Victory Field walking very slowly by the discus area. A man was there talking to his friend. As I passed by, I heard him say, "I believe in God. God speaks to me. And I believe in Sri Chinmoy!"

First he tells his friend that God speaks to him, and then he says he believes in me. I do not know him or his friend, but still he believes in me. Can you imagine!

RB 974. *Thrown out at Delta*

The Delta Air Lines terminal used to be my favourite place to walk in cold weather. All the workers there liked me. One time the main guard even came up and told me that I would get better exercise if I walked at a difference place in the terminal.

But the assistant manager did not want me to walk there, and he threw me out. He said that I was running, but it was not true.

When I used to go there, I would always see two old ladies who worked in the terminal. Every time they saw me, they would talk to me.

Just the other day one of the ladies saw me. She asked, "Why do you not come anymore?"

I told her, "I am not allowed to come. But now I am going to the USAir terminal. They are very nice to me there."

She was so happy that I had found somewhere to walk.

RB 975. *The friendly USAir manager*

The manager at USAir is so nice! He has put in writing that I can come to walk or run there at any time.

The other day he saw me running, so he came up to me and said, "Sri Chinmoy, I am so happy you are using our airline."

Then I said to him, "I am so grateful to you."

He said, "You are coming every day and blessing us."

I said, "I wish to give you a piece of good news. Recently some students of mine from various parts of the world came to New York on your airline."

The manager answered, "I know! Dr. Agraha Levine gave me the list."

Then I talked to him about other things, including my meetings with President Gorbachev.

RB 976. *The Roberta Flack admirer*

Most of the people who work at the USAir ticket counters near the place where I run are black. An elderly black lady is the supervisor, and there are two other black ladies and one white lady.

The other day I showed them some recent pictures of Sudhahota running with me.

I said, "May I show you something? This is Carl Lewis." They were so happy to see the picture.

Then I was telling them about some of the prominent black figures whom I have met over the years. I mentioned Muhammad Ali and "Big Man" Clarence Clemons, Mokshagun. I also mentioned Eddie Murphy, Narada, Reverend Jackson and my hero, Jesse Owens.

Then I said, "I know Roberta Flack; she is a very close friend of mine." As soon as I said "Roberta Flack," how thrilled the ladies were. You have no idea how much people love Addwitiya!

RB 977. *The look-alikes*

After showing the ladies the picture of Sudhahota and me running together, I went back to my chair about twenty metres away and started drawing birds. After a few minutes, the elderly black lady, the supervisor, came up to me and asked to see the picture again. She had brought with her a young white lady who worked under her.

The young lady said to me, "I want to tell you something, but I am afraid and embarrassed." Then she looked at me and said, "You and Gorbachev look alike." Immediately she put her hands over her face and turned away in embarrassment.

I said, "You are right. He is my friend. I have received many letters from him and just the other day I met him in Washington." She said, "But you two look alike!" Look at this! I was only telling them about my black friends. I had not mentioned Gorbachev at all. But this was her intuition.

RB 978. *The lost birds*

The other day I went to the USAir terminal to run around 6:15 in the morning. After running, I started drawing.

When I finished drawing, I went to a gift shop fifty metres away to buy a T-shirt for one of my disciples that said "Titan" or something like that, since that particular disciple likes this kind of thing.

When I came back to my seat, I saw that my notebooks were missing! One contained 5,000 bird drawings and the other had 3,000 drawings.

I went to the nearest ticket counter and asked the lady there, "Did you see anybody take my notebooks?"

She said, "Perhaps the trash collector took them and threw them away."

I said, "They are so important."

She said, "Ask the trash collector."

Then I went to another counter. The man there was so nice. He said he would page the trash collector. Finally the trash collector came. He was Puerto Rican. Unfortunately, he did not speak much English and the man who was helping me did not speak Spanish. He was calling the Puerto Rican an idiot, while the poor fellow looked so innocent. He definitely was not the one who had taken the notebooks.

Then I went back to my original seat. By then, the elderly black lady who likes me so much had come to her counter, which is near where I sit. I said to her, "You have to help me."

She said, "Of course!"

I told her, "I have lost two notebooks."

Then she started searching for my notebooks here, there and everywhere. Finally, she found my notebooks on somebody else's counter. I was so moved and grateful.

RB 979. *A way of saying thank you*

Later that day I went back to the USAir terminal to give the elderly black lady a big scarf. She knows I am a big shot because she has seen my picture with Sudhahota. But this time I also took the blue book, which mentions all our different activities. I took Govinda as my assistant, along with Sagar and Databir.

When we arrived, the lady who had been so nice to me was busy. From her counter she kept running into the plane and back again. I was wondering when she would be free. When she finally was free, I gave her the scarf.

She said, "Oh, you shouldn't have done it!"

I said, "You were so kind to me. You found something very valuable to me."

Again she said, "But you should not have done it." She was very happy.

I had also brought gifts for the others who had helped me, but I felt miserable because I had not brought anything for the innocent Puerto Rican who got such a scolding. When I was leaving USAir, he happened to walk by, and he raised his broomstick. He did not know that we had found the notebooks. So I said to him, "Gracias, gracias!" Next time I go, I will give him something very nice.

RB 980. *A new kind of candy*

A few days ago, as usual, I went to USAir to run. After I had done my running, I went to my favourite gift store, where I go every day. The man who works there comes from Pakistan. He welcomed me.

I bought a copy of Time magazine and a British newspaper, The Sun. It had an article about somebody who had heard the voice of Jesus Christ.

Every day I buy a piece of candy for whoever drives me. I usually do not eat any myself, but today I wanted to have some. So I said to myself, "Today I must buy something really new."

I saw something new that looked like chocolate with birds on it. It looked very nice. I said, "One for me and one for Maral!"

Then I said to myself, "Yesterday I promised Saroja that the first thing I would eat today would be one of her brownies." She had baked them for her birthday and left one for me in the refrigerator at my house.

I said, "I have to be a sincere person at least one time." So I decided not to eat the candy until after I ate her brownie.

When I got home, I ate Saroja's brownie and then I said, "Now let me have this candy." But when I opened it up, I saw it was not candy at all. It was a bunch of cards with the pictures of basketball players, saying how great the players were.

O God, this was the candy I got for Maral and myself!

RB 981. *The soul of the shoe*

When I was ready to go out walking the day before yesterday, it was quite dark. But I did not turn on the porch light when I put on my shoes. As a result, on my left foot I put a Nike shoe and on my right foot I put something else. Believe it or not, a shoe not only has a sole but also a soul. The soul of one shoe was telling me, "I will hurt you if you wear me." It was addressing me very devotedly.

I asked, "Why?"

The soul said, "Look at your shoes."

When I looked, I saw that I had two different kinds of shoes on. One was already starting to hurt because it was new. The right one was perfect, but the left one was the wrong shoe. So I went back and put on another shoe.

On that day I walked four miles, so definitely the shoe would have hurt me.

RB 982. *My favourite gift shop*

I buy such simple things at the gift shop, but they are so expensive. On that day, the magazine, newspaper and two pieces of candy came to $10.59. When the man said, "$10.59," I said, "Stop, stop! I do not have that much. I have only $10."

The Pakistani man said, "Do not worry. Every day you come."

On another day I was going to buy three ties for Gorbachev. The three ties, plus candy and newspapers had come to a little over $40. I only had $40 with me, so I decided to buy only one tie and the other things. Then it came to only $20.

I said to the Pakistani man, "The other day when I did not have enough money, you did not give me a discount. So I had to return something."

He said, "What could I do? That fat lady Louise, was here." He himself is very fat.

I said, "That lady is so thin!"

He told me, "She calls me fat, so I also call her fat."

Then he said, "You come from India and I come from Pakistan, and we are friends. But if you had been living in India and I had been living in Pakistan, no good!"

I said, "So many times we have had wonderful conversations. Here there is no India or Pakistan. Here in America we are one."

Then I told him, "Tomorrow I am not going to come. I will be in Canada."

He said, "Do not worry about the 59 cents!"

RB 983. *The useless water bottle*

Yesterday I walked four miles. After I had covered two miles, I felt thirsty. I am supposed to drink every two miles; otherwise, I get cramps. In my pocket I was carrying a small water container. It says, "Press and then turn to open." So I pressed and turned once, then twice. Two or three times I tried to open it, but I could not do so. I was in a very high consciousness. After trying to open it three times, I threw it away.

Then I said, "O God, what am I going to do?"

When I go out walking, I usually take a small amount of money with me. Before I left the house, I had said, "Since I am carrying water, what is the use of bringing any money?" But I took a twenty dollar bill anyway.

I found a small store selling donuts and pretzels. I said, "This place should have something for me." I asked for a Snapple and gave the man my twenty dollar bill. He asked me, "Do you have anything smaller'"

I looked at him pitifully. Then he put his hand inside his pocket and brought out a bundle of one, five and ten dollar bills. So we exchanged smiles.

RB 984. *Afraid of the dogs*

Sometimes dogs can frighten me. When I was out walking the other day, a huge dog started walking alongside me.

The owner was about ten metres behind. The owner said, "Do not be afraid; he is very gentle."

He was speaking to me in such a compassionate way, but I was praying for him to come and take the dog. Then the owner went ahead of me and the dog went with him.

RB 985. *The secret prasad*

The other day I walked six miles. After two miles I entered into a small grocery store and bought a Snapple, an Orangina and a corn muffin. They put it all in a paper bag.

When I was near Suradhuni's bakery on my way back, I said to myself, "Let me have some fun with the bakery."

I had eaten a little more than half the muffin. The rest I put in the brown bag, which I left in front of the bakery door. I said, "If Suradhuni or Pratibha come, they will be blessed with my prasad."

I was hoping that they would be in tune with my consciousness and take it. But my hope was not fulfilled. Pratibha came first, and she thought the paper bag with the muffin was left by some vagabond or hooligan. So she threw it away.

Later I called to give them my "blessings." Suradhuni was absolutely innocent, so she escaped my blessings. But Pratibha I scolded to my heart's content!

Once, many years ago, I had left a hat for Lucy on top of the water bottle she had hidden for herself along her running route. I laid the hat out very nicely, so I was hoping she would know I had left it for her.

Afterwards, she said she thought the hat might have come from me. But part of her was afraid it might have been left by some bad person, who might have also drunk from her water.

So she left both the hat and the water.

RB 986. *My surrender is my progress*

I have made tremendous progress in my outer walking. In the past, I used to watch who was going ahead of me. If it was a fat lady, it would make me miserable. If I saw someone going ahead of me whose strides were shorter than the shortest and whose legs were hardly moving, I would be so disheartened.

The day before yesterday a young boy passed me near Thomas Edison High School. I said, "Here is the proof that I have made tremendous progress. Ten years ago I would have tried to compete with him, but now I only surrender."

So my surrender is my progress.

RB 955. *(p. 477)* 8 December 1986
RB 956. *(p. 477)* 18 February 1987
RB 957. *(p. 478)* 18 February 1987
RB 958. *(p. 478)* 28 February 1987
RB 959. *(p. 478)* 28 February 1987
RB 960. *(p. 479)* 28 February 1987
RB 961. *(p. 479)* 28 February 1987
RB 962. *(p. 479)* 28 February 1987
RB 963. *(p. 480)* – 5 March 1987
RB 964. *(p. 480)* 11 August 1987
RB 965. *(p. 480)* 13 August 1987
RB 966. *(p. 481)* 13 August 1987
RB 967. *(p. 481)* 6 September 1987
RB 968. *(p. 481)* 8 September 1987
RB 969. *(p. 482)* 7 September 1987
RB 970. *(p. 482)* 27 November 1988
RB 971. *(p. 482)* 27 November 1988
RB 972. *(p. 483)* 8 September 1992
RB 973. *(p. 483)* September 1992
RB 974. *(p. 483)* 17 November 1993
RB 975. *(p. 484)* 21 November 1993
RB 976. *(p. 485)* 23 November 1993
RB 977. *(p. 485)* 23 November 1993
RB 978. *(p. 486)* 23 November 1993
RB 979. *(p. 487)* 23 November 1993
RB 980. *(p. 488)* 25 November 1995
RB 981. *(p. 488)* 5 April 1995
RB 982. *(p. 489)* 25 November 1993
RB 983. *(p. 490)* 5 April 1995
RB 984. *(p. 491)* 5 April 1995

RB 985. *(p. 491)* 5 April 1995
RB 986. *(p. 492)* 5 April 1995

RUN AND BECOME, BECOME AND RUN

PART 20

Around 7:35 this morning, if not for Divine protection, I would have gone to God! I was jogging very slowly on 150th Street, near my 300-metre mark. I was on the sidewalk, going towards the Grand Central Service Road, when I saw a car approaching from the side street on my right to cross 150th Street. It was coming at about 50 miles per hour. Another car was approaching on 150th Street. It was going towards the 150th Street hill at about 30 miles per hour.

All of a sudden, both cars saw each other and tried to stop. But the car that was coming at 50 miles per hour from the side street lost control of the steering and smashed into a telephone pole less than 10 metres away from me. The car went up onto the sidewalk. It finally stopped when it hit the fire hydrant which was right in front of me.

The whole thing was over in a matter of seconds. If that car had gone a little more to the left, I would definitely have gone to the other world. But at the moment before the car hit the fire hydrant, my whole body was lifted up over a little hedge and a part of the lawn belonging to the house on the corner, and I landed on the first step of that house. You all know the story about the time in India when I jumped from a moving train and landed quite safely far away in a paddyfield. This time there was no jumping on my part. My body was just lifted up and I landed in a standing position on the first step of the house, about five or six metres away.

What a crash there was! You have no idea what a loud noise it made. The sound was so terrifying. But the man who lived in that house did not come out to see what was happening. I was the only witness and I was also almost the victim.

The car that had been travelling on 150th Street collided with the one that hit the fire hydrant, but not seriously, and it stopped about five feet away. It was driven by a gentle, old lady. Her car was slightly damaged but, fortunately, she was not injured.

The old lady got out of her car in an absolutely panicky way and started screaming at the Puerto Rican lady who had been driving the other car, "What made you drive so fast?" Alas, the Puerto Rican lady could not come out of her car. The lower part of her face was covered with blood.

While the accident was taking place, these ladies did not see me standing there. But afterwards, the old lady was looking at me. I would have been another victim, like them. There was broken glass everywhere and parts of the first car had also flown all over the area. The first car was totally smashed.

I prayed in silence for a few moments.

Then I said to myself, "What am I doing here?"

So I started jogging again. I went to my 800-metre mark and started coming back. Usually I never talk to anybody while I am running, but when I came to the accident place I saw Pragati. I asked her, "What happened?"

Pragati said, "O Guru, there was a terrible crash!"

Then I told her the whole story. She was so horrified. When I was talking to her, my physical body was shaking. If not for God's Protection I would have been in Heaven. Then I also saw Anna, Aaron and Sulochana at the place where the accident was.

By that time, quite a large crowd had gathered. You cannot imagine how many people had come in five minutes' time. They were all discussing the accident. I saw an ambulance, but there were no policemen. They took the Puerto Rican lady out of her car and put her in the ambulance. They did not put her on a stretcher, but they carried her into the ambulance. One man was holding her head. Perhaps her neck was broken. There were two or three more people in her car, but they were all right.

Afterwards, I took Databir, Radha and Nilima to see the place where the accident happened. The owner of the house was sweeping up the glass. I could still see pieces of glass near the step where I landed. Another old man said that he has been living there for thirty-five years, and he has been trying to get the city to put a red light on that corner. So many accidents take place there, according to him.

So I always say to meditate for one minute before you drive or before you do anything. The old man who was fighting to have a red light installed said to me, "You should pray to God and thank God that you are still alive."

RB 988. *A fellow runner's greeting*

This evening, at about 5:30, I went out for a run. When I crossed my 800-metre mark, I saw a tall, black girl wearing an absolutely flamboyant outfit. She was running quite fast towards me. She started screaming, "Hi!" When she screamed, "Hi!" to me, I asked myself, "Who is she? She is not one of my disciples, but she is speaking to me as if she knows me quite well." I was guarded because I did not know her at all. Perhaps she was happy to see another runner.

RB 989. *Looking for the bakery*

Last Saturday I ran to my three-mile mark on Union Turnpike. While running, I remembered that Suradhuni's bakery is at the two-mile mark. I was looking and looking for her bakery, but I did not see it.

RB 990. *In memory of that fateful day*

A few days ago, while I was running, I noticed that some flowers had been placed on my 300-metre mark where there was a terrible car accident two weeks ago. I have been praying that the Puerto Rican lady will recover from her injuries, but usually flowers signify that someone has died at that place.

RB 991. *A special prize for Snigdha*

I ran six and a half miles altogether today. Early in the morning, while I was running on 150th Street, I am sure I saw Snigdha. She was behind me on the other side of the street. Then she went ahead of me so fast. Such long strides she was taking! I will give her a special prize. She is injured and cannot run the marathon, but she is very good over short distances. Later I went to watch our marathon in Flushing Meadow Park. There they were playing the tape of me singing *Nayan nehari*. I was admiring my soulful performance.

RB 992. *A pack of cyclists*

I was running on my course near Jones Beach. There were five cyclists in a single line, all perhaps in their thirties, wearing uniforms. One by one, as they passed by me, they said, "Hi, Sri!" Each one said exactly the same thing. I was on my third mile and they were going quite fast when they saw me. How did they recognise me?

RB 993. *Not afraid of Billy*

I went out to run at five o'clock and around five-thirty I was returning home. I saw a middle-aged man with a small dog that looked like Kanu, but it was even smaller than Kanu. The dog was on the sidewalk. I said to myself, "I do not want to be bothered by the dog." So I came down from the sidewalk and entered into the street.

The man said, "Why are you afraid of this puppy?"

I said, "I am not afraid. I was smiling at the dog and I came very near it."

I asked the man, "What is his name?"

He replied, "Billy."

I smiled at Billy and at the owner. Then I continued on my way.

RB 994. *My fellow runner becomes a seeker*

The other day I was telling you that I saw a tall, thin, black girl running on 150th Street early in the morning. Her outfit was very flamboyant. She was very happy to see me. During our Wednesday night meditation at PS 86, I was so surprised and happy to see that this same girl came up to meditate with the seekers.

RB 995. *Saved by the hood*

Yesterday, as soon as I started the very first step of my run, rain had to come and bless me. Before that, there was absolutely no rain. But, as soon as I came out of the front door, my very first step was blessed by rain.

I said, "O God!" Then I felt something very thick and heavy on the neck of my jacket. I said, "That means there is a hood there." So I opened it and found a hood to protect me from the rain. Even that little jacket had something!

RB 996. *The shopkeeper admires my jacket*

After I finished running, I went to buy a new tennis racquet. The shopkeeper said that he wanted my jacket. It was the jacket with the hood. He asked, "Where did you get it from?"

I said, "I do not know. It was a gift." This was the jacket that Nilima gave me.

The man said, "I want to keep it and sell it in my store."

RB 997. *My race walker friend*

While I was watching the New York City Marathon, I saw the race walker Tom Klein twice. I took his picture and I will give him copies of the picture.

RB 998. *Conversations with the runners*

One man came up to me during the New York City Marathon and said, "I run your races. They are the best! I understand that you do not run nowadays because you have injuries and also you have taken up weightlifting. I saw in the newspaper that you have lifted 600 pounds."

I told him that I had done 7,000 pounds, but he thought I was saying 700 pounds.

RB 999. *A U.N. worker recognises me*

Another man came up to me. He works at the United Nations. He asked, "Where are your people? They work at the U.N. and I work at the U.N."

I have never seen this man at our meditations there. He went and told his wife, "This is the meditation teacher." He was looking at me with such admiration.

RB 1000. *Seeing me at different places*

One man came up to me and asked, "How come I see you at different places along the course?"

I told him that I watch the marathon from many different points along the way.

This time I received so much inspiration from the New York City Marathon. I have decided to start practising 30 miles a week. Every Monday I will run 13 miles. Then next year I will run marathons. I will start with the Chico Marathon.

In a marathon, no matter what speed you go, something becomes tired. If you go fast, your legs become tired, and if you go slowly, your mind becomes tired.

RB 1001. *Nemi's former boss*

During the marathon, I saw Sandy, Nemi's former boss, and his wife. Sandy was so happy to see me but when I was taking their picture, the wife deliberately bent down. She did not want to be in the picture.

RB 1002. *I become the marathon photographer*

At the finish line I was taking pictures of disciples' heads and their finishing times. I took a very nice picture of Boiragi and Databir running together.

RB 1003. *My running courses*

Each of my running courses has a name. Vinaya's course is full of hills. Dhanu's course is in Yonkers and Pulak's mother's house is on that course.

Today I ran on Vinaya's course. A battalion of fifteen people followed me, so afterwards we all enjoyed ice cream.

RB 1004. *Gary Fannelli stops to chat*

Gary Fannelli was running among the lead runners in the New York City Marathon. When he saw me at the three-mile mark, I was begging him to continue. But he stayed and talked and talked and talked. He was telling me that he had a vision of me and that he meditates on me. He said that he is so grateful to me. Like this, he went on and on talking. Finally, he continued running, but by that time many runners had gone by.

RB 1005. *The mystery of the red car*

This morning, I was on my way running to our half marathon in Flushing Meadow Park. At my one-mile mark, somebody in a red car was trying to draw my attention. Who was in that red car?

RB 1006. *The brave soldiers*

I am extremely grateful to and extremely proud of those who ran
our half marathon this morning. You are really brave soldiers.
It was so cold! I ran four miles and walked four miles. That was
enough.

Many years ago in Boston I had frostbite. My nose was seriously affected. So I was getting frightened that again I would
have frostbite. You are all really brave!

Ninety-five non-disciples came to run in this weather! I am
so grateful to them.

RB 1007. *Missing one husband*

The other day, Anna and her husband were running together.
Then what happened? I did not see Aaron any more. I thought
that perhaps he had become tired. Later he told me that he had
to go to work.

RB 1008. *Running twice in one day*

On my trip to Australia and New Zealand I walked and ran
every day, except one. Yesterday I ran in Australia. The date was
December 3rd. Then, when we arrived in Los Angeles after so
many hours in the plane, it became the 3rd once more. Again I
ran. So on the 3rd I ran twice.

Tomorrow, no matter what happens, even if it rains or snows,
I will definitely run.

RB 1009. *Niriha's intuition fails*

This morning when I ran two miles and walked two miles, Databir followed me in the car. Then I saw Niriha. I thought that her intuition was working and she would go home and bring her video camera to take pictures. But Niriha never came back.

My second mile timing was 8:30 in spite of one long hill. As soon as I go over five miles, my left leg suffers so much!

RB 1010. *Morning aphorism-meditations*

Today, here in Japan, we started our morning aphorism-meditations. This morning, as I was going out to run, I saw Vijali and then Pratap. Then I got the inspiration to give aphorisms.

When I was returning, I saw Pratap and Vijali once again. When I came back into the hotel lobby, Chetana had joined their company.

RB 1011. *Saved by Ila*

During my run this morning I saw two more soldiers: Ila and Nirvik. Ila saw me first and her soul saved me from imminent death. I was about to make a left turn, but I did not see that one car was coming behind me. I would have crossed in front of the car, but Ila called out to me and saved me.

A little farther on, I saw Pradhan and then I saw Agraha. I ran for twenty minutes and then I came back to the hotel following the same route. On the way back, it was less than eighteen minutes. So, while coming back, I ran faster.

RB 1012. *Little children running*

This morning, when I went running in Jakarta, I saw little children running. They were all about three or four years old. Some of them were wearing sandals, but most of them had no shoes at all.

How I wish my spiritual children would get up early in the morning at 4:30 like these children and run! Savyasachi told me that the main street would be blocked off for joggers and walkers this morning. So many people were out running so early in the morning!

RB 1013. *Pragati runs inside my heart-corridor*

Pragati is one of the very few disciples in the New York area who is so kind to me to give me expressions. Almost every day she gives me ten expressions.

Then, when she sees me early in the morning, running or walking, she puts both her hands over her chest. Her humility is very sincere, her devotion is very sincere. I feel intensity in her humility and intensity in her devotion.

She runs according to her own pace. Most of the time, it is the pace of an Indian bullock cart. Since she runs at the speed of a bullock cart, my compassion-heart can keep pace with her speed and it blesses her for at least 50 or 60 metres. Then I reach my house-destination. I run towards my house-destination and she runs and runs inside my heart-corridor, which is her destination.

RB 1014. *Running in Bukkuttingi*

Around 6:30 in the morning, it is quite light. Before 6:30 I have asked the girls not to run alone. At least two girls, or preferably four or five, should go together. Otherwise, some serious calamity may take place. Today I was very happy to see four or five girls running together. I saw Bigalita and quite a few others.

While I was running, little vans were inviting me. They were literally stopping the vans to ask me to come inside. Perhaps they thought that I was lost.

RB 1015. *Running in nature's beauty*

I was running and walking early in the morning in Yogyakarta. It gave me such joy. Today, for the first time, I walked for one hour. On other days, I walked for forty or fifty minutes. Today it was one hour.

After I crossed over the mile mark, I saw Savita and Ankhi. Then I went a mile and a half and I saw Indu and another girl.

Running here is so beautiful. Farmers are ploughing their paddyfields and nature's beauty is all around. I was walking and walking so happily.

RB 1016. *"Amitabha, Amitabha!"*

As I was walking on the beach this morning, I saw that six or seven Balinese men had gathered to play volleyball. When I walked by, the leader came up to me, folded his hands, and said, "Amitabha, Amitabha!"

I said also, "Amitabha, Amitabha!"

Then, in case I did not understand, the man told me, "Lord Buddha, Lord Buddha."

Soon after that, a Balinese lady saw me and said, "Wise man, wise man."

RB 1017. *Running and shopping at the same time*

When I went out running this morning, I said, "At least there will be nothing open, so I do not have to take money." So I put only 10,000 rupiah in my pocket.

I was walking and meditating. All of a sudden, I saw a little shop there in the sand. When I enquired, the man said that everything was fixed price.

The Balinese man who owned the little shop spoke English. I wanted to buy three or four things. Each time he said that something was a fixed price, I bargained with him. Finally, when I said, "All right, then I will not buy it," he lowered the price. This happened with each item.

So I took 10,000 rupiah with me and I spent it all.

RB 1018. *Meditating on the pier*

While I was walking on the beach this morning, I saw a pier, ending in a circle over the water. So I went out on the pier. I liked it very much. There was water all around and I was meditating.

At one point I was thinking of Niriha. She should have been there to catch it on video. Quite often she has excellent intuition, but this morning it was not working.

RB 1019. *The green light vanishes*

Am I too slow or is it true that the green light does not last as long as the red light? This morning I was on Main Street. I was waiting and waiting for the red light to turn green. As soon as the green light came, I started walking. But before I had crossed half of the road, it started blinking.

RB 1020. *Going out in vain*

This morning I went out, only to come back. It was raining heavily. I wanted to go out running, but I saw that it was useless. Students were wearing raincoats and holding umbrellas. I said, "Let me take exercise indoors today!"

RB 1021. *The vibration of Savitri's soul*

Once Savitri, the leader of our Vancouver Centre, fell down on one of my running courses and her soul went up into a particular tree. Then I put the soul back into the body. This happened on my old course at two miles and 1,300 metres. The mark is in Flushing Meadow Park near the highway, not near the lake. At that point, there are a few trees.

Now, whenever I pass by that place, immediately I feel the vibration and Savitri's soul comes to me. Not even a single time do I pass the tree and the tree does not respond, because the soul left the body and it was in the tree.

Sometimes, when souls leave the body, they do not want to come back. But when there is pressure, the soul does come back. Had Savitri's soul left the body at that time, it would have been an untimely death. That is why I compelled the soul to come back. Then Savitri stayed on earth for at least ten or twelve years more. Her soul got the opportunity to love God more and manifest Him more. So that tree is always so grateful to me.

RB 1022. *Stuck in the snow*

Usually I see quite a few people in the street when I run. This morning I did not even see Sulochana on her famous block. Then I saw Nemi's car. Nemi was probably going to our Runners are Smilers race. Quite a few cars were having problems because of the snow. It was very dangerous. Some buses were stuck at the top of 150th Street. They did not dare to go down 150th Street hill!

RB 1023. *The great runner Calvin Smith*

The great runner Calvin Smith needs no introduction. Today he was at Annam Brahma restaurant for forty-five minutes. Instead of allowing the disciples to ask him a volley of questions, I asked him one question after the other. I was very pleased to see him. He is simplicity incarnate. All his childlike qualities deeply impressed me and the disciples who were present.

Strangely enough, some of his pictures are quite similar to mine when I was younger, and I also felt in him the same type of shyness that I had when I first came to America.

RB 1024. *The jumping dog*

On 150th Street, near my 200-metre mark, there is a big, huge dog. How high he jumps! Once he grabbed my glove and took it. How I wish the fence around his house could be a little higher!

RB 1025. *Calvin Smith's smile*

Our prayer for Calvin Smith was fruitful. He stood third in his race in New York and also that was his best timing for the entire year. Usually he does not do well in just 50 or 60 metres. So God listened to our prayers.

Bhashwar has taken a very nice picture of Calvin Smith. Look at his innocent smile — how simple and childlike it is! His whole face radiates with his simplicity-smile. His smile comes spontaneously.

RB 1026. *Not allowing Savita to defeat me*

In Chico I ran my first marathon. I will never forget my very first attempt. One San Francisco girl instigated me or inspired me to run. During the marathon, I made a gesture and this girl thought I was getting a heart attack. Garima came and said, "O Guru, Guru!"

I said, "I am not getting a heart attack," but they thought I was getting one. As a matter of fact, I enjoyed the marathon.

This year I wanted to do Chico again. My hope and promise never die. They are always immortal in the loving hearts of my spiritual children. There are many, many things I may not be able to perform on the physical plane, as old age is shattering the body's physical capacity. But my spiritual children are still young, physically young, and I do want them to remain spiritually young. Your loving feeling of oneness I most deeply appreciate and admire.

So this year I could not go because my legs are not allowing me to walk or run. But Garima is so kind. She wanted to pay for Savita to run. She bought the ticket plus Savita was ready. I said, "No, I do not want Savita to go. Then she will defeat my timing." I am so clever!

RB 1027. *The Bengali-speaking American*

As I ran past my 700-metre mark, I saw a middle-aged man riding a bicycle. He had his helmet on. He stopped cycling and came up to me and said, in Bengali, "Keman ache?" which means, "How are you?"

I said, "Bhalo, bhalo." I thought that perhaps he knew only one phrase, so I added in English, "Good morning!"

Then, still in Bengali, he said, "Suprabhat," which means good morning in Bengali. He looked like an American. How did he know Bengali?

Then I smiled and went away. This happened on 150th Street and 84th Drive. He lives there. He spoke to me in pure Bengali and I had to tell him good morning in English!

RB 1028. *Am I tired of running?*

When I was running today, an old man came up to me and said, "Are you tired of running? Do not worry, my dog is doing it for you."

At that very moment, when he was saying this, his dog came near me running.

RB 1029. *The Parks Commissioner's strength*

Today was the start of our Ultra Trio Race. How strong the Parks Commissioner was! When Gary Ackerman was shaking my hand, he was trying to show his strength. But the Parks Commissioner with both hands pressed my hands so hard! He was very nice. He is also a runner. He told me that he has run a 10-kilometre race.

RB 1030. *The grateful runner*

Among the non-disciples in the Ultra Trio Race, the best is Tom Klein. Two or three times, he grabbed me and said how grateful he is for this kind of opportunity to run and also to have such excellent organisation. Again and again he has told me. With other runners, we have to please them in millions of ways because quite often they feel they are doing us a big favour. We have to appreciate and adore them because they have come. But Tom Klein was deeply appreciating our activities. This time he has appreciated us and felt our sacrifice the most.

RB 1031. *The Father's Day Marathon*

In our Father's Day Marathon, one Swedish girl was so strong! She was wearing trousers, thicker than the thickest. She was trying to lose weight and not going fast. But she was very, very strong. And it was so hot, so hot!

Of all the runners, Surabhi should get a prize for her style.

RB 1032. *Ready for the lunatic institute*

Yesterday my pace was 18:40 per mile walking. Today it became 17:30 — so I am progressing. And yesterday somebody insulted me very badly. I was struggling and struggling. After my two-mile mark, each stride was agony.

An elderly white man passed by me and said, "Why don't you go to a lunatic institute?" He was very serious. It was not a joke. His voice was full of contempt.

I thanked him.

RB 1033. *My early morning adventure*

Yesterday, early in the morning at 4:35, I left my house to go walking. When I came to my 500-metre mark on 150th Street, I saw a car coming towards me. I was on the sidewalk and the car was on the same side of the street. Someone in the car called out, "Stop, stop!"

I stopped and I saw that two young men were in the car. The driver was drunk. He said to me, "Shrai, Shrai."

The other one was Puerto Rican. He said to me, "Sri Chinmoy, you are a man of wisdom. Please give me some wisdom."

The driver screamed, "No, man, he is a man of light, light, light. Give me light, light." He was screaming very loudly. This drunk one was quite aggressive.

I said to myself, "Oh, what an experience to have at this hour!" Just then a bus came up behind them and chased the car away. So I continued walking. Then, when I came to my 700-metre mark, the same car came back in the other direction, on the other side of the street from me. This time the Puerto Rican was driving. He said, "Sri Chinmoy, is it true that you have lifted such heavy weights?"

I said, "Yes."

He went on, "I see your picture all around." Then he added, "I trust you."

Just at that moment we reached the Grand Central Service Road. I made a left turn and the car made a right turn. I did not see them again.

RB 1034. *The friendly jogger*

When I came to my 1200-metre mark, right near Main Street, one American man was jogging. He was behind me, but he passed me. As he went by, at least six or seven times he said, "Good morning, Sri, Sri, Sri."

Then I said "Good morning" several times.

At Main Street, he made a left turn and I kept going straight.

RB 1035. *The car thieves*

How much can happen in one day! I crossed Main Street and I was coming towards Queens Boulevard. When I came to my 1500-metre mark, I saw a tall, young man and a girl near one of the cars up ahead. All of a sudden, they left that car and went to the next car right in front of that one. Perhaps they were opening the car. Then I started walking a little faster towards them and the girl ran away in the direction of the side road that goes to Union Turnpike. So I suspected something.

When I came near the man, I said, "What are you doing?"

The man repeated, "What am I doing?"

He had something with him, an iron instrument. He immediately put his hand inside his pocket and brought out a cigarette. He said, "Man, can you give me a match?"

I said, "You are planning to break into this car. I am going to bring my students to thrash you."

He said, "No!"

Then I said, "I am going to this house to inform them."

He looked at me and I looked at him. Then he said, "Damn you!" He did not break into the car. He just went away. I saw the number of the plate on the small grey car — LOX 118. When I saw that this fellow had left, I continued walking.

RB 1036. *"Lord Jesus, save me!"*

My walking experiences were not yet over. I continued to my mile and a half mark. I was walking slowly, since I can barely walk. I reached the mark and I was returning the same way. When I had gone another 100 metres, an old, black man with short, grey hair came from behind me and passed me. He was carrying newspapers. He was about thirty metres ahead of me when, all of a sudden, he stopped. When I came near him, he asked, "What is the matter with you? You cannot walk."

I said, "I have a very bad knee injury. That is why I cannot walk." I placed my hand on my right knee.

The old man was very sympathetic. He said, "Let me accompany you." So we started walking together. At first he was walking fast, but when he saw that I was struggling, he slowed down to accompany me. I gave him a smile.

He started saying, "Lord Jesus, save me! Lord Jesus, cure me!" Then he said, "Now say this with me." So I joined him. Nobody was there to hear us.

He started accompanying me at my one mile plus 600-metre mark. At the 300-metre mark, he started chanting out loud. Both of us were saying, "Lord Jesus, save me! Lord Jesus, cure me!" together. When we came to the one mile and 100-metre mark, he turned down the side street going towards Union Turnpike, near the Motor Inn. I thanked him profusely. He was such a simple man, with such faith in Jesus. But Lord Jesus did not listen to my prayer.

So all these things happened in one day.

RB 987. *(p.497)* 6 October 1987
RB 988. *(p.499)* 20 October 1987
RB 989. *(p.499)* 21 October 1987
RB 990. *(p.500)* 21 October 1987
RB 991. *(p.500)* 27 October 1987
RB 992. *(p.500)* 30 October 1987
RB 993. *(p.501)* 30 October 1987
RB 994. *(p.501)* 30 October 1987
RB 995. *(p.501)* 30 October 1987
RB 996. *(p.502)* 30 October 1987
RB 997. *(p.502)* 1 November 1987
RB 998. *(p.502)* 1 November 1987
RB 999. *(p.503)* 1 November 1987
RB 1000. *(p.503)* 1 November 1987
RB 1001. *(p.503)* 1 November 1987
RB 1002. *(p.504)* 1 November 1987
RB 1003. *(p.504)* 2 November 1987
RB 1004. *(p.504)* 2 November 1987
RB 1005. *(p.504)* 22 November 1987
RB 1006. *(p.505)* 22 November 1987
RB 1007. *(p.505)* 22 November 1987
RB 1008. *(p.505)* 4 December 1987
RB 1009. *(p.506)* 6 December 1987
RB 1010. *(p.506)* 18 December 1987
RB 1011. *(p.506)* 18 December 1987
RB 1012. *(p.507)* 27 December 1987
RB 1013. *(p.507)* 31 December 1987
RB 1014. *(p.508)* 2 January 1988
RB 1015. *(p.508)* 9 January 1988
RB 1016. *(p.508)* 20 January 1988

RUN AND BECOME, BECOME AND RUN

PART 21

RB 1037. *An all-German day*

I was walking around Jamaica High School. All of a sudden, out
of the blue, a soul came to me for blessings. I blessed the soul
so happily. Then I said, "Today I am going to invite him to my
place to eat."

Not even three seconds later, a runner came around the corner
near Thomas Edison High School and ran towards me. The
distance was about 200 metres, but I saw immediately that it
was the same person: Aviram.

This is an all-German day. Before that, when I was making a
right turn, I saw a German lady, Rose.

RB 1038. *The soul and the body*

I always say that if someone's soul comes to me, I invariably see
the person a few seconds later. This time it was at least seven
minutes. The incident happened three days ago, early in the
morning.

At least seven minutes before I saw her, Vijaya's soul came
to me and I blessed her. It was at my 1500-metre mark. Then
when I had gone another 800 metres, I saw Vijaya running. I
said, "I never thought she would run at this hour by herself."
On other days, I have seen Nilima with her. But on that day she
was alone.

No matter which way I go, Sulochana is available, either here
or there. Usually, I do not draw attention from people. But in
her case, she runs looking down. So I have to scream and draw
her attention. She is in another world.

RB 1039. *My sympathetic friend*

An elderly man who is very tall often sees me at my 800-metre mark. He is usually accompanied by his small dog. Whenever this gentleman sees me, he has to greet me. A few days ago, he said with such sympathy, "When are you going to start running again?"

I was walking, but for years and years he has seen me running. He was not joking. He feels genuinely sad that I cannot run. So I gave him a very grateful smile.

RB 1040. *A warning from Dipali's soul*

I was at my 1400-metre mark. Dipali's soul came to me. Her soul was telling me, warning me, that she has to reduce her mileage and also be more careful with regard to her running — careful is the right word.

I said, "All right, I shall tell her." My eyes were half-closed. Then, three or four seconds later, I saw one girl with folded hands. I was on the pavement walking and she was in the street. I said, "Who is this?" I opened my eyes wide and I saw Dipali. First I saw Dipali and then I saw Snigdha. Snigdha and I greeted each other.

Every day I take an oath that I will not look at anybody; I will only remain in my highest meditation. Then, as soon as I go out, I see someone this side and someone else that side. They are expecting my greetings.

RB 1041. *Hawaii anecdotes*

At 1:30 a.m. on the first day in Hawaii, I went out walking in Honolulu. A young man came up to me. He said, "Sir, Sir, what are you doing at this hour?" He wanted to know why I was moving around at this ungodly hour. I was meditating, so I just smiled at him. Then he continued, "It is not safe." Again I smiled at him. Once more he said, "This is not safe. Please!" He was worried about me.

*

The second day I went out a little after two o'clock in the morning. I was walking and meditating as usual. Ahead of me I saw a tall man who was drinking. I passed by him and did not pay any attention to him. Then he came chasing me. He said, "Why are you afraid of me? Why are you running away? I am only drinking Diet Coke." Then he showed me his paper cup. He said, "You do not have to be afraid of me. I am not drinking liquor. I am taking Diet Coke."

I was walking fast, but he thought that I was afraid of him. This is how people catch me when I go out early in the morning.

*

The third day I went out at 1:30 a.m. One man came up to me and said, "Can you tell me the time?"

I replied, "It is a quarter to two." He went on his way and then, a few minutes later, he came back.

"How do you know?" he asked.

I said, "I know that I came out of my apartment at 1:30. Now I have walked for fifteen minutes."

Then the man took his watch out of his pocket and checked the time. He said, "Right!"

If he had a watch, why did he challenge me? But he did not want to take the trouble to look at it.

*

Every morning some experience I get when I walk. For three mornings I saw Vijali's soul eight or ten metres ahead of me. Three days her soul was there facing me and each day I blessed her. Many years ago, when I used to walk along the canal at four or five o'clock in the morning, she used to be there.

Yesterday I went out at 12:45 a.m. I was having a very high meditation while I was walking. All of a sudden I saw the soul of an ex-disciple. The soul was asking for a blessing. I blessed the soul and went on my way. After some time an idea came to me: perhaps it is this person's birthday. Later that day I asked somebody to check and it was true. Then I discovered that it was also Rijuta's birthday. Rijuta's soul did not come at that time. After four or five hours, her soul came.

RB 1042. *A near collision*

This morning at 7:35 I went out for a walk. When I was coming back, I was reaching my 1200-metre mark when I saw one girl running towards me very fast. She was running at least a seven-minute pace and taking long strides. I saw that we were almost going to have a collision. So I stopped and waved at her. Then I moved my left shoulder away from her path. My left shoulder escaped by an inch or two. She acted as if she did not see me, but I knew that she was only showing off. She ran on and did not stop.

When I was on 150th Street, I saw another disciple on my side of the pavement coming towards me. She immediately stopped and entered into the street with folded hands to allow me to pass.

Then, when I was very near my house, I saw a third one. It was Dipali. She stopped and put her hands on her heart chakra.

RB 1043. *Pragati catches my hat*

Yesterday I was walking and it was so hot. I took off my hat as I was walking. As soon as Pragati saw me, she ran into the street and I threw my hat to her. I thought she would miss it and have to pick it up, but she was able to catch it.

RB 1044. *Taking pictures at the marathon*

At the New York City Marathon I was taking pictures of the disciples as they went by. Everybody was deaf, specially at the finish line. Sometimes I shouted their names three times, but they did not hear me.

After fifteen miles, Saroja and Sulochana were crying and dying. Then they got a second wind. Some people become miserable at the end of each mile, but Saroja and Sulochana were becoming happy.

RB 1045. *At the finish line*

After a marathon, almost everybody is happy. Only those who were fighting against time are miserable. But thousands and thousands of runners come only to finish. They come only to complete the race.

One fellow was dancing and jumping at the finish line. Another man was running back and forth at the end.

Sujata's strides are so short, but she finished in 4:30 or so. Whoever thought that seven or eight of my Japanese disciples would come to run the New York Marathon?

RB 1046. *Offering prasad to the runners*

I wanted to buy Tootsie Rolls to give to the runners, so Ranjana went into two or three stores and found them. She also bought doughnuts and so many disciples took from her a half or a quarter.

RB 1047. *My vision*

In the New York Marathon, the first mile is horrible for everybody. Then, from the second mile, the lead runners go really fast.

This year Steve Jones ran 2:08:23, but Salazar's record is still 13 seconds better.

Somebody has to come from Africa and break the record. Under two hours — I envision it. Somebody will run under two hours.

RB 1048. *Determined to do well*

Gary Fanelli was running very seriously in the second batch of lead runners. This time he was not joking or fooling around. I called his name, "Gary, Gary!" but he did not hear me.

In Harlem the spectators were telling the runners, "Everybody is a winner."

RB 1049. *Insults from the wives*

When I ran the New York Marathon some years ago, I noticed that in the beginning, on the hill, the runners enjoy talking. All ridiculous things they tell each other. But most of them have the same story: their wives are laughing at them or their wives have predicted that they will not be able to finish the race.

RB 1050. *An enthusiastic spectator*

I do not have speed, I do not have stamina, I do not have the determination to run, but I do have the eagerness to watch the marathon. I like it so much. Everybody is like a beautiful flower. While they are crying, we smile. While they are smiling, we cry. If somebody is crying, in order to cheer the person, we smile. If they are smiling, we say, "We know that you are crying inside." We identify with their smiles and with their tears.

RB 1051. *Life is the same*

The other day I went out to run at a quarter to four in the morning. I could not believe so many shops were open at that hour here in Bangkok.

Everywhere life is the same. On 150th Street there is construction and here it is the same story. Wherever I tried to run, there was construction.

RB 1052. *A change of mind*

This morning, I went out to run. As I was leaving the hotel, Adhiratha's soul came to me. Then just as I turned the corner, I immediately saw him standing there, looking at his watch. He was all ready to start running. He did not see me.

For some reason I changed my mind and went back into the hotel. Adhiratha also changed his mind and went back into the hotel. When he entered the lobby, at that time he saw me.

RB 1053. *Ready for the ambulance*

This morning, when I was out running, I heard the siren of an ambulance. It was coming nearer and nearer. I decided to go up onto the footpath. An old Chinese man was nearby. I have seen him many times. He said to me, "I thought the ambulance was for you!"

"I am ready," I told him.

He was joking about the way I was running. He used to see me running before I injured my leg. Now I go very slowly.

RB 1054. *Experiences at the gym*

Let me tell you an amusing story with regard to my age. Perhaps most of you know that I go to a gym to take exercise, specially for my running, my sprinting. This gym has a smaller than the smallest running track. If you complete four corners, then it becomes one hundred metres.

Anyway, I run that course thirty-two times, so it makes practically two miles. The track is on the third floor and on the second floor there are all kinds of machines, heavy-duty machines, where people can take exercise.

This morning I did my running to my satisfaction and then I came down to the second floor. A middle-aged woman came up to me and said, "Sir, Sir, is it true that you are eighty-one years old?" I think from the second floor she had seen me running.

I said, "I am only fifty-eight."

"But these people are saying that you are eighty-one," she replied. "Even then, you look so smart, so trim. You look very strong. Please tell me what you eat."

I said, "I am a vegetarian, a strict vegetarian."

"But what do you eat?"

"I take tomato, potato and so on," I explained.

"That is what you eat?" she said. She simply could not believe it.

Databir had taken me to the gym and I was trying to draw his attention, but he was in trance. He has two eyes and one pair of glasses, so four eyes plus his third eye makes five and still he could not see me.

Finally, he came up to me to tell me that he was going to the car to get a press release to show one man who was taking exercise. He said, "I am going to get material for him. I spoke with him a few days ago. He is so nice. He had the same tennis coach as you did."

This world is so small! This man's tennis coach was Ronnie, the same one who was my tennis coach. Two weeks ago, the man saw me running and he could not believe that I had so much speed and energy.

When Databir came back, I said to him, "Before you show it to that man, I want you to show it to this lady." So Databir showed the lady the press release and also my picture. She was very pleased. She said to Databir, "I see an aura on his skin." She has started meditating, so one day perhaps she will come to meditate with us.

RB 1055. *Databir's super-trance*

Databir is wonderful! He was absolutely sure that the man he saw working out was the same man with whom we spoke a few days ago, whose tennis coach is Ronnie, my coach. So he went to him with the press release and other material. But the man could not recognise Databir. He said, "I am not the right person."

Then Databir was insisting that he was the person! Can you imagine? The funniest thing was that that man knew nothing about us.

I said, "Let me go and see him for myself." I walked about twenty metres so that I could see the man properly and I discovered that it was a totally different person! His hair was different, the structure of the face, everything was different.

Today Databir was really in trance, super-trance!

RB 1056. *Embarrassed by his tears*

About a week ago, I was running along the track at Harbor View Gym. Another gentleman was also running. He was twice as big as me. He was running very slowly, but he saw something in me. When he stopped running, he started talking and talking to Databir. He told Databir that he deals with retarded children. He feels he is taking their karma. A while ago he had a mental breakdown. Now he has just started taking a meditation course.

Databir said to him, "Here is a meditation teacher." Then Databir invited him to come that evening to our Wednesday night meditation. He came and brought his wife and I gave him a flower. Then he came to our New Year's Meditation in Manhattan. As soon as he heard me playing my esraj, something happened. He started crying and crying and crying. He was so embarrassed. Right after the esraj, he left. His wife wanted to stay, but he said, "No, I am embarrassed. How can I cry in front of so many people?"

Look at his interpretation! His soul came to the fore and was offering gratitude to the Supreme because he was getting such light, such peace, from Above. But he thought it was unmanly to cry, so he disappeared.

Today he was here at the gym. He said to me, "Sir, how are you?" I smiled at him. Then, for forty-five minutes, he and Databir enjoyed a marathon conversation. I told Databir to tell him that his soul was deeply moved and that is why he cried.

RB 1057. *Advice from a Mr. Universe*

There is an instructor at the gym who happens to be a Mr. Universe. He is very, very kind to me. Alas, now he has come to realise that I am the worst possible student. On his own, for a few days, he tried to come to me when I was working out, telling me that the exercises I was taking were all wrong, wrong, wrong. My position was wrong, my form was wrong and so forth. He wanted to correct my exercises on his own. He is such a nice man, but I am a hopeless case! I continued doing everything in my own way. He greets me now, but he does not come and advise me when I am taking exercise.

One day Databir showed him the picture where I lifted up the police officer who won the bodybuilding contest "New York's Finest." So he said to me, "We bodybuilders work so hard, so hard, to develop strength and muscle. But you do not work hard."

I said, "I do work hard."

"No, no," he answered. "You do not stay here, inside the body. You stay a few inches above your head. We stay inside the body, but you stay right over it, a few inches above. That is why it is possible for you to lift such heavy weights. Otherwise, if you lived inside the body, you would not be able to do this kind of thing."

RB 1058. *A good vibration in the gym*

One day Rupantar took me to the gym. Somehow the owner of the place had come to learn that I am well-known. He came to greet me and then he talked and talked with Rupantar. Rupantar gave him our philosophy. The gym has a bulletin about all their activities, so he wanted my resume. They are going to put it in their magazine.

I must say, the staff are very, very nice there. I have been to quite a few gyms, specially in New York. Sometimes it is very difficult for me to breathe when I go inside. As soon as I get there, I suffer so much from the atmosphere, the vibration. But here the place is neat and clean, and the people are very good. I am very happy to be a member of that gymnasium. It is Harbor View.

RB 1059. *"God is always with you"*

This morning I was walking in front of my house. A police car stopped right at the corner and honked. I said to myself, "I am doing nothing wrong; I am only walking."

When I came near the car, I stopped. The policeman said to me, "Good morning, good morning!"

I responded, "Good morning, good morning!" Then he opened his door and came out of the car. He said to me, "Sri Chinmoy, God is always with you."

I said, "So is He always with you as well!"

He said, "No, no. God is always with you." He was not saying "God bless you," or anything, but "God is always with you."

Then he said, "You have made my day," and he went back into his car. This is a policeman whom I have never met before. He was so nice.

RB 1060. *An announcement*

I have a piece of good news: today Sri Chinmoy jogged a little. Fourteen years ago today, in Connecticut, I did my best performance for two miles: 13:42. Fifteen years ago I did my best seven-mile performance: 51:18. So, for me, the past is not dust; the past is gold, gold, gold!

RB 1061. *The alert driver*

Near my house, I saw a boy coming along the street towards me on roller-skates. He was moving very restlessly. He was going forwards, but all of a sudden, what happened? He started skating backwards.

There was a car just three metres behind him. The driver was a Chinese lady. What could she do? There was only a three-metre gap, but she stopped her car immediately. How alert she was! Otherwise, this boy would have gone to God.

I was about twenty metres away, so I saw everything. If anything had happened to the boy, it would not have been the driver's fault at all. Fortunately, she stopped in time. This is how careless children can be.

RB 1062. *Pure joy*

For the last few days I have been running. After a long time I have started again. It is pure joy! Today Databir and the guards gave me a cake to celebrate the start of my long-distance running in June 1, 1978. When I think of my long-distance running, I remember only cramps, cramps, cramps. When you have cramps, your life-breath disappears. When I run a short distance, I do not have a problem with cramps.

RB 1063. *My progress report*

I would like to show you a video of my recent running performances. This is specially for those who belong to my Inspiration Club and who encourage me every week to continue. This is my progress report. I may not run fast, but I am very devotedly and diligently practising. I practise whenever my legs permit me. I have done 400 metres in 1:34.53. When I come back from the Christmas holiday, I hope I can make some progress.

RB 1064. *Turned away at the door*

Today I was thinking of one unfortunate experience I had in Fort Lauderdale many years ago. One night I had run quite a few miles and I became very hungry. Luckily I had money with me, so I stopped at a restaurant. Because I was wearing running shorts, they would not allow me to enter. So I decided to try another restaurant. Again, the same story: my clothing was not suitable. They told me to go home and change. Then I tried another restaurant and again I was turned away. I was so hungry. By then it was only a matter of half a mile to go home and change and come back, but I did not do it. My pride was hurt.

RB 1065. *Taking my guards with me*

This morning I took my tennis court guards to guard me while I was running. I was walking and running. The Mother Earth felt how happy I was! I saw one elderly gentleman running. He was wearing a headband. My guards were watching me with such compassion and he was observing everything. He came up to me and said, "It is so nice of you to take care of so many young men!"

RB 1066. *Pulak's pictures*

This morning I ran three miles. Pulak drove me to the course. The scenery was very good and the place was very beautiful. I like that course so much, but today there were so many people playing this game and that game.

Pulak took millions of pictures. He would go ahead of me and take pictures. Sometimes he would be down on the ground as I ran past. But then nothing came out and I felt very sorry for him.

RB 1067. *Unexpected applause*

Today when I was running, one non-disciple saw me and he started clapping and clapping. He is older than I am, but I do not know who he is. Perhaps he also does not know who I am. Yesterday I saw many disciples, but today I saw only this older man.

RB 1068. *Followed by fans*

Today, when I came back from the UN, I went for a walk. On the way, I saw two young girls who were very tall, very thin. They were about to cross the road in front of me, but then they felt shy and they waited for me to go by.

As I was passing them, one of them said, "You are very strong. Is your name Sri Chinmoy?"

I said, "My name is Sri Chinmoy."

Then they asked, "Where do you live? Do you live around here?"

I replied, "I live near 150th Street."

Both of them were very, very nice. Instead of walking to their destination, they followed me for some time, staying about thirty or forty metres behind me. Then they came very close and said, "Bye!"

RB 1069. *Abedan's cycling speed*

After seeing those two girls, I continued walking and walking. As I was returning, I saw somebody cycling very fast. I said, "Who is cycling so fast?"

All of a sudden, he made a left turn and I saw that it was our great Abedan. Then he bowed to me. He was wearing a yellow helmet and a yellow uniform. At that hour our Abedan was riding a bicycle very fast.

This evening we watched an Olympic cycle race. Abedan should have joined! One cyclist was going ahead of all the others. I felt sure he was going to win. Then, at the last moment, somebody came and overtook him.

Cycling is great fun if you watch it, but not if you cycle! If you cycle, you get cramps. Then you cry! I will never forget how many times I got cramps when we joined the 24-Hour Bike Race in Central Park. I still remember my worst cramp. The pain was excruciating. The muscles were all coming out of the body. Arpan came to me as my saviour. He saved my life by massaging me.

I also had the same experience when I used to run marathons. I have long forgotten that I did twenty-two marathons, but I will never, never forget the cramps that I got. The cramps during my marathons will remain immortal, but the marathons themselves I have forgotten. How much I suffered!

RB 1070. *The runaway car*

Yesterday in the morning, when I went walking, I saw Sumadhur crossing the street. He was going towards Agni Press. Then I walked a few blocks to Hoover Avenue. Yesterday I did not even know the name of the street, but today I looked for the street sign.

I was just a few metres from the end of the street. I did not cross the street; I was on the pavement, walking nicely. In front of me, a car was coming towards Parsons Boulevard. When it was about thirty metres from me, all of a sudden, both tyres on the right side gave way. The driver was panicking because he could not control his steering wheel. He was unable to drive the car straight and the car went up onto the pavement. There it did not stop. It was coming directly towards me. O God, what was I going to do?

I was so lucky that I was almost at the end of the street. Immediately I turned left and the car did not turn right. It went straight. After forty or fifty metres, the car stopped. The driver got out of the car and he was shaking all over.

What an experience I had yesterday! They say the sidewalk is safe, but no-where is safe. At any place, something can happen. Yesterday's incident happened in a matter of a few seconds.

RB 1071. *My smile saves me*

Yesterday afternoon I went for another walk. I saw an elderly lady. She looked very, very nice and dignified. She said to me, "Good afternoon, Sir!"

Poor me, nothing came out of my mouth because I was in my high meditation. I tried to say, "Good afternoon," but nothing came out. I only smiled. Luckily, my smile saves me.

RB 1072. *The irate pedestrian*

This morning one lady got a little bit mad at me. She wanted to know the time, but instead of asking me, she was just pointing to her left wrist. I did not understand what she wanted. She was just pointing and pointing. What could I do? Then she got annoyed. I did not know why she was angry. Then afterwards, when I walked away, I realised what she meant. She did not have a watch. I also was not wearing a watch.

This happened when I came to the Grand Central Parkway Service Road and crossed Parsons Boulevard. She was standing on the corner waiting for a car or something. She was pointing to her wrist, but I did not understand what she was asking. I have such funny, funny experiences when I go out.

RB 1073. *Encouragement from a runner*

This morning I walked three miles. The temperature was only 38 degrees! I made a right turn on the Grand Central Service Road and went a mile and a half. When I had come back about 600 metres, I saw a tall, thin, black runner taking very long strides. She said to me, "Okay, Sri Chinmoy!"

She was offering me her genuine encouragement.

RB 1074. *"Salaam, God-man"*

Then I walked another 400 metres, and a small, red car stopped. I was on the pavement, so there was no problem. A tall, stout man came out of the back seat of the car and said to me very respectfully, "Salaam, God-man."

Immediately I knew that he was Muslim. A young man was driving and the stout man was sitting in the back. I smiled at him and he entered into the car again and they drove away.

RB 1075. *Blessing disciples*

Finally, I reached 150th Street. There I saw Carolina on the
other side. This is the third day that I have seen her this week.

At my 200-metre mark I saw Chetana standing on the other
side in a yellow jacket. She was standing there for her birthday,
so I looked at her. I was in a very, very, very high consciousness,
so I was not able to say hello to her. Inwardly I blessed her
profusely.

A few days ago, I saw Nilima on 150th Street also. She has
her own peculiar style.

RB 1076. *Seeking a promotion*

Yesterday, on my sister's birthday, I started jogging again after
one month's vacation. Today also I was able to jog. Soon I am
hoping to get a promotion and start sprinting. This is all due to
the prayers of my disciples.

RB 1077. *Greetings from Coach Hurt*

I was walking at St. John's University track. My friend Coach
Hurt saw me and said, "Sri, Sri!" Again he said, "Sri, Sri!" Then
he added, "You look fit!"

He was ten metres away from me. Three times he said hello
to me. He was coaching two groups of girl sprinters. How fast
they were running! He had a long bamboo stick and he was
using it to illustrate what exercise they should do.

Then I walked on the track for about two miles.

RB 1078. *Appreciating the marathon runners*

All those who ran today's New York City Marathon, please come and announce your times, from first to last. Only for the first person we will clap, and for the last person we will clap — the first person for their speed and the last person for their patience. In between, we will clap in silence; otherwise, it will take a very long time.

RB 1079. *The message of the t-shirt*

During today's marathon, Pulak wanted to give up. His T-shirt said, "Never give up!" An Indian man who was also running saw his shirt and advised him, "Do not give up!" Then he and Pulak finished the race together, talking philosophy for hours and hours.

RB 1080. *"You carry me through"*

During the marathon, I was cheering the runners at different places on the course. One man came up to me, grabbed my hand and said, "Sri Chinmoy, every time I run a long distance, I think of you and you carry me through!"

And he was not a disciple.

RB 1081. *Flute-inspiration*

During the marathon, when I was at our 19-mile aid station, I was deeply admiring Upasana. How long she was playing the flute — and playing such high notes! She was going on and going on, playing so beautifully and powerfully.

Two middle-aged men who were running the marathon were so excited and delighted with her flute playing. They stopped running and started dancing in front of her instead!

RB 1082. *My gratitude and pride*

Those who have run the marathon deserve my most sincere appreciation, admiration and adoration. This sincere appreciation, admiration and adoration I also offer to those who helped in any capacity and specially, most specially, to Sanyogita the Great and, needless to say, to Rupantar, Bipin, Sahishnu, Sandhani and others. If I have forgotten any name, please forgive me. Rupantar and his assistants in the marathon deserve my most sincere, most sincere gratitude and gratitude and pride and pride.

Our Marathon Team has become well known on the strength of your love for me and your oneness, oneness, oneness with my soul, my heart and my life.

RB 1083. *Proud to be an American*

Many of you were there on Saturday morning when I opened the "International Friendship Run" at the United Nations with a moment of silence. There were 12,000 runners! Before the ceremony, I was talking to the world record-holder in the marathon, Khalid Khannouchi. He and his wife, Sandra, came to Annam Brahma a few months ago and we sang a song in his honour. He is originally from Morocco. He was applying to become an American citizen.

This time he himself told me that he is so proud to be an American. We took a nice picture together. He is now also the American record-holder in the marathon.

RB 1037. *(p.523)* 24 July 1988
RB 1038. *(p.523)* 3 August 1988
RB 1039. *(p.524)* 8 August 1988
RB 1040. *(p.524)* 8 August 1988
RB 1041. *(p.525)* 14 September 1988
RB 1042. *(p.526)* 10 October 1988
RB 1043. *(p.527)* 6 November 1988
RB 1044. *(p.527)* 6 November 1988
RB 1045. *(p.527)* 6 November 1988
RB 1046. *(p.528)* 6 November 1988
RB 1047. *(p.528)* 6 November 1988
RB 1048. *(p.528)* 6 November 1988
RB 1049. *(p.528)* 6 November 1988
RB 1050. *(p.529)* 6 November 1988
RB 1051. *(p.529)* 20 December 1988, Ambassador Hotel, Bangkok
RB 1052. *(p.529)* 4 January 1989, Hotel Grand Continental, Kuala Lumpur
RB 1053. *(p.530)* 18 March 1989
RB 1054. *(p.530)* 12 December 1989
RB 1055. *(p.531)* 12 December 1989
RB 1056. *(p.532)* 12 December 1989
RB 1057. *(p.533)* 12 December 1989
RB 1058. *(p.533)* 12 December 1989
RB 1059. *(p.534)* 31 August 1992
RB 1060. *(p.534)* 29 March 1995
RB 1061. *(p.535)* 25 May 1996
RB 1062. *(p.535)* 3 June 1995
RB 1063. *(p.535)* 4 December 1995
RB 1064. *(p.536)* 24 December 1996, Kyoto, Japan
RB 1065. *(p.536)* 28 March 1998

APPENDIX

PREFACE TO ORIGINAL EDITION

Sri Chinmoy's interest in running dates back to his youth. At the ashram, or spiritual community, where he lived from the ages of 12 to 32, he was the top-ranked sprinter and, for two consecutive years, decathlon champion. It wasn't until the fall of 1978, however, that he first became interested in long-distance running. Since then, he has pursued the sport with the same one-pointed intensity that he has brought to his various literary, artistic and musical pursuits. For Sri Chinmoy, running – like writing, painting and composing – is nothing but an expression of his inner cry for ever-greater perfection: perfection in the inner world and perfection in the outer world. "Our goal is always to go beyond, beyond, beyond," he says. "There are no limits to our capacity, because we have the infinite Divine within us, and the Supreme is always transcending His own Reality."

Sri Chinmoy regards running as a perfect spiritual metaphor. "Try to be a runner and go beyond all that is bothering you and standing in your way," he tells his students. "Be a real runner so that ignorance, limitations and imperfections will all drop far behind you in the race." In this spirit he has inspired countless individuals to "run" – both literally and figuratively.

"Who is the winner?" he writes in one of his aphorisms. "Not he who wins the race, but he who loves to run sleeplessly and breathlessly with God the Supreme Runner." As a fully God-realised spiritual Master, Sri Chinmoy has consecrated his life to this divinely soulful and supremely fruitful task. At the same time, on an entirely different level, he has made some significant contributions to the sport of running. He was the inspiration behind several long-distance relays, including a recent 300-mile run in Connecticut and the 9,000-mile *Liberty-Torch* run through all the states held during the 1976 Bicentennial. He has composed several running songs, which his students have performed at a number of races. His students have sponsored *Sri Chinmoy Runs* throughout the U.S., Canada, Europe and Australia as an offering to the running community. Moreover, Sri Chinmoy has encouraged his followers around the world to take up running as a means of overcoming lethargy and increasing their spiritual aspiration on the physical plane. Two hundred of his disciples, for example – most of whom were novice runners – completed last years's New York City Marathon.

In the year he has been running, Sri Chinmoy himself has completed seven marathons. He averages about seventy to ninety miles a week, with most of his running done late at night or in the early hours of the morning. During his runs he has been chased by dogs, accosted by hooligans, greeted by admirers and cheered on by children. Sometimes he has had significant inner experiences; other times he has suffered deplorable outer experiences. As a spiritual Master of the highest order, Sri Chinmoy views these experiences – both the divine ones and the undivine ones – with a unique perspective. The running world is nothing but the human world in microcosm, and Sri Chinmoy's reminiscences stand as a remarkable commentary on the whimsical, poignant, funny, outrageous and, above all, supremely significant experience we call life.

BIBLIOGRAPHY

SRI CHINMOY:

–*Run and become, become and run, part 1*, New York, Agni Press, 1979.

–*Run and become, become and run, part 2*, New York, Agni Press, 1979.

–*Run and become, become and run, part 3*, New York, Agni Press, 1980.

–*Run and become, become and run, part 4*, New York, Agni Press, 1981.

–*Run and become, become and run, part 5*, New York, Agni Press, 1981.

–*Run and become, become and run, part 6*, New York, Agni Press, 1981.

–*Run and become, become and run, part 7*, New York, Agni Press, 1982.

–*Run and become, become and run, part 8*, New York, Agni Press, 1982.

–*Run and become, become and run, part 9*, New York, Agni Press, 1983.

–*Run and become, become and run, part 10*, New York, Agni Press, 1983.

–*Run and become, become and run, part 11*, New York, Agni Press, 1983.

–*Run and become, become and run, part 12*, New York, Agni Press, 1983.

–*Run and become, become and run, part 13*, New York, Agni Press, 1983.

–*Run and become, become and run, part 14*, New York, Agni Press, 1985.

–*Run and become, become and run, part 15*, New York, Agni Press, 1985.

–*Run and become, become and run, part 16*, New York, Agni Press, 1985.

–*Run and become, become and run, part 17*, New York, Agni Press, 1986.

–*Run and become, become and run, part 18*, New York, Agni Press, 1996.

–*Run and become, become and run, part 19*, New York, Agni Press, 1996.

–*Run and become, become and run, part 20*, New York, Agni Press, 2004.

–*Run and become, become and run, part 21*, New York, Agni Press, 2005.

Suggested citation key is RB.

POSTFACE

Publishing principles

This edition of *The works of Sri Chinmoy* aims to obey the Author's wish: scrupulous fidelity to his original words, use of typographical style by him selected, specific spelling choices, end placement of any editorial content (i.e. not written by Sri Chinmoy himself), particular treatment of some personal nouns in special cases, etc.

Textual accuracy

This edition has been checked to ensure faithful accuracy to the originals. Although much effort has been put in proofreading and comparing different versions of the text, this print may still present lingering errors. The Publisher would be grateful to be apprised of any mistypes via postal mail or facsimile, possibly with scan of the original page where the text is different. Please use original books only, specifying the year of publication, as no online version can be considered authoritative.

Ongoing reprints will include any revised text from these errata.

Acknowledgements

The Publisher is very grateful to the late Professor Lambert and his équipe for his invaluable advice. For many decades Prof. Lambert conducted a small publishing house specialising in hand-made prints of philological edition of the classics. The standard of this edition would not have been the same without his scholarly advice.

The Publisher is also grateful to the international team of collaborators that spent countless hours proofreading and checking the current text against the originals.

Our deepest gratitude to Sri Chinmoy. His living presence can be felt breathing throughout his writings. It is a privilege to be involved with his works, in any form.

Citation keys

Citation keys are used throughout *The works of Sri Chinmoy* to allow accurate cross-reference of texts across titles and editions. Examples: EA 13, ST 50000, UPA 7.

Sri Chinmoy Canon

We could not use better words than Professor Lambert's, who kindly offered the name *Sri Chinmoy Canon*:

«By defining Sri Chinmoy's first editions as *editio princeps* we chose to follow classical scholarship criteria, not because we consider Sri Chinmoy's work antique, but because we believe it is among the few post ‹classical antiquity› works to rightly deserve to be considered a *classicus*, designating by that term *superiority, authority* and *perfection*.
«The monumental work Sri Chinmoy is offering to mankind is awe-inspiring and supremely pre-eminent in proportions and quality. It is manifest that Sri Chinmoy's work — which we feel right to call *The Sri Chinmoy Canon* — will be of profound help and source of enlightenment to anyone seeking a higher wisdom, truth and reality supreme.»

[Translated from French by M. G.S.]

TABLE OF CONTENTS

*Composition typographique par imprimerie
Ab Academia Aoidon, Paris & Lyon.*

*Un grand merci à Prof Knuth pour
l'utilisation avancée de TEX.*

A LYON, LE 27 DÉCEMBRE LXXXVII Æ.G.

www.ingramcontent.com/pod-product-compliance
Lightning Source LLC
Chambersburg PA
CBHW020814300326
41914CB00075B/1771/J